ST. MARTIN'S

TRUE CRIME
CLASSICS

The cops approached the mansion's rear doorway, a bit uncertain. They had their guns drawn. Who knew what was going down? Knock and announce? No way, the cops decided. The estate was huge—three acres, heavily treed, and the house itself had thirty-three rooms. Who could say for sure what might be inside—a multiple murderer maybe, some crazed Manson-style maniac? The cops had already decided to go through low and fast, ready to shoot first and ask questions only after the smoke had cleared.

Just after 5:20 a.m. on February 3, 2003, they crashed through the door, ready for the worst. There, sprawled in a chair near the stone entryway, the police saw the body of a woman who had obviously been shot in the face. Across the foyer they saw a short, disheveled man clad in what looked like a white nightshirt. His eyes beneath his long, thin gray hair looked wild.

The cops told the man to put up his hands—right now!—but the man started to argue with them. That was when one of the cops zapped the man with 50,000 volts from a Taser gun. Down went the man in the nightshirt. . . .

DON'T MISS THESE OTHER TRUE CRIME
TITLES BY CARLTON SMITH . . .

AVAILABLE FROM ST. MARTIN'S TRUE CRIME LIBRARY

RECKLESS

Millionaire Record Producer Phil Spector
and the Violent Death of Lana Clarkson

Carlton Smith

St. Martin's Paperbacks

RECKLESS

Copyright © 2004 by Carlton Smith.

Cover photograph of house © W. Mancini/*Pasadena Star-News*/ZUMA Press. Photo of Lana Clarkson © Scott Weiner/ZUMA Press. Photo of Phil Spector © Ringo H. W. Chiu/Getty Images.

ISBN: 0-312-99405-2
EAN: 9780312-99405-1

Printed in the United States of America

St. Martin's Paperbacks edition / October 2004

St. Martin's Paperbacks are published by St. Martin's Press, 175 Fifth Avenue, New York, NY 10010.

10 9 8 7 6 5 4 3 2

Acknowledgments

The author wishes to thank a number of people who helped make this book possible. Some asked not to be named, but were nevertheless instrumental in helping to unravel the events that led up to the death of Lana Clarkson. They know who they are, however, and it is my hope that this brief note will let them know how much their assistance is appreciated.

Among the many others who can be acknowledged by name, I especially wish to thank the Honorable Michael E. Pastor, Judge of the Superior Court, who patiently and courteously heard my arguments for why the warrants authorizing the Los Angeles County Sheriff's Department's search of Phil Spector's castle should be disclosed, and who finally did approve their release. Special thanks is also due to Anna Gorman of *The Los Angeles Times*, and Susan Seager, of the law firm of Davis Wright, for their support and assistance in the same endeavor.

Thanks are also due to Roderick Lindblom, attorney at law, who patiently answered many questions over the intervening months; Mick Brown of the United Kingdom's *Daily Telegraph*, who freely shared many of his own insights into the events; Sandra Gibbons of the Los Angeles County District Attorney's Office, who helped me keep track of the calendar of the Spector court proceedings; and Harry Phillips of ABC News, who helped compel the Los Angeles County Coroner to release its suppressed report on the shooting, and who freely shared some of his own thinking about the events in question.

Finally, I also wish to thank singer/songwriter Carol Connors for the extensive and detailed interview she provided on the early Phil Spector; and actress Sally Kirkland and Foley artist Rick Partlow for their recollections of their very good friend, Lana Clarkson.

Carlton Smith
South Pasadena, California

Contents

SPIN CYCLE

RECKLESS

THE CASTLE

1

SEVEN DWARFS

There was only one word for the house at the top of the hill, the one surrounded by all the trees and the electrified fence: spooky. What else could it be, with its dark shadows, its gothic turrets, its forbidding forest, its warning signs to "KEEP OUT"? The only things missing were the moans, the rattle of chains, and the sepulchral laughter of an Igor.

The cops drove up the hill and came to a stop in front of the heavy iron gate, the one with all the spikes on top. There they stopped, unsure of what to do next. The sign on the gate warned of a high voltage greeting to the uninvited. They decided to call for reinforcements. Six minutes later they were joined by paramedics, and ten minutes after that it was decided to storm the house. One team went up the long series of steps that led up the hill to the front door, while another forced the gate and drove farther up the ascending blacktop to the vehicular circle at the top, the place with the fountain that couldn't be seen from the street down below. They parked their cruiser and prepared to go in. On a lawn nearby, hidden from the prying eyes of the world, were seven small shapes—statues, the cops realized in the pre-dawn darkness. It was only later that someone identified them—Dopey, Sneezy, Sleepy, Bashful, Happy, Doc and Grumpy—Walt Disney's seven dwarfs, each of them frozen in rigidity, as if embarrassed at being caught at the scene of a crime. The reporting person, cell phone in hand, was waiting near the black luxury Mercedes parked not far from the back door of the gloomy mansion. It was in the house, he told the cops—the gunshots.

The cops approached the mansion's rear doorway, a bit uncertain. They had their guns drawn. Who knew what was going down? Knock and announce? No way, the cops decided. The estate was huge—three acres, heavily treed, and the house itself had thirty-three rooms. Who could say for sure what might be inside—a multiple murderer maybe, some crazed Manson-style maniac? The cops had already decided to go through low and fast, ready to shoot first and ask questions only after the smoke had cleared.

Just after 5:20 A.M. on February 3, 2003, they crashed through the door, ready for the worst. There, sprawled in a chair near the stone entryway, the police saw the body of a woman who had obviously been shot in the face. Across the foyer they saw a short, disheveled man clad in what looked like a white nightshirt. His eyes beneath his long, thin gray hair looked wild. The cops told the man to put up his hands—right now!—but the man started to argue with them. That was when one of the cops zapped the man with 50,000 volts from a Taser gun. Down went the man in the nightshirt.

Phil Spector, the one-time legendary rock-and-roll music producer, had finally done it. The proof was right there in the chair, breathing her very last. After decades of bizarre behavior, he had finally, really killed someone.

Or so the cops believed. As the dawn arrived, and with it more and more cops, it seemed like an open-and-shut case: there in the chair was one dead woman, along with a handgun that seemed to belong to Spector, and Spector himself, in a highly agitated state. There was no one else in the entire mansion. Who else could the killer be?

Spector refused to say what had happened. The cops put their cuffs on him and tried to sort things out. The paramedics came and went. One thing was for sure, and if they hadn't known it when they went through the door, the cops knew it now: Phil Spector was a big wheel, and a squeaky one at that. Whatever had happened inside the hidden mansion atop the small hill in suburban Alhambra, California, it was about to become big news: another celebrity murder case for the Los Angeles area, which seems to have them with some regularity.

The Alhambra police had a reputation for being a competent, professional department. But this thing had all the earmarks of something that promised to mushroom out of control. For one thing, there was Spector himself, still handcuffed, with a reputation for suing when he thought he was being wronged, and who now had been Tasered and arrested. After a few minutes' discussion among the Alhambra department's higher-ups, it was decided to toss the case over to the far-larger Los Angeles County Sheriff's Department. If this thing grew, no one wanted it said that the Alhambra police had decided Spector was the culprit simply because he might otherwise have grounds to accuse them of incompetence. Besides, it looked like this might take more resources than the Alhambra department had at its disposal.

At 6:25 A.M., the woman was officially pronounced dead, just as the first of three teams of investigators from the Sheriff's Department arrived at the scene to spread through the sprawling house on a search for evidence. One half-hour later, Phil Spector, the producer behind some of rock-and-roll's biggest hits of the early 1960s, was placed under formal arrest on suspicion of having committed homicide. Within an hour after that, Spector was on his way to the Alhambra City Jail.

In a way, despite Spector's reputation for bizarre behavior in the past, the entire scene was incongruous, not least the house itself. Nestled amidst a tract of middle-class homes just east of the Long Beach Freeway, the Spector house stuck out like the oddity it was—a huge mansion, almost a castle, surrounded by and towering over the ordinary dwellings of middle-class wage earners that lapped all around the edges of the wooded hill. It was not for nothing that one of the nearby residents, when later asked about their reclusive celebrity neighbor, said she rarely saw him—except when he was driven by, "waving, like the feudal lord to the serfs."

But even more disconcerting was the question of why? Why was a woman dead in Spector's sprawling castle-like house, and in Alhambra, of all places? Why was a man who, by all accounts, had everything but peace of mind, now in jail on suspicion of murder, and in a place so far removed from the tony locales of Hollywood and Beverly Hills, where he had once been famous? What had happened in that house, with its gates and turrets and statues of cartoon dwarfs, that seemed so far removed from ordinary reality? It was, some thought, a case of fame, or rather notoriety, relentlessly pursuing a man who had tried with all his might for years to get it, and at the same time, to leave it far behind.

2

BEAUTY AND THE BEAST

As one of the world's mega-centers for the manufacture and distribution of popular culture, Los Angeles and its environs has long been an epicenter for high-profile criminal cases involving celebrities. As far back as the 1920s and 1930s, the fatal follies of the famous provided regular grist for the nation's newspapers and airwaves, a sort of fun-house mirror to the more prosaic felonies and misdemeanors of the rest of the country. Over the years, people like silent actress Mabel Normand and director William Desmond Taylor, theater owner Alexander Pantages, bandleader Spade Cooley, actress Lana Turner, show biz mobster Johnny Stompanato his boss, gambler Mickey Cohen, and his rival, Bugsy Siegel, had all at one time or another provided the nation with a peep show into the lives of the rich and famous, and their crimes, deaths or accusations. It was something of a tradition. More recently the trials of O. J. Simpson, Winona Ryder and Robert Downey all became grist for the popular media, elevating them into a new category of defendant: the star as the accused, manifesting the fundamental truth that a culture driven by celebrity creates its own gods, and as quickly devours them. Or, as accused wife-killer Robert Blake might have put it: that's the name of that tune.

It wasn't even necessary for a body to be involved: fifty years earlier, when actor Robert Mitchum was arrested for smoking marijuana, it was national news, so that Robert Downey's own battle with drugs two generations later had a sort of derivative quality to it, an echo, or more accurately, a burp, from the culture-making machinery. Even when a star couldn't be the protagonist, an ordinary person could be made to serve as a stand-in, because the armies of cameras and microphone holders could transmute even the baser element into something akin to stardom. Long ago, for instance, the efforts of the state of California to execute the so-called "Red Light Bandit," Caryl Chessman, made Chessman himself into a sort of celebrity, as did the later effort to convict John DeLorean on drug charges. The Menendez brothers, Lyle and Erik, tried for the murders of their parents, were just another chapter in the book of alchemy that made ordinary criminals into public figures, staples of the celebrity-creating culture.

Thus the arrest of Phil Spector, the one-time "tycoon of teen," the legendary progenitor of the "Wall of Sound" that had revolutionized rock-and-roll music in the early 1960s, was the opening act of yet another media-driven criminal case, another wild ride toward the crossroads of fate and fame. But to borrow the words of later rock-and-roll icons, what a long, strange trip it had been—getting there, at least, if not the final, fatal destination.

The news of the arrest of Phil Spector seeped into the public awareness slowly at first, then with stunning rapidity. Just after 7 A.M. that gray Monday morning, over the very radio waves that had once made Phil rich and famous, the word went out: Phil Spector, the legendary record producer, now a supposed recluse in suburban Alhambra—*Alhambra?*—was in jail in connection with the shooting death of a woman at his sprawling castle-like mansion. The news readers told what little they knew, and by eight that morning, a substantial portion of the Los Angeles–area drive-time population, who had once drummed their teenaged fingers on steering wheels to the Crystals' "Da Doo Ron Ron," or the Ronettes' "Be My Baby," now found themselves musing that somehow, somewhere, perhaps, Phil Spector had lost that lovin' feelin'.

Soon that morning, helicopters were circling Spector's

castle, reporters gave their stand-up reports in the driveway in front of the large iron gates, while their camerapersons shot close-ups of signs warning trespassers to keep out, or the fearsome-looking bits of jagged metal set along the tops of the estate's walls. A gaggle of grim-visaged, silent men, some in uniforms, made their way in and out of the gate, followed by the departure of the ominous gray van. A television reporter for the NBC affiliate in Los Angeles interviewed one of the neighbors, Terri Arias: "I heard the boom, boom boom," Arias told the television station. "It was about three or four shots."

Later in the morning, a spokesperson for the Los Angeles County Sheriff's Department confirmed the news that Spector had been arrested, while declining to say who had been killed.

"Shortly after five o'clock this morning, officers responded to a shooting call and discovered a female shot inside the location [sic]," said Faye Bugarin of the sheriff's department. "She was pronounced dead at the scene and suspect Phillip Spector was taken into custody and is currently being detained."

Eight time zones away, in London, England, a reporter for the United Kingdom *Daily Telegraph* newspaper, was just about to leave the newsroom for the day. An editor asked writer Mick Brown, the paper's cultural affairs expert, just what he had done to set Phil Spector off.

"What?" Brown asked. The editor told Brown that Spector had just been arrested in connection with the shooting death of a woman at his mansion near Los Angeles. Because Brown had written a lengthy profile on Spector that had run only two days before the shooting—in fact, Brown had obtained the first face-to-face interview that Spector had given in decades—the editor kidded Brown that his just-published profile had made Spector mad enough to murder.

Brown was flabbergasted, especially to hear the news that the dead person was a woman. He tried to imagine who had been killed, and could only think of two names: Phil's personal assistant, Michelle Blaine, the daughter of storied drummer Hal Blaine, and also the young woman who had helped him secure the prized interview; or—and here Brown gave himself a mental double-take—the woman Phil had been seeing socially in recent months: Nancy Sinatra.

Brown turned around, went back to his desk, and started making telephone calls.

But it wasn't Nancy Sinatra, and it wasn't Michelle Blaine. Late that day, while Brown and other newspeople on two continents tried to figure out who Phil Spector was supposed to have killed, a man named Rick Partlow received a telephone call of his own. A friend had just heard the news: the woman shot dead at Phil Spector's house was none other than their mutual good friend, the actress Lana Clarkson.

Partlow, a veteran actor and Foley artist—an expert in sound effects for movies and television—couldn't believe it. In fact, he refused to believe it. He had known Lana Clarkson for more than twenty years, ever since she had first become involved in show business in her late teens. He was very good friends with Lana, her mother Donna, and her brother and sister. He was, in fact, very nearly a member of the family. His mind racing, Partlow dialed Donna Clarkson, who lived not far away.

It was true, Lana's mother told Partlow; Lana was dead. Donna had just been notified by the authorities. It had been Lana who was shot down in Phil Spector's house.

Partlow's mind kept slipping gears, even as Donna's pain came over the line. It didn't seem possible: Lana, so bright, so upbeat, so personable, so close a friend . . . how could she be dead? Partlow's mind refused to accept it. It was as if some new, alien reality had taken over, some force that had wrenched the entire universe into an inconceivable new channel. Numbly, Partlow went through the particulars of getting the information necessary to deal with what had happened; he would help Donna make all the funeral arrangements.

Replacing the telephone, Partlow struggled to make sense

of everything; it was as if all that he had known, everything that he had accepted as a given, had been thrown into confusion.

His mind filled itself with images: Lana during all the years he had known her, in all the various incarnations he had seen her go through as an actress: ingenue, action heroine, star of television commercials, and most recently, a promising stand-up comedienne. And beneath those images: all the times that Lana had flopped on his couch, hair in curlers, watching the old movies they both loved so much, and the actresses Lana adored: Jean Harlow, Carole Lombard, Myrna Loy, Marilyn Monroe, and others, all of them light, comedic geniuses who had delighted millions over the years, just as Lana herself had yearned to do. It seemed impossible that she could be dead.

But by that evening, the news was out, which somehow seemed to make it more real: the dead woman on Phil Spector's floor *was* Lana Jean Clarkson, a 40-year-old actress most famous for her role as the prototype for Xena, Warrior Princess, as the female lead in producer Roger Corman's 1985 cult classic film, *Barbarian Queen.* By that evening, in fact, Lana's life had been weighed and assayed against the balance of Spector's own: *B movie actress found slain at Phil Spector's house* was the story line that led the evening news. The unstated subtext was that somehow, desperate for success, Lanan Clarkson had put the moves on Spector, and had been killed for her trouble. **Fatal Attraction,** the *New York Post* headlined. Why else would she have been at his house all night?

Inside, Partlow seethed: that was just like the media, he thought, just like Hollywood, to sum up an entire life with a simplistic tag line. "B movie actress," indeed, as if the woman he had come to love over so many years was nothing more than a Hollywood wannabe, a second-rate player of no significant value, and to use it to cast an implied sneer at her virtue. The more he thought about it, the angrier he got. It was as if the television was in effect saying, B movie actress, big deal; as if it somehow made it more *acceptable* that she was dead, since she wasn't a big star. Partlow knew that wasn't true, that they weren't actually saying anything like that, but the feeling was hard to get rid of. And when he thought about Spector—rich, famous, successful beyond anyone's dreams—he got even madder.

Just who the hell does he think he is? Partlow thought. *Does he think he can just shoot somebody down in his house and get away with it? Does he think he can murder my friend and walk away from what he did, just because he's rich and famous?*

But there it was, also on the news that night: Phil Spector, the famous rock-and-roll producer, had been released from jail on $1 million bail. Phil, a police officer just behind him, was shown making his way out of the Alhambra police station. He was still in his nightshirt, his eyes unfocused, his thinning hair waving wildly and his ferret-like face looking pinched, an aging legend, now caught in the strobe lights.

3
BACK STORY

Spector's release on the evening of February 3, 2003, caught many people off guard. One thing was sure, if Spector hadn't had access to a million dollars, or at least property worth that much, he would never have been released; the average person arrested in connection with what appeared to be a homicide in Los Angeles County, and almost everywhere else, would have been in custody for weeks, if not months, and probably never released at all. Even Robert Blake, the actor, had to sit in jail for months while the authorities tried to figure out what to do in the homicide of his wife. But *Spector* got to walk, and it wasn't very long before people began to suggest that either he hadn't done anything wrong, or he was getting special treatment from the authorities.

Phil had spent much of the afternoon before his release at a nearby hospital, being treated for the effects of the Tasering, among other things. Later, the police would seize a videotape of Phil's arrival at San Gabriel Valley Medical Center; they apparently believed that the tape would indicate something of Phil's state of sobriety, even twelve hours after the arrest. Before going to the hospital, however, he had been in contact with prominent Los Angeles lawyer Robert Shapiro, who had once defended O. J. Simpson. Shapiro, a long-time acquaintance of Phil's, went to the Alhambra police station to talk to Phil after his booking. Shapiro helped Phil make the bail arrangements with Chickie's Bail Bonds, owned by a Los Angeles woman, Chickie Leventhal, who had been in business since 1984. Chickie's son, Mitch, helped run the business, which boasted a testimonial from Shapiro himself on Chickie's Web site: "I never want my clients in jail. With Chickie, they are out instantly." To secure the bond, Phil gave Mitch Leventhal and his mother a deed to his castle.

By the following morning, February 4, the news media had fanned out across the celebrity landscape to scoop up bits of information about Spector: having celebrities talk about other celebrities was always good for ratings. Anyone who knew anything substantive, however, was keeping mostly mum. The Associated Press had already tracked Shapiro down at the Alhambra police station just hours after the reported shooting, while Phil was at the hospital, and before his release on bail. Was it true that Phil Spector had been arrested for murder? What was going on? Shapiro was equivocal. "I don't know answers to any of this," Shapiro had told the AP.

Another enterprising reporter lassoed famed palimony lawyer Marvin Mitchelson, who was said to be a close friend of Spector's. Mitchelson expressed incredulity at Phil's arrest. He'd seen Phil fairly recently, Mitchelson said, as they worked to try to put together a proposed movie on Phil's life. "His mental state has been great—very rational, very together, super intelligent, a very funny man," Mitchelson said.

Short of useful facts, the news people did what they always do in such situations: cobble together a short, shallow history of the subject, with particular emphasis on facts that might purport to shed light on the current situation. Thus, the quick version of the Spector legend was wired together: how young Phil Spector had first burst onto the public stage as a performer, one of the Teddy Bears, a two-boys-and-a-girl trio who recorded a Number One teen hit in 1958, "To Know Him Is to Love Him"; how Spector had gone on to become a successful behind-the-mike producer in the early years of rock-and-roll, packaging hits for the Crystals and the Ronettes, among others, and then the Righteous Brothers. Spector was credited with developing the "Wall of Sound" recording technique, in which rock-and-roll songs were assembled like collages, with instruments and vocals layered onto recording tracks like thick swabs of auditory paint, over and over again, until the finished product was less a performance than it was almost a sculpture.

Then, according to the legend, Spector had gone into temporary eclipse in the second half of the 1960s, only to emerge as a producer for the Beatles' contentious last album, *Let It Be*, later followed by stints as a producer for John Lennon and George Harrison, after both went on to become solo artists. Still later, Spector did some producing for the Ramones, and after that, for Celine Dion. It was as if, every ten years or so, Phil emerged from his self-imposed seclusion to attempt to get back to the top of the popular music scene, with only minimal success. Only two or three months before the shooting, in fact, Spector had tried to produce some tracks for the British band Starsailor. It appeared that when earlier efforts to make the movie of Phil Spector's life had fallen flat—Tom Cruise and director Cameron Crowe were said to have abandoned the project, apparently because there was no discernible ending—the notion of an ending with Phil returning in triumph to the recording studios and the top of the pop charts with a band like Starsailor had been pitched by Spector and Mitchelson, but the Starsailor gig hadn't worked out either. Now it appeared that there would be an ending, all right—just one that no one, least of all Mitchelson, had anticipated.

But this was all on the front side of Phil Spector, the professional side. What engaged the newspeople's attention that first week of February was the far more colorful back story, as they called it in Hollywood—Spector's nasty divorce from his second wife, Ronnie, the former lead singer of the Ronettes; the long, convoluted history of Spector's legal battles with the Crystals, the Ronettes, the Righteous Brothers and others, over the ownership of the music and royalties; the time that Spector had supposedly fired a gun into the ceiling at a recording studio at a session with Lennon, prompting the ex-Beatle to plead with Phil to "save me ears";

or the time that Phil had purportedly held the Ramones captive in a studio at the point of a gun, insisting that they keep on recording until they got it right. And even deeper in the background was the general consensus that Phil Spector was a deeply disturbed personality, someone with a fetish-like attachment to firearms, a man with a long history of drug and alcohol abuse, a man given to high heels and capes, near histrionic fits of temper, a phalanx of bodyguards behind him, an overweening ego, and extended bouts of reclusiveness.

Much of the reportage focused on Phil's fascination with guns. The U.K. *Daily Telegraph*'s man in Los Angeles, Oliver Poole, reprised the band-as-hostage story, and quoted one band member, Dee Dee Ramone, as calling Phil a "crack shot." According to Poole, Dee Dee Ramone had said he'd once seen Phil "hit a fly at fifty yards." But another member of the Ramones disputed Dee Dee's description of Spector, and used the same insect to do it: "I don't think he would hurt a fly," drummer Marky Ramone told Fox News. "Until anything happens, you're innocent until you're proven guilty. I don't think Phil had it in him to murder anybody."

Other reporters unearthed a 1977 interview with Spector by *Los Angeles Times* music critic Robert Hilburn, in which Phil admitted that he had, in the past, acted in eccentric ways, including costuming himself as Batman for forays out onto the Sunset Strip. "It had to stop," Phil had told Hilburn in this quarter-century-old interview. "It wasn't healthy." Others noted that Phil had occasionally refered to himself as "the Mozart of rock-and-roll," which was about as insightful about his own feelings of self-importance as it was insulting to Mozart.

Having hit the high (and low) spots of Spector's four-decade career, the newspeople next turned their attention to the victim, Lana Clarkson. The *LA Times* made one of the first attempts to explain who Lana Clarkson was, and to try to shed light on her fatal conjunction with Spector.

"The victim of Monday's shooting," the paper's Geoff Boucher, Richard Winton and Andrew Blankstein reported,

"Clarkson left behind a long filmography heavy on such 1980s B-movie fare as *Death Stalker*, *Blind Date*, and [film producer Roger] Corman's *Barbarian Queen*, in which she played the sword-wielding title character. She claimed she was the prototype for the TV show, 'Xena, Warrior Princess.' "

The newspaper went on to characterize Lana as "holding on by her fingernails" to a show business career that had begun when she was still in her teens. Despite her early success in films, she had found parts harder to come by as she neared, then passed, the age of 40. Still, the paper reported, her close friends considered her a cheerful, ebullient personality, someone who was rarely discouraged by the difficulties of earning a living as an actress. "She ran through life, one of them said, at 11 on a scale of 10," the paper reported. Over the past year, friends said, Lana had been working to develop her comedic talent, and had prepared a demonstration video of herself performing various stand-up roles, à la Lily Tomlin; those who had seen the tape were certain that Lana was on the verge of a major breakthrough as a comic actress.

Still, one had to eat and pay the bills while waiting to be discovered, or in Lana's case, re-discovered. Over the prior month, the paper continued, Lana had obtained a job as a hostess at the House of Blues, one of a chain of nightclubs partially owned by actor Dan Aykroyd. It was at the House of Blues, at the club's VIP Foundation Rooms, that she had first encountered Spector, the paper reported.

"Detectives are still trying to figure out how Clarkson met Spector and wound up dead on the floor of his home [actually, seated in a chair when first discovered by the police] after accepting a ride in the music producer's Mercedes early Monday," the paper continued. "But the killing has called attention to the frustrating existence of B-movie actresses: performers who star in cheap, mass-appeal films without ever securing a definitive role."

Here it was again: the subtle suggestion that the fact that Lana Clarkson was dead was somehow related to her career.

To Partlow, and others among Lana's many friends, both in and out of the film industry, it smacked of blaming the victim—as if, had she been the recipient of numerous Academy Awards, she would never have been shot. As far as they were concerned, Lana *was* a successful actress—one of the very few who actually made a living at it. The paper tried to leaven this erroneous portrait of Lana as a desperate out-of-work actress by referring to her four years' volunteer work with Project Angel Food, which the paper described as an "AIDS [patient] meal delivery service," and described her as a highly spiritual person with a naturally sunny outlook. Still, the chasm between the public image of "a B movie actress" and the actual person of Lana Clarkson was too large for the paper to jump. Focused on the two-dimensional picture manufactured mostly for theaters and television screens, the portrait never really came into focus. Certainly those who had known the real Lana Clarkson, such as Partlow, or Lana's lawyer, Roderick Lindblom, or her agent, Ray Cavaleri, or many of her other friends who had known her as the tall, blond, terrifically funny and personable lady she had been, never recognized her at all in these public descriptions.

While most news outlets were content to weave this pastiche of legend and gossip, at least one was more interested in developing the salient facts that lay behind the news: just what had actually happened to land Phil Spector in jail, even if temporarily? In a story published three days later, *Los Angeles Times* reporters attempted to reconstruct the events that had led up to the fatal shooting and arrest. One of the facts that jumped out was that Phil had been doing some serious drinking on the night of the shooting.

The newspaper picked up Phil's trail late Sunday night at Dan Tana's, a west Los Angeles restaurant popular with Hollywood people. Phil was with a woman, another customer told the paper, but the woman was not Lana Clarkson. The couple had salads and drinks, and appeared to be getting along well. Then, shortly after midnight, Phil and the woman left the restaurant. Phil put down a $500 tip on a bill of about $55, the paper reported.

Somewhere between 1 and 2 A.M., the paper continued, Phil arrived, alone except for the chauffeur driving his limousine, at the House of Blues. The paper reported that it was at least Phil's second visit to the club within the past month. There, about 2:30 A.M., closing time, Phil left, apparently taking Lana with him after she had finished her work.

"Among the mysteries still facing investigators," the paper reported, "are when Spector met Clarkson, what he was doing before his visit to Dan Tana's, and what occurred between 2:30 A.M., when he left the House of Blues, and about 5 A.M., when she was shot."

But by the time this information was reported, the rest of the news media had discovered the complete text of Mick Brown's interview of Phil Spector, the one that had been published in the early morning hours [in Britain] two days before the shooting—the publication of which, Brown's editor had half-joked and half-suspected, had made Phil murderously crazy.

4

"I HAVE DEVILS"

This was, by all accounts, an extraordinary interview, and it took very little for a reader to wonder whether its publication hadn't played a role in the events that soon followed.

Published in *The Daily Telegraph*'s Saturday magazine, and titled "Pop's Lost Genius," the piece represented publication of the first major interview that Spector had granted since Hilburn's sit-down more than twenty-five years earlier. The interview itself had been conducted the previous November, shortly after Spector had returned from the United Kingdom after the attempt to produce the Starsailor tracks. As such, it represented a sort of core sample of Spector's brain just after the attempt to get back to the top of the musical heap, represented by Starsailor, and the alleged nadir to which Spector had subsequently descended.

"I have not been well," Mick Brown said Spector told him, during his November visit to the castle. "I was crippled inside. Emotionally. Insane is a hard word. I wasn't insane, but I wasn't well enough to function as a regular part of society, so I didn't. I chose not to."

Brown reported that, at that point, Phil had paused.

"I have devils inside that fight me," Brown said Phil told him.

Well, here it was, for anyone who cared to hazard a guess as to what had happened to Lana Clarkson: Phil Spector had not been well, and if he wasn't crazy, at least he was "crippled . . . emotionally . . ." And there were "devils inside that fight me . . ." Then, three months after he'd made these statements, an actress winds up shot dead at Phil Spector's house. Q.E.D.: Phil Spector went nuts and killed her.

Brown was later to say that he'd been trying diligently for some weeks, if not months, to obtain the interview. It appeared that at least part of the genesis of the request had come from Spector's decision to produce tracks for the Starsailor group. Phil had traveled to the U.K. in the late summer of 2002 to do this, partly at the suggestion of one of his children, his daughter Nicole. By all accounts the producing session was something less than a success, and Phil had to wonder if it was because today's musicians were less talented than those he had worked with in the past, or if the old magic had left his brain forever, sometime back in the early seventies.

Then, on the return from the U.K., a strange incident had unfolded at the airport. As the customs people went through the luggage of one of Phil's long-time bodyguards, they discovered a cache of soap and shampoos, apparently from the hotel where Phil had been staying while in London. According to those familiar with the scene, Phil was embarrassed: he was sure that someone was going to accuse him of having ordered the bodyguard to rip off the hotel on his behalf. Phil fired the man on the spot, or so the story went.

The tale is instructive for several reasons, not least because of what it seems to indicate about Phil: mostly, his belief that his employee was some sort of robotic extension of himself—that people would think the employee had only acted at Phil's direction, that it was *Phil* who wanted the hotel trifles, and had used his minion to get them. So much for free will, especially among those who put themselves under Phil's control.

Secondly, the firing of the long-time bodyguard was very likely a seminal event in the run-up to the tragedy that was to take place three months later. For years, Phil's bodyguards had served a double purpose: while they were ostensibly employed to prevent Phil from being threatened or harassed by the public, their second and more important job was to prevent Phil from doing the same *to* the public. In other words, the bodyguards helped save Phil from his own excesses.

Now, with the bodyguard getting his pink slip, Phil was left without his bumperpads.

So, into this murky atmosphere, as it existed in November of 2002, came *The Daily Telegraph*'s Mick Brown. Brown said later that he'd tried to arrange the interview with Michelle Blaine over a period of several weeks prior to his arrival in Los Angeles. Then, when he finally landed, he was told that the interview had been cancelled.

Brown wasn't surprised to discover that he'd passed over eight time zones, nearly seven thousand miles, only to find that his subject had reneged. That was Phil, Brown knew: at best, mercurial, at worst, extremely self-centered. If Phil didn't want to do the interview, why hadn't he called before Brown had left London? Brown checked into a hotel and waited. Sure enough, within a day there was another call: the interview was back on again.

At length, as Brown described the events later, he was told to go to his hotel's entrance. There, a white 1964 Rolls-Royce Silver Cloud, bearing the license plate "PHIL 500" was waiting to pick him up. A chauffeur opened the rear door, and Brown took a seat inside an interior richly appointed in walnut and leather. The Rolls left the hotel, headed for the freeway, and eventually arrived at the wrought-iron gates in front of the castle, the same barrier that three months later was to be featured so prominently on the evening news. The gates opened, then closed, and the Rolls stopped. The chauffeur opened the rear door and gestured to a series of steps leading upward. The driver explained that Phil liked to have his visitors approach the castle by climbing the stairs.

"The summit seemed to be wreathed in mist," Brown wrote later, "out of which the shape of the castle loomed, grey, turreted, imposing. I felt I was being watched. I might have been imagining this."[1]

---

[1] Quoted excerpts from Mick Brown's interview with Phil Spector, published in the UK *Daily Telegraph* Feb. 1, 2003, are used by permission of UK Daily Telegraph Co.

Probably not, though. If there's one thing that Brown's contrived arrival—being made to walk up all the steps when the car could easily have driven all the way to the top of the hill to deposit him in front of a far more convenient door—seemed to suggest, it was that Phil wanted to inculcate a feeling of humility on the part of his guest, sort of like making a commoner grovel while approaching the throne.

The castle's front door opened, and Brown was greeted by someone he described as Phil's assistant, "a vivacious woman in her early 40s," Michelle Blaine. Blaine gave Brown a quick tour of the lower level of the castle: a "cavernous hallway," as Brown described it, carpeted in red, with wood paneling on the walls, and two suits of medieval armor standing sentinel, as Brown put it. A quick glance at the "music room," where Brown's guide pointed out John Lennon's old guitar on a stand, and a photo gallery showing Phil with various music personalities, a drawing room with a Picasso next to an original sketch by Lennon. A maid arrived with ice water for Brown. In the background, classical music played continuously.

After about half-an-hour, the assistant's cell phone rang. Phil would be arriving shortly, the assistant told Brown when she'd hung up.

Soon thereafter, Phil made his appearance at the top of the stairs—"to the strains of Handel," as Brown put it. "A small, slight figure, he was wearing a shoulder-length, curled toupee, blue-tinted glasses, a black silk pyjama suit with the monogram PS picked out in silver thread, and three-inch, Cuban-heel boots. He looked bizarre, yet at the same time curiously magnificent," Brown recorded.

Phil seated himself on a large white sofa, hunched as if in pain. Brown noticed that his hands seemed to be trembling. He sipped from a glass of something red, whether wine or cranberry juice, Brown couldn't tell. Brown noticed that Phil was wearing an unusual watch that gave out whirring noises, then spoke the time in words—"It's three o'clock."

As the interview began, Phil seemed intent on trying to explain himself, particularly his behavior over the years, especially the reclusiveness. Brown formed the impression that Phil wanted people to understand him, while at the same time he wanted to convey a combative attitude—sort of, "I am who I am, take it or leave it, but please take it." There was a strong note of self-justification, almost defensiveness in his approach that seemed to be at war with his desire to be understood. Brown formed the impression that Phil, at least, considered himself a genius, and a misunderstood genius at that. As Brown took Phil over the past—the forty years since he had been "the first tycoon of teen," as Tom Wolfe had described him back in those innocent years—the outlines of Phil's persona began to emerge, along with the reason for the interview: Phil wanted people to know he was back.

"I am trying to get my life reasonable," Phil told Brown. "I'm not going to ever be happy. Happiness isn't on. Because happiness is temporary. . . . Orgasm is temporary. But being reasonable is an approach. And being reasonable with yourself. It's very difficult, very difficult to be reasonable."

Reasonable? Even Brown thought that was an impossible word to describe Phil. Here was a man who had feuded with nearly everyone who had ever crossed his life's path—including his own children—and who had a history of vituperative litigation with former friends and associates, even his wives, that revealed him to be neurotic, if not quixotic. He was convinced that people hated him because he looked strange, because he acted strange. "I just felt I didn't fit in," he told Brown. "I was different. So I had to make my own world. And it made life complicated for me, but it made it justifiable. 'Oh, that's the reason they hate my fucking guts; I look strange, I act strange, make these strange records,' so there's a reason [for them] to hate my guts."

This was why he had withdrawn from the world, from all the success of the early years, he indicated: because he felt that people hated him, and as a result, he had to find some reason for the hatred—that he looked "strange," acted "strange," that he never fit in. He'd always felt poor, Phil said, even when he was rich.

Here was a case of alienation writ large, compounded by

an early run of phenomenal cultural and financial success that had hardened into narcissism, abetted by a dollop of acute paranoia. But Phil made it clear to Brown that he was well aware of his psychological infirmities, that he had been battling them for over forty years, and that now he was ready to cope.

"Spector talks of his psychological problems with remarkable candour," Brown wrote, "struggling, it seems, to find some explanation for all the phobias, the irrational behaviour, the need for control, for approbation." The root of all this was deep inside, Phil acknowledged: "There's something I'd either not accepted," he told Brown, "or I'm not prepared to accept, or live with in my life, that I don't know about, perhaps; that I'm facing now."

Phil told Brown he thought part of his psychological problems might have come from his genetic inheritance. He said his father and his mother were first cousins, and suggested that part of his mental difficulties may have stemmed from this close degree of blood relation. "I would say," Phil told Brown, "I'm probably relatively insane, to an extent. To an extent. I take medication for schizophrenia, but I wouldn't say I'm schizophrenic. But I have a bipolar personality, which is strange. I'm my own worst enemy." Right at that point in his life, Phil told Brown, he was suffering from acute boredom and restlessness. "But not crazy anxious. Not desperate." He was taking medication for his psychological disabilities, Phil told Brown.

"Listen," Phil said. "People tell me they idolise me, want to be like me, but I tell them, trust me, you don't want my life. Because it hasn't been a very pleasant life. I've been a very tortured soul. I have not been at peace with myself. I have not been happy."

5

THE LEGEND, THE LIES, THE FACTS

"I have not been happy," Phil told Brown. Played back in the aftermath of the shooting death of Lana Clarkson, the words seemed prophetic, as well as a possible explanation for what had taken place at the castle on the night of February 3. The possibility that Phil had flipped out, that his devils had finally overtaken him, was played big across the news over the next few days. Here was a simple answer to the puzzle, a sort of ribbon that could be tied around the otherwise inexplicable. But this only prompted a new question: had Phil confessed?

"No," said Lieutenant Dan Rosenberg, the Los Angeles Sheriff's Department detective supervisor in charge of the investigation. "There has not been a confession by Mr. Spector." Indeed, it appeared that Phil had made no statements at all about the shooting, at least to the police. Following his release by the Alhambra police on Monday night, in fact, Phil had departed to places unknown. His house, the castle, had been thoroughly searched by sheriff's detectives all day Monday and well into Tuesday before it was released back to Phil's custody. But it appeared that Phil had not gone back there.

Brown's very excellent interview of Phil, while conducted months before the shooting, nevertheless seemed to cast a penetrating light on the events; indeed, there was speculation that the publication of the interview two days before the shooting had in some way triggered the incident—as if being thrust back into the limelight, with all his self-confessed flaws, had somehow driven Phil into an uncontrolled manic frenzy.

But Brown's interview, sharp as it was when it came to Phil's own description of his present mental state, was actually erected on the scaffolding of three earlier written assessments of Phil Spector, all of them books. The first, *Out of His Head*[2], was essentially a paean to Phil's musical brilliance by British music critic Richard Williams, published just after Phil's second heyday in 1972; the second was a richly detailed, unauthorized biography of Phil, *He's a Rebel*[3], by Mark Ribowsky, published in 1989; and the third, *Be My Baby—How I Survived Mascara, Miniskirts, and Madness, or, My Life as a Fabulous Ronette*[4], was an acidic if often comic memoir by Phil's second wife, the former Veronica Bennett, "Ronnie" of the Ronettes, published in 1990. All three books helped form the backbone of the Spector legend.

The last two books took their titles from Spector rock-and-roll hits from the early 1960s—"He's a Rebel," by the Crystals in 1962, and "Be My Baby," the Ronettes' Number One of 1964. While Veronica Bennett Spector's book is a terrifically colorful, often tragicomical account of life with Phil, it can't be relied upon as utter gospel, in part because of the bitterness of the couple's 1972 divorce, and also because Ronnie, as she was known, sometimes got her facts and time frames mixed up.

Ribowsky's book, *He's a Rebel*, is more reliable than either Williams' generally admiring *Out of His Head* or Ronnie's caustic *Be My Baby*, principally because Ribowsky made a valiant effort to separate the legend from the true facts, in the process coming to the conclusion that there was

---

[2] Outerbridge and Lazard, Inc., 1972.

[3] E. P. Dutton, 1989. "Unauthorized" in this context means that Phil Spector did not cooperate with Ribowsky, the writer, and does not in any way indicate something that was illegal or even unfair.

[4] Harmony Books, Crown Publishers, 1990.

both more and less to Phil Spector than met the public eye. As Ribowsky acknowledged in his introduction to *He's a Rebel*, "I think it necessary to say that I hold Spector in the highest regard. From my place in the legion of baby boomers who reached teenhood in time to appreciate, and be affected by, Spector's music in its original issue, he is a stately, heroic figure."

Still, said Ribowsky, that admiration did not obscure the fact that his biography was "replete with examples of Phil Spector's aberrance, his intimate pain, his manipulation and deception, his greed and his anxieties . . ." But all of these negatives, in Ribowsky's view, were less evidence of a se-verely disturbed personality than they were a manifestation of Spector's obsession with creating cutting-edge rock-and-roll music—his "genius," using Ribowsky's word. "Whether he was good or bad," Ribowsky concluded, "it is my hope that history will note that America had its own Mozart and his name was Phil Spector."[5]

Apart from Ribowsky's hyperbole, his look at the life and times of Spector up to 1989 remains the single best source of insight as to the subterranean origins of Phil's well-documented, self-destructive behavior. Whether it also sheds light on the death of Lana Clarkson is an unavoidable corol-lary question. In the course of researching his book, written more than a dozen years before the events that were to bring Phil before the bar of justice, Ribowsky tracked down and in-terviewed scores of people, some now dead, from all walks of life, particularly the music industry, and as such, compiled a vital resource in understanding just how Phil Spector ar-rived at the place, where, in his own words, he was not happy. Nevertheless, for anyone who seeks to understand the origins of Phil Spector's life-long angst, and what happened on the night of Lana Clarkson's death, all three books remain a cru-cial template, or more accurately, a Rosetta Stone to translate between the facts, the legend and the lies.

---

[5] *He's a Rebel*, Cooper Square Press edition, 2000.

Or, as New York music producer/songwriter Doc Pomus told Ribowsky: "Phil always told a lot of stories, but here's the reality: what actually happened, what Phil wished could have happened, and what he *says* happened." At the time Pomus said this, it was a joke with a needle of truth. But by the spring of 2003, with a woman shot to death in Phil Spector's house under mysterious circumstances, with the stage set for contradictory stories about what had actually happened, it seemed ominously appropriate.

6

THE FAMILY SPECTOR

Harvey Phillip Spector was born the day after Christmas in 1939,[6] the second child of Benjamin and Bertha Spektor Spector of the Bronx in New York. Bertha and Benjamin were both children of immigrant Jewish families from Russia, and were apparently cousins, if Phil had the story straight.

The cousins angle, with its implication of potential genetic damage from inbreeding, had long been a part of the Spector legend, even before Mick Brown's interview. For his mother and father to be first cousins, that would mean that two of Phil's grandparents would likely have been a brother and a sister, because it isn't likely that one family would have had two sons both called George, which was the first name of both of Phil's grandfathers. That suggests that one of the Georges must have married into the family; in other words, became the spouse of Phil's grandmother, thus becoming grandfather George number two. Later, after coming to the New World, the son and daughter of each side of the family, Ben and Bertha, would have married. Such intermarriage between first cousins was not unusual in insular European or Middle Eastern communities, particularly at a time when such marriages were arranged by matchmakers. The

---

[6] Ribowsky's biography, as well as other sources, say the year was 1940, but Spector's arrest sheet has the year as 1939. In addition, when gaining court approval for the Teddy Bears' contract in August 1958, Spector's birth year was listed in court documents as 1939.

relationship between marriages of first cousins and mental illness is mainly anecdotal, which is not to say it isn't true. In fact, there is some evidence of mental illness in the Spector family even before the supposed marriage between the cousins.

In the version of events published by Ribowsky in his 1989 biography of Phil, Benjamin Spector was born in Russia in January of 1903, and came with his parents, along with a number of brothers and sisters, to the United States at the age of three. Ribowsky asserted that Ben "fought in World War One," which seems a bit unlikely, if indeed Benjamin Spector was born in 1903—that would have made Phil's father a 15-year-old doughboy at war's end, since the United States did not enter World War I until April of 1917, when Ben would have been 14. But there is some tantalizing evidence to suggest that Benjamin Spector was actually born in 1899, as we shall see.

The first independent record of Benjamin Spector—that is, a record that is not based on anecdotal recollection and later disseminated to Ribowsky and others like Mick Brown, by either Phil himself or his acolytes—can be found in the federal census of 1920. That census shows a Benjamin Spector, age 17, enumerated as an ordinary seaman assigned to the U.S.S. *Eagle*, a destroyer–minesweeper based in Portsmouth, N.H. Curiously, the record shows that this Ben Spector enlisted in the Navy at St. Louis just a few weeks before the census was taken. Exactly why Phil's father would have been in St. Louis when he enlisted is a mystery. The 1920 census lists no other Benjamin Spectors born in 1903.

The next record of Benjamin Spector—or, at least *a* Benjamin Spector—is found in the 1930 federal census. This census recorded fifteen Benjamin Spectors throughout the entire United States—none of them born in 1903. There was, however, a Benjamin Spector born in 1899, who would have been 18 or 19 years old in April of 1917, and thus old enough to have served in World War I. In 1930, this Benjamin Spector was listed as a patient at the Brooklyn State

Hospital—a mental patient. Whether this is the same person as Phil's father can't be determined with accuracy, but it seems a possibility, given that none of the other fourteen Benjamin Spectors in the census had a birth year anywhere near 1903. It's also possible that the 1903 Benjamin Spector simply wasn't counted in the 1930 census, and that therefore there is no connection between the mental patient of 1930 and Phil's father.

Regardless of which Spector was in the Brooklyn State Hospital in 1930, one of the other unanswered questions about Phil's parentage is the whereabouts of Benjamin Spector throughout the 1920s, the years of speakeasies and rum-runners, along with his occupation during his years as a single man. This, too, is a mystery.

In 1934, when Benjamin would have been 31, or possibly 35, depending on his true birth date, Benjamin Spector married Bertha Spector, or Spektor—Ribowsky says Bertha's family spelled their surname with a *k*, although the census records seem to show that it was also spelled with a *c*. Bertha, born in Paris, France, in 1911 as the family was making its way toward America from Russia, according to Ribowsky, would have been 23 at the time of the marriage. The following year brought the birth of a daughter, Shirley, Phil's older sister.

According to old telephone directories on file with the New York Public Library, by the time of Phil's birth in either 1939 or 1940, Benjamin, Bertha and Shirley were all living at 1048 Manor Avenue in the Bronx, in the heart of a lower-income district just south of the rusty, noisy elevated train over Westchester Avenue. The Soundview neighborhood followed the classic New York pattern: first a community of Irish immigrants, giving way gradually through the twenties into the thirties to a Jewish enclave. By the time the remnant of the Spector family moved to Los Angeles in the 1950s, it was becoming a neighborhood of Puerto Rican immigrants, as it remains today. Years later, when he was a wealthy, successful music producer, Phil would return to the old neighborhood, just to see what it looked like, according to a close friend. There, as he gazed at the front door of the tenement, a gang of young boys from the neighborhood surrounded his luxury car in a menacing fashion. Phil broke the antenna off the car and started banging it across the hood in an equally menacing fashion, according to the friend. Impressed, the gang left him alone. Or so the story was told—by Phil.

The Manor Avenue address was a tenement housing four families. It served as the Spector family residence throughout the years of World War II, and after, when Phil was growing up. Ribowsky notes that Phil's older sister Shirley was "tall and blonde," in sharp contrast to the short, heavy, more darkly complected Benjamin and Bertha. By the late 1940s, according to Ribowsky, the five-foot-seven-inch Benjamin Spector weighed over 220 pounds—a body type distinctly different from either of his children. Thus, there is some room for conjecture that possibly Benjamin and Bertha adopted both of their children. Records of such adoptions are not public, of course.

Also according to Ribowsky, there seems to have been some sort of desire or intent on the part of Bertha and Benjamin to make Shirley into a movie star or a model.[7] But by the spring of 1949, Shirley would have been only 14 or 15 years old, a bit young to be working as a model or actress. This may have been anecdotal information that developed later, however, because on April 20, 1949, Benjamin Spector allegedly killed himself by way of carbon monoxide poisoning.

The death of Benjamin Spector has to be seen as perhaps

---

[7] Shirley's unfulfilled desire for a movie or modeling career, and the fact that she, like Lana Clarkson, was "tall and blonde," along with Phil's sometimes fractious relationship with his sister, may have some psychological significance in the events that were to take place at the castle so many years later; thus, there is at least some possibility that Phil may have projected some of his long-suppressed resentments of Shirley onto Lana, which might stand as a possible theory for what took place.

the pivotal event in the life of Phil Spector—a root cause of much of the psychological trauma that would later seem so evident throughout his life, almost certainly the thing Phil was referring to in his interview with Mick Brown: "something I'd either not accepted, or I'm not prepared to accept, or live with in my life."

The accepted version of this event—accepted by Ribowsky and Brown, among others, that is—is that Benjamin Spector, a unionized "ironworker" (Ribowsky) or "steelworker" (Brown), was under enormous financial stress by the spring of 1949. Ribowsky's version of the event, apparently taken from interviews of acquaintances of Benjamin Spector, is that Phil's father drove toward his job in Brooklyn, stopped short some distance away from a factory where he worked, then ran a hose from his car's exhaust pipe into the front seat of the car. By 9 A.M. on the morning of April 20, 1949, Benjamin Spector was declared dead of carbon monoxide poisoning, a suicide, at 1042 Myrtle Avenue in Brooklyn.

But this version leaves a number of questions unanswered: for one, where is the evidence that Benjamin Spector was under "severe financial distress"? A check of the court records for the Bronx shows that there were no liens or judgments against him at the time of his death, and indeed, as an employed member of a well-paid union, the ironworkers, it seems unlikely that there was much ordinary financial stress. Moreover, the fact that he apparently owned a car, something of a luxury for a resident of mass-transitized New York City in 1949, seems to suggest that Benjamin Spector wasn't anywhere near stone broke.

A second question: why did Benjamin Spector drive all the way to Brooklyn from his residence on Manor Avenue in the Bronx to do himself in? Was there something significant about the location for the suicide—a rather busy intersection? A third question: how was it possible for him to kill himself with carbon monoxide poisoning on a busy street during rush hour without anyone stopping to intervene, especially with the tell-tale hose running from the exhaust pipe? Isn't it possible that the carbon monoxide death occurred somewhere else, and that the car, with his body in it, was moved to the place where he was found? In that case, one might also consider his death a possible homicide, not a suicide; which in turn would raise questions as to his activities in the months or years before his death. If, for example, Ben Spector owed substantial gambling debts, to the mob, say, that might account for both the unusual circumstances of his death and his supposed "severe financial stress." It's worth noting that in later years, Phil Spector often made references to his own fears of organized crime, which otherwise seem to have been more imaginary than anything else.

Unfortunately, at this point, the records on Benjamin Spector's death are very sketchy. The New York Medical Examiner's Office notes only that the cause of death was carbon monoxide poisoning, along with the rather curious time and location of the event, and the information about Bertha as the new widow at the Manor Avenue address in the Bronx. The New York Police Department, which came to the scene when Benjamin was finally noticed by passersby, threw out all its own records of the event decades ago.

If Benjamin Spector wasn't murdered, but *did* commit suicide, why did he do it? That there was "stress" would seem obvious, but what sort of stress if not financial? These are unresolved mysteries, so long after the event that was to shape Phil Spector's life. But based on Phil's own mental torments, one might conjecture that *if* Benjamin Spector was the biological father of his son—and *if* the Benjamin Spector who was in the Brooklyn hospital in 1930 was the same man as Phil's father—there is the possibility of an inherited mental illness, such as schizophrenia and/or bipolar disorder, as Phil himself suggested in his interview with Mick Brown.

Here there are two additional clues to consider: the location of Benjamin Spector's suicide was less than a mile due north of the Brooklyn State Hospital, still the in-patient care facility for New York City's mentally ill in 1949; and the fact that, according to Phil, his older sister Shirley, "tall and blonde" like Lana Clarkson, would, according to both Ribowsky and Brown, spend much of her own adult life in mental institutions.

7

CALIFORNIA DREAMING

The death of Benjamin Spector was a devastating psychological blow to the young Phil. In the portrait drawn by Ribowsky, until the death of his father, Phil—9 years old at the time—was a normal, healthy, outgoing kid with a talent for music, the apple of his father's eye. Then almost overnight, Phil became a weak, asthmatic, withdrawn, and, it appears, angry boy who craved indulgence from adults, and whose fears seemed very nearly pathological.

The death of Phil's father was quickly put into the box of things not talked about in the households of the extended Spector families in the Bronx. Indeed, it wasn't until years later that Phil learned that the official cause of the death had been listed as suicide. It was as if there was something shameful about the tragedy. After the funeral, Ben's body was buried in a Long Island cemetery, under a headstone that read: "TO KNOW HIM WAS TO LOVE HIM," an epigrammatic enigma that seems to have haunted Phil for years afterward.

But the repression of the facts would have long-term consequences on Phil's own mental stability, as the death became more and more a secret obsession. Always there was the question which had no answer: why? Why had his father abandoned him? What was wrong with him, that his father didn't value him enough to go on living? What was the secret about life—or death—that his father had known, but never shared with his son?

These are powerful riddles that affect the unconscious, and left unaddressed, they can seep into everyday behavior,

warping the way a young boy interacts with the world. Often
an abandoned son will internalize the unexpressed emotions
that swirl unspoken around such an event, and begin to feel
estranged. Or, as Phil would put it later to Mick Brown, "I
never fit in . . ."

A few years after the death of Ben Spector, Bertha Spector
decided to break from the ties that held her in the Bronx. Perhaps with an idea of facilitating her daughter Shirley's desire
for a career in movies, Bertha decided to move to Los Angeles, where an uncle in the Spector family had made his own
home some years earlier. Bertha, Shirley and Phil—he'd
given up the Harvey after his father's death—found housing
in a wood-framed fourplex at 602½ Spaulding Avenue, just
south of Melrose Avenue in the Fairfax district of Los Angeles. Bertha, according to Ribowsky, obtained work as a seam-
stress.[8] Money was apparently very tight. It appears that
sister Shirley's ambitions to break into the modeling/acting
field were thwarted, because she eventually found work as a
secretary.

After a short stint at Laurel Elementary School, Phil enrolled at John Burroughs Junior High School, then, in the fall
of 1954, at Fairfax High School.

Changing schools is always traumatic for adolescents,
and when mixed with changing cultures—from the edgier
East Coast neighborhood of the Bronx to the palm-lined
streets of Southern California was a culture shift of the first
magnitude—there are really only two pathways for a new-
comer to take: either dive into the new culture and take it on
as a full participant, or stand back as a loner, adopting a sardonic, hipper-than-thou detachment from the values that the
majority espouses. Phil saw himself as different from his
fellow students—he was poor, most of them were rich; they
drove cars, he had to take the bus; they were wild about

---

[8] At some point, however, Bertha apparently gave up the sewing machine for a sharpened pencil—the court record of a 1958 traffic accident
involving Bertha lists her occupation as a $90-a-week "bookkeeper."

sports, he could care less. He was from New York, they were goofy Californians. Mostly, though, they had fathers and he did not. Phil's defensiveness as a transplant seems apparent from a story he would tell Mick Brown in the November 2002 interview: as a boy, he always brought along a stash of extra Monopoly money when he played the game with other kids. "An extra $100 or $500 and I'd win every time," he told Brown. "Same with the X's and the blanks in Scrabble." If it was all about winning, Phil told Brown, why not do everything possible to win—even if it meant cheating?

But Phil had a yearning to achieve something, some sort of distinction that would validate his differences in more dramatic ways. In junior high school he had begun trying to learn the guitar. Here was something that was cool, that not everybody could do, that promised to mark him as an *artiste*, thereby justifying his disinterest in malt shops, football scores and jalopies. By the time he was in high school, Phil was an accomplished guitarist, drawn to the complicated rhythms and leads of jazz. In junior high school he met and befriended Marshall Lieb, the son of a wealthy Los Angeles car dealer. Like Phil, Marshall was interested in making music; the two took guitar lessons together from a teacher in Hollywood. But where Marshall was tall, muscular and handsome, Phil was short and skinny, with a disappearing chin and an adenoidal voice; worse, he was already beginning to lose his hair. While Marshall had the potential of being an on-stage performer, even Phil realized that he himself was hardly the image of a fifties rocker.

Few of his fellow students knew or cared about Phil's talent for the six-stringed instrument. Caught up in their own social circles, if they thought about Phil at all, it was as a sort of early-day dweeb—not exactly a nerd, but someone who was outside the social mainstream, and therefore, not worth paying much attention to. Singer Bobby Sheen, who would later perform for Phil as "Bob B. Soxx" and who knew him slightly when both were in school, told Ribowsky that in those days he'd thought of Phil as a "doofus."

And here Phil's alienation, his estrangement, came to the

fore. As an outsider, his quick wit often segued into a smart
mouth. As Lieb put it later, to Ribowsky,[9] "Someone would
say something to Phillip and he'd mouth right back. That
would instigate a problem, and then it would be, 'Marsh!'
and I'd have to turn around from what I was doing and go
bail him out. . . . I was really his first bodyguard, when you
think about it."

This would be a pattern that would be repeated for decades after Fairfax—Phil's habitual reliance on others to
fight his battles for him. Sometimes, in fact, even after he
was a successful music producer, Phil would pick a fight
with someone, then call in his bodyguards to intimidate the
opposition. At one point, in fact, while he was producing the
Ramones, Phil was reputed to have told Joey Ramone, "My
bodyguards want to fight your bodyguards." Here it seems
obvious that it wasn't the prospect of combat that Phil relished as much as the demonstration of control over the instrument of physical force, a sort of projection of power that
took the place of actual physical prowess; this was a theme
that ran through Phil's life right up until the night of February 2, 2003, as we shall see.

Besides having a smart mouth, Phil was also very intelligent, probably brighter than most of his high school contemporaries. But as the youngest in a household that was barely
making ends meet, the idea of college was something of a
fantasy. Who could afford it? Bertha pressed her son to consider business as a career, or even better, something in the
government, which promised financial stability.

When Phil was in high school, the Spectors moved to a
new apartment, this one at 726 North Hayworth Avenue, just
north of Melrose Avenue about five blocks away from
Spaulding. It appears that this was about the time that Bertha
began her new job as a bookkeeper; likewise, it appears that

---

[9] Marshall Lieb went on to a career as a successful businessman. He
died in March of 2002, eleven months before his old friend Phil was arrested in connection with the death of Lana Clarkson.

sister Shirley found her own apartment around the same time.

Lieb would later recall for Ribowsky, as would others, that Phil's life with his mother was less than tranquil. Both tended to be loud and confrontational, adept at using passive-aggressive techniques on the other. Visitors to the household recalled many arguments, often punctuated by slamming doors as one or the other of the combatants withdrew in a huff. There was little affection demonstrated. "The most vivid memories I have of them," Lieb would later tell Ribowsky, "was just a lot of bitterness, a lot of intolerant conversation. I didn't see a lot of endearment. I never really had the feeling of any kind of togetherness among the three of them."

Bertha tended to be particularly controlling of her son, wanting to know where he was going at all times; others recalled that both Bertha and Shirley were famous for tracking Phil down by telephone, then demanding that he come home immediately. The general impression among those who knew the family was that Phil was under his mother's thumb. "To be honest, I thought of him as sort of a momma's boy," Annette Kleinbard, who would later achieve her own fame in music, recalled.[10]

When Phil was a junior at Fairfax, he began a relationship with a sophomore at the school, Donna Kass, who was Annette Kleinbard's best friend. Donna was attracted to Phil precisely because of his status as an outsider. In Donna's eyes, Phil's non-conformism seemed to indicate some sort of genius. Donna's mother didn't think much of Phil, however. "My mother always felt Phil was crazy," she told Ribowsky. "She thought that some day he would end up committing suicide."

---

[10] Annette Kleinbard, who would later change her name to Carol Connors and gain fame as an Oscar-winning songwriter for the theme "Gonna Fly Now," from the movie *Rocky*, graciously provided an interview to the author, in which she confirmed many of the assertions first published in Ribowsky's unauthorized biography of Phil.

Whether this was some sort of spillover from rumors about Ben's demise wasn't clear; but Phil was not the run-of-the-mill Fairfax student, that was obvious. From being an introvert with most fellow students, Phil went over to the other side with Donna, tending to try to dominate her with his intellect and his conversation; it was as if, realizing that he couldn't impress anyone else, he put all of his effort into trying to control his 15-year-old girlfriend.

Bertha was jealous of Phil's attention to her, Donna told Ribowsky.

"Phil was very insecure," Donna said. "And the reason was his father. He told me his father died of a heart attack, but I found out that was not true." Donna said she couldn't remember how she discovered the truth, but that she thought Phil carried his father's suicide as "a horrible stigma."

Despite his mother's insistence that he prepare himself to earn a living, Phil found himself focusing more and more on music as his years in high school progressed. He wanted to be a jazz guitarist—not for Phil was the simple three-chord strumming that most of his contemporaries were practicing. Phil wanted to push the line on his music, stand out from the crowd, break down barriers of convention.

In the afternoons and evenings, Phil found himself drawn to the Lieb home, not far from Fairfax High School, where he and Marshall fooled around with the Lieb family piano, trying to work out new songs. Eventually they joined another budding musician, Michael Spencer, who had a well-developed background in classical music; it was Spencer's notion that the themes of classical music could be threaded into mainstream pop. Though Phil was normally introverted, Spencer would later recall, his aggressiveness would come out when he played the guitar; it was as if the guitar were his weapon against the world.

At night, though, Phil found himself drawn to a different type of music—rhythm and blues. The mid- to late fifties was a sort of a special era for black musicians, just before the dawn when African-American music would go mainstream, a time when jazz and R & B flowed together in the primordial mix that would soon be known as rock-and-roll.

"Sitting cross-legged on his bed, he cradled the guitar and played it to the sound of a transistor radio,"[11] Ribowsky wrote in *He's a Rebel*, "tuned to a jazz or black music station."

At the time in Los Angeles, there were several low-wattage Los Angeles stations that catered to black R & B audiences. One, KFOX, featured a show by Johnny Otis. Otis was a band leader and nightclub owner in Los Angeles who later became a highly successful disk jockey. Otis' show featured such artists as Little Willie John, Jackie Wilson, Big Mama Thornton, Etta James, and the Robins, who later became the Coasters. Phil was entranced by the power and the raw emotion of the music, which made most popular tunes broadcast on white-dominated stations seem simply sappy.

Today, almost half-a-century later, people have forgotten the controversies that attended the birth of rock-and-roll, and the relation of the music to the breaking down of three centuries' worth of racial barriers. There was, in much of the country, particularly in the South, the notion that rock-and-roll was a corruption of white youth by black mores. The sexual suggestiveness of rock-and-roll, and the implied repudiation of authority, gave many church-going people the darkest sort of fears about desegregation—read *miscegenation*. The Little Rock school integration drama was in the air, and its double meaning as a political crisis point, and its use as a symbol standing for the liberation of young people from outworn often racist traditions, inflamed people on all sides.

---

[11] This is probably a simplification; it isn't likely that Phil learned to play his guitar to the music coming from a transistor radio, since the first mass-production of the transistor radio didn't take place until 1957, and didn't become commonplace until around 1959. However, the arrival of the transistor radio would later play an enormously important role in Phil Spector's success as a music producer, as we shall see.

In finding a way to introduce African-American music into the popular music mainstream, the early pioneers of rock-and-roll, such as Alan Freed, were igniting a cultural revolution. Phil, the outsider, the weirdo of Fairfax High, was caught up in the possibilities of the sea change. Eventually, Phil would climb to the top of the rock-and-roll mountain and dominate it—at least until another cultural earthquake, called the War in Vietnam, came to throw him off.

TO KNOW HIM

8

RADIO WAVES

The era between the end of World War II and the rise of television a decade later was probably the golden age of radio. After all the years of privation during the Depression and the sacrifices required by war, America was at last suffused with peace and prosperity. The first years of the Pax Americana were at hand, with all the nation's factories humming, nearly full employment, and a Baby Boom on the way.

By this time, virtually every American home had a radio, or even several. As a mass culture entertainment center, the large floor-model radio quickly assumed a place of primacy in living rooms across the nation, the purveyor of everything from music, comedy, action-adventure, soap opera, news— in fact, all manner of culture for brows high and low. Because of frequency limits, the number of channels for this vast dissemination of culture was itself limited, and the radio had to serve a wide audience. Music was therefore mainstream—big band music, leavened with pop stars, sandwiched around *The Lone Ranger*, *The Jack Benny Show*, *Fibber McGee & Molly*, *Kukla, Fran and Ollie*, or sports broadcasts, all tied together by news feed from New York, Washington and local stations. Musical tastes were therefore much more homogenous than what would be experienced later. More to the point, popular music was infused with romantic themes, packed with imagery suggesting love, marriage, home life—all the ideals that had been yearned for during a terrible depression, followed by a cataclysmic war.

The driving sexual energy of rock-and-roll was completely absent.

The comparatively narrow bandwidth of broadcast culture rewarded performers and songwriters who could keep to the center, where the mass appeal was widest. Thus, by 1952, about the time that Bertha, Shirley and Phil had moved to Los Angeles, the biggest popular music hits included singers like Nat "King" Cole, with "Unforgettable," Frankie Laine's "High Noon," Rosemary Clooney with "Blues in the Night," and Doris Day's "When I Fall in Love." The Four Aces, with "Heart and Soul," along with Nat Cole, represented a stylized version of African-American singing that was very nearly white in its arrangement, however smooth and melodic.

Throughout most of the early 1950s, in fact, popular music tended to be mid-road, and certainly not controversial. But the world began to turn in 1955, when rock-and-roll finally began to make commercial inroads. Thus, 1955's greatest hits compiled by *Billboard* magazine include such standard performers as the McGuire Sisters' "Sincerely," the Four Aces' "Love Is a Many Splendored Thing," "Unchained Melody" by Les Baxter, along with the first rock-and-roll hit to be included in the magazine's annual rankings: "(We're Gonna) Rock Around the Clock," by Bill Haley and the Comets.

For someone accustomed to listening to popular music over the radio while waiting to get a weekly haircut at a local barber shop, the wild guitar riff in "Rock Around the Clock," along with the driving bass beat, probably seemed like the end of the world, a musical expression of drugged-out psychomania. It was hard for people used to crooners crooning or warblers warbling to fathom. Whatever its origins, it was swiftly repudiated by the mainstream. To admit that one liked it was the same as confessing that one had a screw loose. Then, "Crazy, man," may have been a watchword among off-center beatniks, but to most of America, it said it all.

The advent of rock-and-roll was the inevitable outgrowth

of a demographic factor that was little understood at the time—namely, the arrival as consumers of a large cohort of teenagers and near-teens, the front end of the Baby Boom. In contrast to their parents, who had grown up during the money-scarce Depression, these new teens were the first beneficiaries of the material blessings of the Pax Americana. They had money to spend, and were gaining their first measure of economic autonomy just as the cornucopia of consumer goods (and advertising) that resulted from the post-war boom was opening up. Not the least of these new consumer goodies was the automobile. By the mid-1950s, the surplus of cars in the nation drove prices downward, putting transportation independence within reach of teenagers for the first time. And many of the cars sold to teenagers, while "pre-owned," contained radios.

It wasn't very long before the radio stations realized that the middle-of-the-road fare they had offered audiences for the better part of thirty years simply wasn't going to attract the emerging teenage market, with all of its disposable income. As a result, many stations began selecting music that appealed to teenage listeners, forgoing the old standards of the McGuire Sisters, Doris Day, Nat Cole or the Four Aces. In a word, the radio market for the first time became segmented, just about the same time that car radios began arriving with "pre-sets," buttons used to instantly tune to the favored frequency. As the market became segmented, it also became obvious the growth potential for sales of products—from music to pimple cream—to teenagers was enormous.

Almost as important, the autonomy afforded to this emerging market by the car fueled a sense of separateness among teenagers, with its resulting impact on cultural mores. Racial attitudes, for example, that might have been more rigidly enforced in the twenties, thirties and forties began to loosen in the 1950s. Where jazz was eschewed by the churchgoing mainstream in the 1920s as morally corrupting, by the 1950s, music by African-Americans, even that originally germinated out of rhythm and blues, was moving into marketing center, in large part because of teenage preferences.

By 1955, for example, while *Billboard*'s list of the top hits represented mainstream music (with the exception of "Rock Around the Clock"), the teenaged market was already focused on such non-*Billboard* hits as "Earth Angel," by the Penguins, "Only You" by the Platters, and "Maybellene" by Chuck Berry. Significantly, Fats Domino's "Ain't That a Shame" was "covered" by Pat Boone in a white-toned version. Boone's cover made the *Billboard* list, Domino's did not.

The year 1955 also foreshadowed a split in rock-and-roll itself, this between crooning rockers and the beat-heavy sound, with its emphasis on drums and bass. The crooners, typified by the Platters, soon gave rise to the mixed black–white groups later called doo-wop: Little Anthony and the Imperials, the Diamonds, the Crests, the Elegants, Dion and the Belmonts, and Frankie Lymon and the Teenagers, among others. The other emerging side was the harder rock of Buddy Holly, Eddie Cochran, Jerry Lee Lewis, Danny and the Juniors or Chuck Berry, where the driving beat presaged a later generation's heavy metal. Sandwiched around these were novelty acts like the Coasters, whose "Yakety Yak" provided a musical yuk at authority.

Faced with the rise in popularity of black and mixed-race groups among the teenage market, record labels sought to cash in by "covering" many of the songs with performances by white singers. The idea was that those who didn't want to buy the records of black performers could get the same—or somewhat similar—product from a "safe" white artist. Thus Pat Boone and Gale Storm both "covered" Fats Domino's hits in 1955, a practice that would grow throughout the rest of the 1950s.

As Phil Spector came of age, then, in the middle 1950s, the popular music scene was in a state of tremendous flux, with new opportunities opening for those who could capture the attention of the holy marketing grail of the teen audience, the leading edge of a cultural revolution that upset a generation's worth of assumptions about race, sex, authority and aesthetics.

9

DON'T BE LATE IN '58

In the spring of 1957, Phil and his guitar took the stage at Fairfax High School's auditorium for the annual school talent show. Later, there would be two versions of what happened, one recounted by Ribowsky, and another by Los Angeles writer and humorist Burt Prelutsky, who was actually there.

In Ribowsky's version, a confident Phil "could actually swagger" up onto the stage to play and sing Lonnie Donegan's "Rock Island Line." "It surprised nobody that Spector won the contest," Ribowsky reported.

That wasn't the way Prelutsky remembered it, however. In a letter to the editor of the *Los Angeles Times*, published in the aftermath of the Lana Clarkson shooting, Prelutsky said he blamed himself, along with all the others in the audience that day, for Phil's legal predicament. If only they hadn't encouraged him, Prelutsky said, with his tongue firmly planted in his cheek, maybe none of the events at the castle ever would have happened.

"I hold myself partially to blame for Phil Spector's current problems," Prelutsky wrote. "As a classmate of Phil's, I was in the audience the first time he performed at a school assembly. We sat, stunned, as he strummed on his guitar and sang. The idea that anyone with that nasal, New York wheeze would sing outside the confines of his shower redefined chutzpah for us. The end of his performance was greeted by absolute silence. After a few moments, moved by compassion for a fellow human being, my friend and I started to applaud. Soon the rest of the student body joined in. To our collective horror, this so buoyed Phil's spirit that he did an encore . . . If my pal and I hadn't encouraged Phil that fateful day, I find myself wondering if he might not have become an accountant and been spared the drugs, booze and now his arrest for murder. At the very least, we'd have been spared that really awful encore!"

Prelutsky was joking, right? No, he said later in an interview. Well, not really. Phil's singing was truly dreadful, Prelutsky said. Of course, this *was* 1957, years before the nasal wheezing of someone who took the name Bob Dylan would become popular.

And it isn't likely that the applause, whether a gesture of compassion or appreciation, really had that much to do with Phil's life choices. By 1957, Phil was already determined to make his mark in music, if he could only find the way in.

By his senior year in high school, Phil was playing in several teen bands that had begun to spring up as the rock-and-roll revolution caught on, usually joined by Marshall Lieb, Michael Spencer and others from Fairfax. Phil and his pals often practiced in his girlfriend Donna Kass' garage, where Donna's best friend, Annette Kleinbard, was also often present. These groups, like many teen bands, were constantly forming and reforming, picking up gigs at parties, dances, bowling alleys and the like. The money earned was very small—sometimes not even enough to pay for the gas to get there, Lieb later told Ribowsky. One such gig took place at El Monte Legion Stadium ("Be there or be square!"), then a popular venue for quasi-professional performers; according to Ribowsky, Phil and his buddies played in a show sponsored by the fabled Johnny Otis himself.

But by the spring of 1957, as he graduated from Fairfax, Phil knew he was going to have to get ready to earn a living. That fall, he enrolled at Los Angeles City College with Marshall Lieb. According to some accounts, Phil decided to take business courses, while in others he decided to learn court reporting. At least one account has Phil toying with the idea of becoming an official U.N. stenographer, which would combine the court reporting with the French his mother had tried to teach him. In the afternoons, to practice his skills, Phil would transcribe the broadcast of Dick Clark's televised rock-and-roll show, according to Ribowsky. He might wind up getting stuck in a courtroom or a government hearing room for the rest of his life, but even if that's what happened, he had no intention of giving up his ambition to be a star.

By the spring of 1958, popular music had reached the peak of its schizophrenic state, a maelstrom of styles that embraced such pre–rock-and-roll stalwarts as the McGuire Sisters, with "Sugartime," The Tommy Dorsey Band's "Tea For Two," or Tommy Edwards' "It's All in the Game," along with crooners like Frank Sinatra, with "Witchcraft," or Connie Francis' "Who's Sorry Now." Then there was the driving teen beat of Danny and the Juniors' "At the Hop," Eddie Cochran's "Summertime Blues," and "Maybe Baby" by Buddy Holly and the Crickets. Elvis Presley—"Elvis the Pelvis," some called him at the time, the quintessential fusion of black and white—had arrived on the scene as the virtual embodiment of the bad boy of rock-and-roll. Instrumentals were gaining in popularity, such as the Champs' "Tequila," which bespoke a wry sort of anti-authoritarianism savored by teenagers trying their wings. In the sidecar with the instrumentals, which would include Duane Eddy's weirdly twanging "Rebel-'Rouser," were novelty songs calculated to amuse the listener, like Sheb Wooley's "Purple People Eater," or the Chipmunks' "Chipmunk Song," in which the voices of the singers were speeded up to sound like, well, furry little rodents, that is, if they sang, and did it in English.

Later, 1958 would probably stand as one of the most prolific years for popular music hits, with more songs recorded in this year making it to the golden oldies' list than any other. Part of this was due to the explosion in revenue that the emerging teen market was experiencing: the front edge of the Baby Boom had arrived at the age where their discretionary spending was assuming significant proportions, and many of them were spending the money on records. In addition, the technology of the phonograph had changed—old 78 revolutions-per-minute records, the mainstay of the industry for decades, were giving way to smaller 45 revolutions-per-minute disks, which were far less expensive to produce and ship. That made the product more affordable for the emerging market. For most of the 1950s and well into the 1960s, 45-rpm records sold for just less than a dollar each.

With the market in such a state of flux, the opportunity for new, untested musicians to produce a hit was greater than it had ever been in the past, or probably would be in the future. No one who knew anything about the market could say for sure what would sell, and what would not; in effect, all bets were off. Labels were willing to take a chance on just about anyone, because, who knew?

That spring, Phil and Marshall Lieb were determined to try to crash the party with their own record. In May, Phil dropped in at Gold Star, a recording studio on Vine Street near Hollywood Boulevard. The studio, established in 1950 by Stan Ross and Dave Gold, had peculiar acoustics, primarily from the fact that the place had a fourteen-foot ceiling left over from its prior incarnation as a retail store. Most studios had twenty-foot ceilings. The lower ceiling caused sound to do strange things at Gold Star. That meant the music had to be recorded, then manipulated in an echo chamber, which turned out to be the studio's bathroom.

Gold Star co-owner Ross had come to know Phil over the preceding year, as Phil dropped around every so often to watch recording sessions. Ross was also a graduate of Fairfax. Phil kept pestering Ross to give him some studio time, but Ross wouldn't do it. Once the word got out that Gold Star was giving its services away for free, the studio would be inundated with wannabes.

It's only $15 an hour, Ross kept telling Phil; surely he could find a way to dredge up that little money, if he wanted to make a record so bad. Phil didn't want only one hour, though; for what he had in mind, he guessed at least two hours would be needed.

Money for the Spectors was always in short supply. Just a few weeks earlier, Bertha had been in a car wreck. Driving eastbound on Clinton Street, her 1952 Dodge collided with a new Ford driven by a man named Robert Levine. It appears from the court records that Bertha was injured to the extent that she was unable to work, at least for a while. Two months later she sued Levine, asking for $15,000 for "severe pain and mental anguish." Bertha was listed as a bookkeeper earning $90 a week, and her lawyer asserted that she had been unable to work since the May 14, 1958, accident.

As it happened, this was the second car wreck involving the Spector family in less than a year. In July of 1957, Phil's sister Shirley was riding in a car driven by one Gloria Aron. As Aron approached a stop-sign near Fourth Street and Wilton Place in Hollywood, a car driven by a man identified as J. R. Carlson rolled through the intersection, striking Gloria's car in the left side. Shirley, identified as a $425-a-month secretary in the lawsuit, was ejected from the car by the force of the collision. The following month she sued her fellow secretary Gloria, Carlson and Carlson's employer, claiming "serious injury to her body and nerves." She wanted the defendants to pay her $25,000. The lawsuits, both of them, dragged on for the rest of 1957 and well into 1958.

So here was Phil, trying to raise money for a recording session, with both of the significant women in his life involved in litigation over their respective car wrecks. It was hardly like either Bertha or Shirley could afford to waste money on Phil's fantasy of becoming a big-time rock-and-roll star.

Nevertheless, Phil was able to wheedle $10 from Bertha, and of course, Marshall was good for ten, with his car-dealer father. Phil hit up another school pal, basso Harvey Goldstein, who had sung with them at various gigs in the past, and he put in $10. Then he thought of his girlfriend Donna's best friend, Annette Kleinbard. Phil knew Annette loved to sing—in fact she was a naturally gifted soprano—and he thought he might be able to convince Annette to kick in 10 bucks if he promised her she could participate. The record Phil wanted to make was one of his own original song,

"Don't You Worry My Little Pet," a sort of Chuck Berry–esque rock ditty that would call for a minimal background contribution from Annette. Phil's idea was to get the song recorded in the studio, then to play around with the recording levels and overdubbing to bring out a lead. Lassoing Annette, who was just finishing her junior year in high school, for her $10 was almost an afterthought, sort of an insurance policy in case the session ran slightly longer than two hours.

Years later, Annette—by that time known as Carol Connors, with her own successful career as a songwriter and singer well established—could look back on the scene with a sort of wry wistfulness.

"He asked me if I had ten dollars," she recalled. "And I went, 'I don't have ten cents!' And he said, 'Well, if you can get together ten dollars, you can come cut a record with us.'

"So I went home to my mom and dad, because remember, I used to sing all the time. And I said to my parents, 'May I have ten dollars?' And my mother said, 'Go do your homework!' And remember, this was when ten dollars—that was a lot of money then. And we were poor."

Carol's father was a man named Julius Kleinbard, who had emigrated from Poland around the turn of the century, and then had become a racing jockey. "He was very handsome, a very dapper young man," Carol would recall of her father, "looked a little like Bing Crosby." Throughout the 1920s and 1930s, Julius raced Thoroughbreds at Saratoga, Pimlico, Hialeah, all the East Coast tracks. In 1938, he returned to Poland and married Carol's mother, Gail. The couple got out of Poland the year before Hitler's invasion started World War II.

But once back in America, Gail convinced her new husband to stop racing—she was afraid he might get hurt. Carol was born several years later, just before America entered the war. But Julius had never quite given up his sporting nature, and when his 16-year-old daughter—precocious by almost any standard—asked him for the money after the turndown from her mother, she thought her father might be willing to take a gamble.

"So I went to my dad and said, 'Dad, I've got to get this ten dollars. If you give me ten dollars, we're going to have the number one record in the world, I'm going to buy you a racehorse, we're going to be rich, we're going to move, please tell Mom to give me the ten dollars.' 'No! Go do your homework.'"

But Annette persisted, and eventually wore both her parents down. They gave her the $10, and Annette returned to Phil with the money.

On May 20, 1958, Phil, Marshall, Harvey Goldstein and Annette went to Gold Star Studios, where Phil solemnly laid out the cash for two hours of recording time. Then they started in on "Don't You Worry My Little Pet."

"A dreadful song!" Carol said later. "As a songwriter I can say that. But—my voice kept cutting through. Because my part was [singing it], 'You'll think of me, yes you will.' And I was the only girl."

Phil and Marshall's idea in making their record was to fool the audience into believing that the group was larger than they actually were, in part by taking a tape they had previously made of the song, probably recorded in Donna Kass' garage, then playing it over the studio sound system back to the performers, who would then record a new track on top. Since they had no drummer, he and Marshall had to simulate the percussion part by beating a telephone book with a brush. Later, Phil would insist on adding another guitar and additional background "do-wah-dos." It was tricky, especially the timing, and Phil kept running between the guitar, the piano, and the studio control panel trying to get everything in sync. Ross was willing to try this melange style of making a record, although it was foreign to his experience. He was amused at Phil's take-charge insistence on how things should be.

After spending the two hours on "Don't You Worry My Little Pet," Ross transferred the final overdubbed result from the tape to an acetate, a master copy, and gave it to Phil. The foursome left the studio, then Marshall and Phil went to a nearby record store. There they told the clerk that they'd just made a record. So what? the clerk yawned. Phil and Marshall realized that making a record was one thing, selling it quite another.

Eventually, Phil zeroed in on another teen gigger, Donnie Kartoon, who happened to live next door to the co-owner of a record label, Lew Bedell. Phil pestered Kartoon for an introduction to Bedell. Bedell agreed to check Phil and Marshall's record out, so Kartoon took Phil to Bedell's office at Era Records in Hollywood. At the time, Bedell was riding pretty high in the pop music business, having recently had a number one hit with Gogi Grant's "The Wayward Wind."

Ribowsky would later track down Kartoon to get his version of the historic encounter.

"I took Phil down there," Kartoon said, "and as soon as we got to the reception window, he tried to ace me out." Kartoon told Ribowsky that Phil wanted him to wait outside while he went in to see the big man himself. Phil told the receptionist to announce him. The receptionist told Phil she'd never heard of him.

At that point, according to Kartoon, he stepped forward and identified himself. His name seemed to be the magic word, because the receptionist waved them in.

In his office, Bedell took the master copy of "Don't You Worry My Little Pet" and played it. Then he called in his co-owner, Herb Newman. The two men played the recording numerous times as Phil got increasingly upset by the machine's inadequacy and rough treatment of his product. Finally Phil could stand it no longer, and told the two men that their phonograph was out of adjustment, that it was playing the song too slow.

Phil's outburst impressed the two moguls. It apparently helped that Phil was Jewish. "I liked him," Bedell told Ribowsky. "I liked all Jewish kids."

After discussing the matter for a bit, Bedell and Newman decided to take a flyer on the foursome. They offered Phil and his co-recorders a "lease of master" agreement, in effect gaining control of the master recording of "Don't You Worry My Little Pet" for a nominal amount. Besides the demo they'd just heard, Bedell and Newman agreed to underwrite recording sessions for three more sides. If the records sold—that is, if the distributors could find a market for them—the four performing members would split a royalty rate of one-and-a-half cents for each record sold. As a songwriter, though, Phil would also get an additional royalty for the license of his copyright.

On July 3, 1958, the four teens signed the "lease of master" agreement with Bedell and Newman. Because the members of the as-yet-unnamed group were under legal age, they had to get court approval of the document before it became binding. In the meantime, however, Bedell and Newman arranged for more studio time at Gold Star. At that point, the group had to come up with a name. Harvey Goldstein, in what, besides his initial $10 seems to have been his major contribution, suggested the Teddy Bears. At the time, Elvis Presley's song "(Let Me Be Your) Teddy Bear" was popular.

The next week, the four teenagers returned to Gold Star, this time with the intent of recording a new song to occupy the flip side of "Don't You Worry My Little Pet." Bedell chose an Era-owned ballad, "Wonderful, Loveable You." The session for the new song did not go smoothly. Bedell and Newman tried to control the production, but Phil kept elbowing them out of the way. Although they had been booked for only an hour, at the end of two hours the song still wasn't done. Phil and Marshall were still fooling around with their overdubbing tricks. Bedell and Newman were disgusted.

Whether because of this frustrating experience—caused in part by the acceptance of the song from Bedell and Newman's own stockpile of tunes—or because it had been something in his mind all along, Phil by this time had decided to try out another of his own originals.

Carol Connors (Annette Kleinbard) later remembered that the new song seemed to be in Phil's mind almost from the instant they'd finished "Don't You Worry My Little Pet" nearly a month-and-a-half earlier. After that session, she recalled, Phil had told her that he loved her voice, and that he intended to write a song that would feature it.

At some point, apparently in early June of 1958, Phil called Annette at home.

"About a week or two later [after recording 'Don't You Worry My Little Pet'] he called me up at night," Carol recalled. "And I'm doing my homework, just like my mother wanted. And he said, 'I gotta play you something.' I went, 'Okay.' I was really accommodating. And he played me this song, 'To Know Him Is to Love Him,' over the phone, cupping it, playing the guitar, him singing, and it was pretty good. And he says, 'What do you think?' And I went, 'I guess it's okay.' And he says, 'Come over to Marshall's house. Meet me at my house first.' I had to take a bus. So I met him at his house, which was on this side of Fairfax High School. And Marshall's was on the other side. And then we rehearsed in Marshall's garage. And I learned 'To Know Him Is to Love Him.' I don't remember the time frame, but very shortly after that, we went in to cut the song."

Ribowsky sheds some additional light on this. According to his version of the events, the song was to have been recorded on the same day that the quartet tried to make "Wonderful, Loveable You," but the inability to finish that song in one hour made it impossible to start in on "To Know Him Is to Love Him." After two frustrating hours on "Wonderful, Loveable You," Bedell called things off for the day. By then he and Newman were beginning to regret getting tied up with Phil.

The following week, still in July, three of the Teddy Bears returned to Gold Star to finish the work on "Wonderful, Loveable You." Harvey Goldstein was absent; he had to fulfill an Army Reserve commitment. The three Teddys decided to go on without him, and in fact, Phil and Marshall, at least, decided to dispense with Harvey altogether. All of a sudden, Goldstein was out of the group he'd helped to form, and even named. "I wasn't in on it," Carol said later. "I was just a kid! The decisions were not made by me, trust me, they were made by Phil and Marshall."

By now Bedell and Newman decided the telephone-book drumming just wasn't working. They induced Phil and

Marshall to find a drummer, and in turn they recruited Sammy Nelson, who would later record his own drum hit, "Teen Beat," as Sandy Nelson. Newman and Bedell didn't think much of Nelson's effort. It was difficult, with all the piped-in overlays that Phil and Marshall kept trying to weave into the ballad, and took almost an hour-and-a-half. By then Newman and Bedell had had it. They told Ross to cut the Teddy Bears off after two hours. Then they left the studio, doubtless thinking that, in the rock music business, you win some, you lose some.

With thirty minutes left in the session, Phil and Marshall abandoned "Wonderful, Loveable You." They turned instead to "To Know Him Is to Love Him."

Annette sang the lead, and for the first time her sweet voice took over.

"To know, know, know him," she sang, "is to love, love, love him . . . "

Well, was this sappy, or what? But the arrangement composed by Phil, taken in part, according to Carol Connors, from a composition by Wagner, somehow worked. By far the best part of the song was Annette's crystalline voice, which, for the first time in any of the Teddy Bears' efforts, was featured. "To know, know, know him, is to love, love, love him, and I do," she sang, and then Phil and Marshall chimed in on background, "And I do and I do and I do."

The arrangement of the song had a hook midway through, where Annette's voice climbed the ladder in a sort of primal angst, pinpointed by an unusual ninth chord that gave it a tone of melancholy pain: "Why can't he see? How blind can he be?"

After going through Annette's part twice, Phil and Marshall were running out of time. Ross, the Gold Star owner, had already been told to cut the Teddy Bears off from further studio minutes. Phil and Marshall rushed around, overdubbing a guitar, a piano, Nelson's drumming, and their own background vocals. Marshall later told Ribowsky that the whole thing was planned, but the recording quality of the song has always been beside the point. Rough-sounding or not, "To Know Him Is to Love Him" spoke directly to the freshness of unrequited teenage love.

Now, with three songs on tape—"Don't You Worry My Little Pet," "Wonderful, Loveable You," and the Spector-written "To Know Him Is to Love Him," Era Records finally had a product it could take to market. On August 1, 1958, Bedell and Newman pressed 500 copies of the first Teddy Bears record, on a label, Doré, named for Bedell's son. Side A was "Don't You Worry My Little Pet," Side B, "To Know Him Is to Love Him." Neither Bedell nor Newman had any idea which side would play. The 500 copies went to a distributor, and the two impresarios sat back to see what would happen.

But first everything had to be made legal.

10
PAYOLA

On August 14, 1958, Bedell, Newman, their lawyer Lee
Perkal, the four Teddy Bears (Goldstein hadn't gotten the
word yet) and their parents gathered in the courtroom of Los
Angeles County Superior Court Judge Harold Schweitzer.
Under Section 36 of the California Civil Code, minors were
not permitted to make employment agreements in the entertainment industry without a court's approval. This was the
so-called Jackie Coogan law, enacted after the child star's
handlers had allegedly looted all or most of his earnings as a
minor.

Schweitzer noted the presence of all of the Teddy Bears'
parents: Mack H. and Dorothy Goldstein, Leonard and Belle
Lieb, Julius and Gail Kleinbard, and Bertha Spector. Also
present were the four Teddy Bears themselves. "All are
sworn to testify," the court file reported.[12]

But this hearing only took place after an earlier get-
together in the Era offices. Ribowsky later quoted the colorful Bedell: "I had all these people in my office before we
went to the court, all their parents and everybody. I said,
'Look, if I'm gonna have any *tsouris* [Yiddish for *trouble* or
grief or *scene*] down there, I don't wanna even do this thing.'
And they said, 'Don't worry.' And we got down there and

---

[12] The court record lists the birthdates of the four Teddy Bears, including the date of December 26, 1939, for Harvey Phillip Spector, making
him 18 at the time.

there was nothing but *tsouris*, everybody talking all at the
same time. I said to the judge, 'Do me a favor. Just ask 'em
if they want to sign. If they do, fine. If not . . .' He did and
they said, 'Yes.' And that was it."

In approving the agreement for the "master lease" of the
four sides signed the month before, Schweitzer also ordered
that there should be no assignment of the contract to any
other party without his approval. That way, Era couldn't
dump the contract on some other entity that might not have
the wherewithal to make good on it. Nor could the company
itself change owners without the court's approval. If Era
went bust, the court could invalidate the contract. As for any
money earned by the sale of any records, "There shall be no
distribution of any funds to said minors until an order of the
court be made therefor, all payments from ERA Records
Inc. to said minors pursuant to the contracts approved herein
shall be made into a trust account designated as such on behalf of said minors and no such payments made from said
account until court approves and orders such."

Schweitzer ordered Era to impound any royalties, and to
return to the court "when sufficient royalties have accumulated." In other words, Era had to keep its own hands off any
money until the court said otherwise.

Thus legalized, the Teddy Bears went out into the world
to make their fortune.

But at first, no one seemed interested in the Teddy Bears or
their record. A Los Angeles disk jockey for KFWB, B.
Mitchell Reid, listened to the record and decided the A side,
"Don't You Worry My Little Pet," wasn't going to make it.
He flipped the record over and put the B side, "To Know
Him Is to Love Him," on the air. Los Angeles yawned. B.
Mitchell Reid shrugged.

While the song was generally seen as a portrayal of unrequited teenage love, the four Teddy Bears knew better. In
fact, they all knew the story of how Phil had come to write
the song—while lying in bed one night, obsessing on his father's epitaph, the idea had come to him. Like most of those

who were Phil's closest friends back in those years, Carol Connors later came to perceive that the death of Benjamin Spector was the unhealed, perhaps unhealable wound of Phil's life.

"Well, I think that it damaged him," Carol said later. "I think that he probably loved his father a lot, and you know, he [Phil] was young at the time, when it happened. And I think it always left a mark, for the rest of his life, that his father had done this. But then, to write this beautiful song, which, by the way, some of it is based on a Wagnerian opera, I think that it was kind of a tribute to his father. You look at the words, of course, every kid in America thought it was about unrequited love."

But when the words are examined from an abandoned child's point of view, the song takes on a completely different meaning, and in fact, stands as a palpable yearning for the father Phil missed so much. The words are almost a plea for his father to come back, to recognize him, to validate him:

Why can't he see, how blind can he be?
Someday he'll see that he was meant for me . . .

By early September of 1958, Bedell and Newman had grown frustrated that the record wasn't moving. They kept trying to pump it in the LA market, and cajoled the Teddy Bears to call their friends to pepper the radio stations with requests for it, but still nothing happened.

Then, it appears, someone, somewhere, decided to take more direct action.

Later, after the so-called "payola scandal" of the late fifties and early sixties had been aired out before a congressional committee and in the public prints, no one pointed to "To Know Him Is to Love Him" as an example of the nefarious practice. But the circumstances of the record's breakthrough suggest that it was a viable candidate for a prosecution exhibit.

Once again, the legend of Phil Spector has it one way, and the facts another.

According to the legend, the big break on "To Know Him" came when a disk jockey in Fargo, North Dakota, put the song into his regular rotation—that is, played it several times a day. As the legend has it, the song became popular in and around Fargo, and then seeped into Minneapolis, where a program director at KFWB's sister station, KDWB [WB standing at one point for Warner Brothers], Lou Riegert, ordered it put on the air. Carol Connors later said that Riegert had told her that he'd fallen in love with her voice, and so decided to put the record on the station's play list.

But this may be only half of the story. By the time the record made it into the "regular rotation" in both Fargo and Minneapolis, the broadcasting business was hip-deep in the payola scandal that would later surface.[13]

In payola, the old role of the song pluggers of yesteryear was reprised, this time on behalf of the labels and their distributors. In the practice, the labels' representatives plied the deejays with money and gifts to give play time to favored records. This wasn't so necessary for the big stars, like Frank Sinatra or Paul Anka or Bobby Darin, but it could make all the difference for an unknown artist or group. Once the bandwagon (so to speak) got rolling by repetitive plays over the air, sales demand for the record usually tended to follow. If the deejays said a record was hot, kids bought it, if for no other reason than to show they were with it and knew the score.

And even if the demand didn't soon follow the regular airing of a paid-for song, there were other ways to influence a climb up the charts. One was through the distributing company. For a steep discount, or even for an out-and-out bribe, sales records could be manipulated. Once a song achieved

---

[13] It should be remembered that "payola" was not illegal at the time—that is, there was no law against it. It was only considered ethically and artistically improper.

ignition and lift-off, the costs of the "promotion" could be folded back into the production budget and obscured, while covertly being deducted from the net owed to the artists. Some labels, in fact, saw this sort of pump-priming as a legitimate promotion expense.

In mid-September, after a week or so in rotation in Fargo and Minneapolis, orders for "To Know Him" began coming in to Era. "By mid-September," Ribowsky would report, "Bedell and Newman were looking at an order for 18,000 records."[14]

Eighteen thousand records seems very large for one mid-sized Midwestern city, and it seems a particularly large number when no other distribution centers were recording any demand at all. But then, the record wasn't being played much anywhere else.

"Bedell then played his biggest card," Ribowsky reported. "He knew Dick Clark, and he called him in Philadelphia to ask a favor. He pushed hard, saying he had a peculiar problem—a No. 1 record in Minneapolis that he couldn't get played anywhere else. The first thing Clark wanted to know was if Universal Distributors—a giant distributing depot powerful enough to create its own record labels, and closely linked to 'American Bandstand'—was handling the Doré [Era] record in Philadelphia. It was, and that bit of good fortune may have led Clark to listen to it."

Here Ribowsky is being entirely too ingenuous. As author Kerry Segrave would point out in his book *Payola in the Music Industry—A History*[15], Dick Clark actually owned a share of Universal Distributing at the time, along with two other men, Harold Lipsius and Harry Finfer. Only two years later, both Clark and Finfer were called on the carpet by a U.S. House of Representatives committee investigating payola in the record industry, and both were found to have numerous conflicts of interest between the broadcast of records and

---

[14] *He's a Rebel*, page 37, Cooper Square Press Edition.
[15] McFarland & Company, Publishers, 1994.

their distribution.[16] The import of Ribowsky's version of the rise of "To Know Him" is the suggestion that the record only took off when Dick Clark agreed to promote it on his nationally televised *American Bandstand* show, and that Clark only agreed to do this when he learned that Finfer and Universal Distributing, in which Clark held an investment, was handling the record. This is the very essence of "payola."[17]

Having assured himself of his own financial interest in the success of the record, Clark activated his hit-making machinery. In the third week of September, he played the record on his show, and the climb began. It hit number 40 on the Top Forty list on October 11, 1958, then number 16 a week later. By late October it had reached number 4. Two weeks later, Clark called Bedell and asked him if the Teddy Bears would agree to appear on *American Bandstand.*

By this point Harvey Goldstein was definitely out of the group. The other Teddy Bears told him he didn't need to accompany them to the *Bandstand* taping. Later, Goldstein got sore, and sued the three remaining Teddy Bears, claiming they owed him a quarter of the group's royalties. The lawsuit was eventually settled out of court, with Goldstein getting his share. "We were eighteen-year-old kids fighting like animals over a few dollars," Goldstein later told Ribowsky. "There's something extremely sad about that."

Just before Thanksgiving in 1958, Phil, Marshall and Annette boarded an airplane for a flight back to New York, to be followed by a trip to Philadelphia and the *Bandstand* show. For both Phil and Annette, it was the first time they had ever flown. Phil, at least, was nearly petrified. The flight, however, was uneventful. After landing in New York, Phil escorted

---

[16] *Payola*, Segrave, page xxx.

[17] Phil, in his November 2002 interview with Mick Brown, obliquely referred to the questionable provenance of "To Know Him Is to Love Him" when he observed, "I learned a lot by being in the Teddy Bears. I learned I didn't want to be a singer. I learned about payola and distributors and manufacturing. I learned about the Mafia."

Marshall and Annette to see his uncle, his mother's younger brother, who was then living in New Jersey. It appears that Phil also visited Ben Spector's grave on Long Island, although Carol Connors later had no recollection of this.

The next day, November 28, the Teddy Bears made their appearance on *American Bandstand*. They were escorted to the show by Harry Finfer of Universal Distributing. The format of the show was simple: the techs put the record on the sound system, while the talent lip-synched the words to their hit. Meanwhile the camera moved back and forth from the "singers" to the dancing teenagers. As an exercise in the mass inculcation of mainstream mating rituals, the show influenced incalculable numbers of impressionable minds.

One week later, "To Know Him Is to Love Him" reached Number One on the charts.

11

FOLLOW THE MONEY

After the trip to Philadelphia, Phil's ego became severely inflated. And why not? After ten years as an outsider, as someone dismissed as a dweeb or a weirdo by most of his fellow students, Phil now had his revenge. This was more than "I told you so"; this was proof positive that he was special. Hadn't he written the Number One song? Hadn't he (well, with Marshall Lieb's assistance) recorded it, laying in the overdubs *he* knew were just right? Hadn't he found the golden voice of Annette Kleinbard, and wasn't he smart enough to feature it? Didn't he know a prospective hit far better than the so-called professionals like Bedell and Newman and other tin-eared record business types—the "cigar-smoking sharpies," he would later call them—who were just trying to cash in on the teen bonanza? And wasn't the evidence right there for everyone to see, Number One, the holy grail of the teen music treasure hunt?

Bedell and Newman soon found themselves irritated by their protégé. Where in the summer, Phil had often been obsequious, giving Bedell and Newman the courtesy of calling them "Mister," post–Dick Clark he was cheekily familiar, even condescending.

This was something more than the sort of ego boost that might have been expected from sudden success. After a decade of what can only be construed as prolonged depression—first, the death of his father, followed by the move to a strange neighborhood in a different state, social isolation, domination by a mother and older sister, prolonged and persistent poverty—suddenly Phil was liberated. Fed by the pent-up forces of all these years of painful repression, Phil's ego ballooned. "You never saw such a change in a little fuckin' Jewish kid," Bedell told Ribowsky.

If Phil had suddenly become a god, Bertha and Shirley were his priestesses. It was as if in Phil, mother and daughter realized that they had the inside seats on a rocket to the moon. They endeavored to protect their investment, and soon began to interfere with Phil's relationship with his girlfriend, Donna Kass. After one session at the Spector apartment, in which Bertha and Shirley berated Donna for distracting Phil from his music, she left in tears.

Later, Carol Connors couldn't remember the first time she'd met Bertha or Shirley. She had hazy recollections of seeing them at the Spector apartment, usually before or after a rehearsal. Asked her impression of the Spector family, Carol said, "It's very strange but . . . I thought that they didn't take enough showers. But remember, I'm a kid. Strange things stick in my mind. And she [Bertha] and Phil always seemed to be bickering. And getting at each other. You know, I got the feeling that, you know, there was a lot of angst. But I got the feeling that she was very loyal, you know, really loved him. But anyway, there was this sort of maniac attitude . . . I mean, he was always either screaming or getting upset. I remember slamming doors, I mean, not me, but them. But it was like, 'You've gotta take care of this, or do that.' And it was, 'Yes, yes,' that sort of thing."

By this point, according to Carol's recollection, Shirley had moved out of the apartment. Court records show that just as "To Know Him" was moving up the pop charts in November of 1958, Shirley's traffic accident lawsuit against J. R. Carlson and her (former) friend Gloria Aron was the subject of a pre-trial conference. The defendants, who were also suing one another, both wanted access to Shirley's hospital records. Shirley claimed that Gloria had been transporting her for hire—that is, Shirley said she'd agreed to pay Gloria $1 a week to drive her to and from work. "In addition thereto, defendant Gloria Aron was to receive her lunches at the expense of the plaintiff," the court file recorded. Gloria denied that any such arrangement existed. Shirley said Gloria deliberately drove into the intersection to be struck by Carlson's vehicle. That wasn't so, Gloria said; she'd come to a complete stop, then started forward, only to be struck by Carlson's vehicle, which was going between 20 and 25 miles an hour. In the end, the court granted the defendants access to Shirley's medical history. The lawsuit would drag on into the spring of 1959.

In the meantime, Bertha kept up pressure on Phil to do something for his sister. Now that he was Mr. Big, why shouldn't he look out for his own? Sometime in December, Carol discovered that Shirley had become the Teddy Bears' manager.

"All I remember is, we all decided we needed a manager. And we thought that she would be good, because she was forceful," Carol recalled. "And that we could trust her. Remember, we all stuck to each other in those days. I think it was Phil's idea. Or Shirley talking to Phil. She was crazy."

By this time, the Teddy Bears had a professional agent, Ned Tannen, and a New York promotions specialist, Bud Dollinger. As a manager, it would be Shirley's job to smooth the way for the group as they made future live appearances. But Shirley was not the self-effacing type. Over the next few months, conflict over Phil's sister's role with the group would eventually murder the Teddy Bears.

By late in December of 1958, the Teddy Bears' relationship— or rather, Phil's relationship—with Bedell and Newman had reached a nadir. The group owed one more song on their original agreement with Era, and Phil couldn't agree with Bedell on what it should be. Phil wanted to follow "To Know Him" with a somewhat similar song, one with the sort of minor chords that had worked with the big hit. Bedell didn't want to make the record. He thought it wouldn't sell. But Phil had him over a barrel—once the last song was done, there was nothing to keep the Teddy Bears from moving to another label.

That's just what Phil proposed to do. The group had an offer from Imperial Records. Fine! said Bedell. Go! And take your sister with you!

By this time, Bedell and Newman had already had several confrontations with Shirley. In one, according to Bedell, Shirley had arrived at the Era offices late one Friday to demand her brother's money. Bedell had prepared a check for $38,000, which apparently included Phil's cut as both a performer and writer for "To Know Him." He gave the check to Shirley, who hit the roof. She accused Bedell of trying to rip Phil off by giving him a check that couldn't be negotiated, because the banks were all closed. She wanted hard cash. Bedell tried to mollify her by explaining that the banks were open until six on Friday afternoons, whereupon Shirley took the check and left in a huff. "[T]hat's the last I saw of the *meshugenah*," Bedell later told Ribowsky.

And here is another collision between the legend and the facts. While Ribowsky reports that Phil's earnings, by late December of 1958, from "To Know Him" represented $38,000, Mick Brown (and others) would later say that all but $3,000 of Phil's earnings from the Number One hit was ripped off by some sort of recording industry legerdemain. "He made $20,000 on the record and was swindled out of $17,000 of it," Brown reported in his long interview with Phil, the one published just before the shooting of Lana Clarkson.[18] The contradiction seems to indicate that the truth about Phil's early career is pliable—unless, of course, one assumes that Shirley absconded with the money.[19]

But even Phil, by late 1958, was already getting into trouble over the truth. In one incident, reported by Ribowsky and confirmed by Carol Connors, Phil claimed he'd written

---

[18] This information, however accurate or inaccurate, was first reported by Tom Wolfe in his 1963 essay, "The First Tycoon of Teen." It appears that it later became the basis for the assertions that Phil netted only $3,000 from "To Know Him Is to Love Him."

[19] See Page [81], below.

Ritchie Valens' 1958–1959 megahit, "Donna." Phil told Donna Kass that he'd written the song for her. It was only later—on February 3, of all dates, in 1959—when the small plane carrying Valens, Buddy Holly and the Big Bopper crashed in Iowa, killing all aboard, that Donna Kass learned that Phil had lied to her. That happened when she saw the real Donna, weeping, on television.

12

DEATH OF THE TEDDY BEARS

Around the first of the year, newly signed with Imperial Records, the three Teddy Bears embarked on another trip, this one featuring what was to be a live appearance on NBC's *Perry Como Show*. This trip would prove to be the beginning of the end for the group.

By this point, Annette Kleinbard (Carol Connors) had already begun to feel antipathy from Phil's sister, something not unlike the bad vibes that had driven her friend Donna Kass away from Phil. Both she and Marshall tolerated Shirley because of Phil, but both felt uncomfortable around her. "She was really an extension of Phil," Marshall later told Ribowsky, "but a lot more unpleasant. She was a very hyper, very nervous person. She was very loud, very New York."

Tall, blond, brassy and bossy, smoking incessantly, Shirley rubbed Marshall and Annette raw. "I remember she had a very strange face, not much of a chin," Carol recalled. "And that she didn't wear nylons. And her feet were dirty. Isn't that awful [to remember]? And I remember I thought she was very nervous. *Very* nervous. Because I would look at her, and she would, like, be jumping around! And one day, Shirley was there. I don't remember Shirley *not* being there. She was just there, and then she was our manager. And then we went to New York with her. That was a terrible trip."

The three Teddy Bears and Shirley checked into New York's Plaza Hotel the evening before the show's rehearsal at Kraft Music Hall. Unlike *American Bandstand*, this was to be a live performance—the Teddy Bears would actually have to sing, not lip-sync. So everyone was very nervous, especially with a national prime-time audience waiting.

Things began to go wrong almost from the start. In the rehearsal, Annette missed the high note. "I went to the high note of the song and I missed it. My voice cracked," Carol recalled. She was terribly embarrassed.

"I remember that Phil took me aside after I didn't hit the note," Carol recalled. "And he said to me—he sort of had his hand around my throat—I mean, not, I don't mean badly—and he said, 'If you don't hit that high note when we go on TV, I'm going to be—' You know! 'It's my song! You have to get it right!' I said, 'Okay, okay. There's so much pressure on me as it is.'"

That evening, the three Teddy Bears returned to the Plaza. Phil and Marshall shared one room, Shirley and Annette another.

"Then she started in on me," Carol recalled. According to Carol, Shirley began berating her, telling her that she had no talent, that it wasn't fair, "That she should have been the girl [in the group], and not me," Carol said. "You know, and that I was worthless. Just terrible things. And then she called my mother. And she said that I was a slut, and that I was sleeping with the boys."

Annette was devastated by Shirley's sudden verbal assault.

"I called my mother back. And it was not easy to do a long distance call, there were no [direct dial] phone calls. And I was crying on the phone. And I said, 'I think she's going to hurt me.' She didn't really, physically, but she was mentally—and this was like, I think, the night just before we were supposed to go on the show. That night. And I went into Phil and Marshall's room, and I was hysterically crying. And they let me sleep on like an armoire—what do they call it, at the foot of your bed? And I slept there, I wouldn't go back into the room."

Later, Carol wasn't sure whether the episode of missing

the high note had somehow triggered Shirley's already simmering anxiety, or if it only brought to the surface hostility that had been present for months. But that was it, as far as Annette was concerned—in her mind, Shirley was bad news. "She would go from being vicious to not being vicious. And somebody said, I don't remember who, 'Well, of course, Carol, she wanted to be you. She wanted to be singing that song. Remember, it was written by her brother off her father's epitaph, who had committed suicide.'"

But at the time, Annette was mostly aware of Shirley's "Jekyll and Hyde" personality swings, as Carol put it later.

The Teddy Bears returned to Kraft Music Hall the next evening for the show, all of them tired and worried. "So the next day—and I was humiliated that my voice had cracked—when we did the show the next night, first of all, Phil stepped on Polly Bergen's gown, and ripped it. It was a gorgeous gown, and we were all walking, getting ready to go on." The three Teddy Bears felt like stupid kids.

But then they were on, and singing while Annette Kleibard's mother, Gail, sat at home watching on television. "And my mom said that when I went to the high note, I hit it beautifully, but the expression on my face was one of sheer terror! But I hit it. That's all that anybody cared about."

After the trip to New York, the Teddy Bears embarked on a series of "one-nighters," as Carol recalled them, appearances in East Coast and Midwestern cities like Cleveland and Detroit. And it was on this tour that yet another part of the Spector legend was born, or at least conceived. This was the supposed savage beating that Phil took in a men's room, somewhere along the tour, perhaps in Iowa, which he later cited as one of the main reasons for his devotion to guns. But the legend itself mutated over the years, and in retrospect, one has to wonder whether the incident ever really happened.

This story appears to have had its first incarnation in British critic Richard Williams' early authorized biography of Phil, *Out of His Head.*[20] "While the group were touring," Williams wrote, "an incident occurred that seems to have marked Spector for ever." Williams attributed the story to Paul Case, whom Williams said later "became one of [Spector's] closest friends."

"They were doing a one-nighter," Williams quotes Case, "and Phil went to the men's room. He went to the urinal, and four guys who'd come to see the show came in right after him and locked the door. They all urinated on him. I think this was the most shocking thing of his life."

Williams went on to observe: "This indeed seems to have triggered Spector's obsession with his personal security, leading him to surround himself at all times—even in the studio—with bodyguards."

More than thirty years later, the same incident would resurface, this time in a piece written for *Vanity Fair* magazine by Robert Sam Anson in the wake of the shooting of Lana Clarkson.

"During a break in a Teddy Bears show," Anson wrote, "four toughs beat Phil to a pulp in a men's room, then urinated on him." Anson quoted another Spector acquaintance, Dave Kessel, as observing that the supposed incident helped convince Phil he had to have bodyguards, and go armed.

There are a few interesting things about this men's room saga—first, that over thirty years, the assault grows. In 1972, Phil was urinated on; by 2003, not only was Phil urinated on, but he was beaten to a pulp. Like other parts of the legend, it appeared to grow with the retelling.

The other interesting thing about the story is that it never

---

[20] In contrast to Ribowsky's unauthorized biography, first published in 1989, Williams' version included direct quotes from interviews that Williams had with his subject. The book is marred by a number of significant factual errors related to Phil's life, however, including the assertion that Annette Kleinbard was dropped from the Teddy Bears to be replaced by . . . Carol Connors!

made it into Ribowsky's unauthorized biography. There's not a word about it—it's almost as if the entire thing had never happened. And for good measure, there's Carol Connors' recollection:

"No," she said. "I don't remember that. And I would have known that. I would have been there. I don't even remember being in Iowa! Maybe he got picked on, but I never remember seeing Phil beaten to a pulp. Ever."

And finally, there's Mick Brown's interview, the one published just before Lana Clarkson's shooting, which includes nary a word about this incident that supposedly explained why Phil's life was "marked forever."

In March of 1959, the Teddy Bears began work on an album for Imperial. Because the label had an arrangement with a different studio, the group had to leave Ross and Gold Star, with its low ceilings. The new studio wasn't as well equipped as the Gold Star. Phil's obsession with both performing and overseeing the recording continued to get him in trouble. After several weeks, the Imperial brain trust took the recording responsibilities away from Phil, and rushed through the rest of the songs; the last six cuts were recorded in just six days. Worse, Imperial's Lou Chudd, the man who'd signed the deal with the group, forbade Phil from playing the guitar on the record. He was afraid that Phil would fool around with the arrangements, meaning more time in session. *The Teddy Bears Sing!* was a flop.

Meanwhile, the group's troubles over sister Shirley continued to grow. In April of 1959, Shirley finally settled her traffic accident case against her former friend Gloria Aron, and J. R. Carlson; the court records don't show who won. But by then, Shirley was well entrenched as the group's manager, dictating to Annette what she should wear, and how she should act while performing. Finally Shirley wanted the group to sign a formal agreement, making her their official manager. Marshall and Annette refused to sign. Phil didn't know what to do. He wanted to keep the group together, but he also wanted his sister to share in his good fortune. And at home,

Bertha was pushing Phil all the time to look out for his own. "In my mind, it became a matter of integrity and honor," Carol later told Ribowsky. "I said, 'I'm not selling myself to the devil for anything or anybody.' "

As the spring unfolded, the Teddy Bears simply faded away.

13

CRASHING BUT SURVIVING

By the late spring the Teddy Bears were very nearly defunct, and Imperial hadn't even released their record. It appears that most of the money from the big hit from the previous fall had gone to Phil, who by then had acquired a new Corvette to drive around town. Carol Connors and Marshall Lieb got far less. "I recall we got some money," she said. "Not very much. Not *that* kind of money," meaning the supposed $38,000 Ribowsky reported Shirley picking up for her brother, or even the $20,000 cited by Mick Brown.[21]

Phil now began toying with the idea of forming a new group, one that wouldn't have all the internal stresses associated with the Teddy Bears. He continued to hang out with Michael Spencer, and linked up with some other guitarists, trying to move into the jazz field. He reinvented himself as "Phil Harvey," and put together a band including three

---

[21] Ribowsky asserted that Era eventually disbursed a substantial sum to Phil for the writing royalties on "To Know Him," and that the money had been "assigned to" Shirley by Phil. He quoted Marshall Lieb, now deceased, as saying, "It was $200,000. Phillip told me he gave it to Shirley, and it didn't reach him." Lieb indicated that Phil told him Shirley had spent most of the money. Whether any of this actually happened is unclear; again, this is a story that accompanied the growth of the legend, and not necessarily the truth. The issue of payola again arises in this connection, owing to the lack of clarity as to how much Phil actually earned.

guitarists, a pianist and a drummer. The Phil Harvey band
began appearing at teen dance venues, including the Rainbow Roller Rink, dressed like thirties gangsters—wide
lapels, double-breasted suits, long overcoats, snap-brim hats
pulled low over their faces. Phil had the idea of meshing
with the hit TV show of the time, *The Untouchables*. In a
way, according to those who saw it, it was an idea far ahead
of its time, a sort of music video without the video. The trouble was, no one knew what to make of it—a bunch of overdressed teenagers acting like Mafiosi with guitars? What?

With her brother heading in a new direction, it appears
that Shirley became even more possessive. According to Ribowsky, Shirley often called people to see where Phil was. It
was as if she no longer trusted Phil to provide her with the
show business entree that she so desperately craved. And,
too, it appears that Phil was feuding with his mother Bertha
at the same time. Sometime that summer, apparently under
pressure from his mother and sister, Phil co-wrote a song
with Shirley, "Be My Girl." The song had no legs. From that
point forward, Shirley began to fade from the official life of
her brother, but not from real life. For most of the next forty
years, Phil would try to take care of her, even when, as Ribowsky reported, she would reside in an institution in Northern California.

In September 1959, Annette Kleinbard was enjoying some
of her modest new-found wealth as a Teddy Bear. While she
and Marshall Lieb didn't cash in the way that Phil—or his
sister—did, they still earned some money. That September,
Annette bought a new MGA sports car. "It was white, and it
was long," Carol remembered.

Just after getting the car, Annette decided to have seat
belts installed. The cost came to thirteen dollars. "And I didn't
have enough money to put the seat belts in. I didn't even
have a checking account. I was a kid! So they said, 'Come
back after the holiday.' And I said, 'Okay.' So I drove off
with this guy. And my mother said to me, 'Be careful.' And I
said, 'Oh, what's with this "Be careful" stuff?' "

Carol drove up to Mulholland Drive where it winds around the hills above Hollywood and West Los Angeles. "I loved Mulholland. I said, 'Let me take you up to Mulholland, so you can see the way it handles.' And I was probably going a little bit too fast. Remember, we didn't have any seat belts. And we went into a double-ess turn. I know exactly where it is.

"The mountain was on one side, the cliff was on the other. And I swerved away from the mountain and I didn't compensate correctly. And we went flying off the cliff at about fifty miles an hour. And he jumped. There were no seat belts! And I don't know that he jumped. So I go down with the car. And I was thrown out of the car at one hundred fifty feet [down]. The car slams into a tree at three hundred fifty feet. I have a picture of the car, it's like an accordion. And I remembered saying, you know, 'Charlton Heston always told me to come down and visit, and I did!' Because I practically landed in his back yard. And I stood up, and I remember seeing the car hit the tree, and I looked at my hand and it was covered with blood. And I don't think I'd ever even had a cut before. And all of a sudden my hands are covered. And I remember touching my whole body, going up my body, and I got to my face, and I go, 'Oh God, why my face? Why couldn't you scrape my arm? Why does it have to be my face?' It was not that I was the prettiest thing in the world . . . but I certainly was attractive . . . and there was a big fold in the middle of my face where my nose was bent. And the horn of the car had not stopped, so the car was constantly beeping. And sound reverberates in the canyon, and we were one-eighth of a mile from a fire station. And he [her passenger] was on the top of the cliff, and I screamed out, 'Oh my God, I've killed someone!' I saw the car hit the tree, and I was hysterical." Carol was certain that her friend had still been in the car when it crashed into the tree.

"The firemen came, and I'm screaming, 'Oh my God, I've killed somebody!' And he says, 'No! No! I'm alive!' Because he could hear me. He says, 'Are you okay?' And I went, 'I don't know!' So the fire department came and they came down and they said, 'Can you walk up? 'Cause if you can't, it's going to take a long time to get you up with the stretcher.' Actually, it was very stupid on their part, because I could have had internal injuries. And I walked up with them, with their help. And the ambulance took me to the hospital. And it took four-and-a-half hours in surgery to get the dirt out of my face.

"I had cuts here, and there, and a lot of bruises. I remember, this is so bizarre, because my last thought before I, I guess I was unconscious for a couple of seconds, because I don't remember leaving the car, or I blocked it, I only remember standing and seeing the car. And X amount of time had gone by, seconds, I guess. And I remember saying, 'Oh my God, I'm going to die. And there's nothing I can do about it. And what is my mother going to think about this?' "

Annette's recuperation after the accident lasted some weeks after extensive plastic surgery. Phil never came to visit her, and that hurt, she said later. She thought that Phil blamed her for the breakup of the Teddy Bears, because of her conflict with Shirley. Eventually a friend came by and told her that when Phil heard about the wreck, he was supposed to have said, "Too bad she didn't die." He later claimed he'd never said any such thing, but the fact that Annette could believe it only showed how bitter the breakup of the Teddy Bears had become.

Knowing that the Teddy Bears were moribund, Phil began to look around for another way into the record business. As early as April, he made contact with a man named Lester Sill,[22] who was something of a powerhouse in the recording business, having solid connections with industry mavens on both coasts, including Finfer, Lipsius and Clark. He had been involved in the music business in Los Angeles since the late 1940s as a promotions man (a "plugger"), and later had

---

[22] Lester Sill, born in Los Angeles in January of 1918, died in his native city in October of 1994.

managed the Coasters, the act which had scored so big with "Yakety Yak" and "Poison Ivy." Sill had also mentored a hot writing/producing team, Jerry Leiber and Mike Stoller, who had gone on to write hits for the Coasters ("Searchin'," "Yakety Yak"), the Drifters ("There Goes My Baby"), and Elvis Presley ("Hound Dog"). Leiber was, like Phil, an alumnus of Fairfax. So Phil, in making contact with Sill, hoped to hitch his own bandwagon to the same powerful industry engine.

Late in April, Phil sold the rights to "Be My Girl" to Sill's publishing company, Gregmark, which Sill co-owned with Lee Hazlewood, who was then producing the twangy Duane Eddy records.

Sill would later say he decided to get tied up with the 19-year-old Phil after meeting him one day in the studio while Phil was still trying to produce *The Teddy Bears Sing!* He said he was impressed with Phil's grasp of harmonies as the trio labored on the album that would go nowhere.

At some point in the summer of 1959, even before the Teddy Bears were finally, irrefutably dead, Sill signed Phil to a three-year contract as a producer, writer and performer. The deal called for an escalating royalty rate of 6 cents a record, four times what the four Teddy Bears had received for their deal with Era.

Sill later said he wasn't interested in Phil so much for his talent as a performer—Sill thought this was marginal at best—but for his writing and producing abilities. By that point, advances in recording hardware were beginning to make more feasible the sort of complex overdubbing that Phil and Marshall Lieb had favored. Sill perceived Phil as someone who had mastered this technical art. In a way, the job title of producer, which had hitherto simply reflected the task of getting the talent into the studio, was starting to evolve to reflect the actual mixing of recorded sounds, a much more hands-on concept.

While Phil had a lot of ideas on how to produce recorded music, he also had a lot to learn. Here Sill provided an invaluable tutelage for his new protégé, first by letting him experiment inside the studio manipulating various sounds, and second, by introducing him to his partner, Lee Hazlewood. Hazlewood had been a disk jockey in Phoenix when he'd hooked up with Eddy, he of the twangy guitar heard in "Rebel Rouser." Hazlewood's forte, accomplished mainly in a seedy studio in Phoenix, was in manipulating the recorded music by varying its playing speed, or re-recording, often with the effects of echo and reverberation induced with simple materials, such as a piece of pipe. Soon Sill and Phil were visiting Hazlewood in the Phoenix studio, watching Hazlewood tweak Eddy's metallic sound with his innovations.

It appears that Hazlewood had no great affection for Phil. A decade older than Phil, tall and angular, Hazlewood seemed to resent Phil's relationship with his partner. Phil bugged Hazlewood for hours to learn his techniques, then had the effrontery, in Hazlewood's view, to suggest how it might be done better. Eventually Hazlewood told Sill to keep Phil away from him.

By the fall of 1959, Phil had largely given up on performing; he had become much more interested in producing, as the task of assembling the parts of songs was now increasingly being called. The days when a performer came into a studio and simply let 'er rip into a single microphone were over, and had been for some time. Thanks to advances in the recording art, the new product was crafted, component by component; no longer did the result depend on the performance. Now it was the packaging. It was like the difference between live action and instant replay; fashioning the product in a studio, no matter how many times something had to be played (or echoed or overdubbed) meant never having to say one was sorry.

Inevitably, however, the star performer became just another instrument to be manipulated, a lesson that was not at all lost on Phil.

14

LEGALLY SPEAKING

If one believes the legend, in addition to his burgeoning music career, Phil had also continued with his legal reporting. Ribowsky, for instance, asserted that even as Phil shadowed Sill and Hazlewood in and out of music studios in the summer of 1959, he had occasional employment as a court reporter. According to Ribowsky, Phil was "called to do [sic] stenotype when depositions were taken and legal papers filed in the Los Angeles courthouse during the interminable appeals case of Caryl Chessman, the convicted murderer who was sentenced in 1949 to die in the gas chamber."

There are several problems with this recitation of the legend, however. For one, Caryl Chessman was not convicted of murder; in fact, he was never even accused of murder. Instead, Chessman was found guilty in May of 1948 (not 1949) of seventeen counts of kidnaping, rape, robbery, attempted rape, attempted robbery and car theft, as the so-called "Red Light Bandit" who preyed upon lovers' lanes in or near Los Angeles. Based on the state law of the time, however, kidnaping that resulted in bodily harm was punishable by death.

It is true that Chessman's appeals were interminable, just as it is also true that his fight to avoid the death penalty became a *cause celebre* among the cognoscenti of the late 1950s; indeed, one was likely to find the same people protesting Chessman's proposed date with the gas chamber who had previously opposed the Rosenbergs' electrocution as atomic spies, or who would in the future call for Banning the

Bomb. Many people in left-leaning Hollywood jumped onto the pro-Chessman, anti–capital punishment bandwagon, and it appears that Phil was no exception. It is not true, however, that Phil was "called to do stenotype when depositions were taken" in the case, most of which had already been settled long before Phil ever became proficient (if he ever did) as a stenographer.

Ribowsky was not the only person to succumb to this part of the legend; so, too, did Robert Sam Anson of *Vanity Fair* in his long, post-shooting profile of Phil ("Phil made a temporary living as a stenographic court reporter on the Caryl Chessman and Johnny Stompanato cases"[23]), and even Mick Brown of *The Daily Telegraph*, in a long piece on Lana Clarkson published in July of 2003, claimed that Phil was the reporter on the spot when Lana Turner's daughter, Cheryl Crane, was taken before a coroner's inquest in the stabbing death of her mother's mobster boyfriend, Johnny Stompanato, in April of 1958 ("Sitting in the well of the court at the inquest, recording the proceedings, was a young, part-time court stenographer named Harvey Phillip Spector."[24]) But the records of the California Board of Court Reporters show that Harvey Phillip Spector was never licensed as a court reporter in California.[25]

Phil's Zelig-like ability to be on the spot at least had the advantage of being hard to check, particularly by biographers and profilers eager to skip over the provenance of the storied background to get to the main event, Phil's supposed genius at the studio control board.

It was true that as the 1950s segued into the early 1960s, Phil emerged as a particularly outspoken leftist, at least for

---

[23] Anson, *Vanity Fair*, June 2003.

[24] UK *Daily Telegraph*, July 27, 2003.

[25] The California board responsible for licensing certified shorthand reporters has records going back to 1951; according to board officials, no license was ever issued to Harvey Phillip Spector, or even Phillip Spector. There were only two Spectors listed, neither of them Phil.

a while. Sill, in fact, told Ribowsky that other young people, after hearing Phil spout off about Chessman and the evils of capital punishment, thought Phil might be "a communist." Nothing could have been further from the truth, however, as Phil's subsequent career as a ruthless music mogul would illustrate.

But Phil did have a deep-seated affinity for the underdog, doubtless a residue from his years as an impoverished outsider. He was particularly drawn to the barbs of comedian Lenny Bruce. By 1959, Bruce had already become the *bête noire* of the establishment with his recorded anti-hypocrisy monologues, *Interviews of Our Times* in 1958, and *The Sick Humor of Lenny Bruce* the following year. Carol Connors recalled that on one plane trip taken by the Teddy Bears—presumably the road trip to New York, Detroit and Cleveland just after the first of the year—Phil recited almost the entire Bruce repertoire from memory.

Whatever his politics, by the fall of 1959 Phil decided to try to re-create his Teddy Bears success—without the Teddy Bears. He went into the studio and laid down several tracks with a female session singer whom Phil hoped might reprise Annette Kleinbard's magic. The result was a sort of admixture of doo-wop and the cloying sentimentalism that lay beneath "To Know Him Is to Love Him." Next, Phil decided he needed a trio to sing the songs in public. He recruited another Fairfax teen gigger named Russ Titelman, a sort of clone of Marshall Lieb; Titelman's pretty blond girlfriend, Annette (another Annette!) Merar; and a third Fairfax alum, Warren Entner. The public group—as opposed to the trio recording in the studio—was called "Spector's Three." By this time, according to Ribowsky, Phil had realized that he was never going to make it himself as a performer. By naming the new group after himself, however, Phil hoped to keep his own name in the public eye.

"Spector's Three" made three records, and all of them flopped. The style that had moved "To Know Him Is to Love Him" (or the creative accounting, if one prefers) to the top of the charts had already evolved to a new form even before the close of the decade.

Sill wasn't discouraged by the "Spector's Three" flops. He still had hopes for his new protégé, despite Hazlewood's carping. For one thing, Sill was impressed with Phil's intense obsession with the music business. Phil spent hours and hours in the studio, and when he wasn't there, he spent more hours trying to think of new and better ways to make music.

It also seems that something transpired around this point between Phil and his mother, Bertha. Ribowsky contends that as the fall unfolded, Phil actually moved in with Sill's family in Sherman Oaks, "sharing a room with Lester's ten-year-old son, Joel."

These last few months of 1959 exposed Phil for the first time in years to what might be referred to as a normal family life. Sill's three sons treated Phil with brotherly camaraderie, even as Sill himself indulged Phil as some sort of long-lost nephew who had wandered in from the cold. As Sill recalled it later, Phil steered clear of Bertha and Shirley as much as possible. But the thawing process had a long way to go before Phil could escape the grip of the demons bedeviling him. Sill would tell Ribowsky that when his wife, Harriet, reached out to touch Phil with an affectionate gesture, Phil jerked away. "She thought he didn't know *how* to be close to anybody," Sill told Ribowsky.

But Phil still couldn't seem to bring in any hits for Sill, and by the spring of 1960, Phil was anxious to get out of Los Angeles. At the time, there were three main centers of activity in the music business, Los Angeles (with its proximity to the movies), Nashville (with its country roots), and New York City. Of the three, New York was then the biggest, and the brashest. Phil convinced Sill that he needed to get to New York if he was going to make his mark, and the ever-obliging Sill agreed to run interference for him. That spring, Sill called up his old friends, the red-hot songwriting/

producing duo of Jerry Leiber and Mike Stoller, and asked them if they would take Phil on as a $150-a-week songwriter and apprentice producer.

Probably because they figured they owed Sill one, Leiber and Stoller sent airfare for Phil to come to New York.

15

TEEN PAN ALLEY

In the first year of the decade of the 1960s, the nerve-center of the popular music business in New York was located in the Brill Building at 1619 Broadway, near West 51st Street and not far from Rockefeller Center.[26] As the 1950s unfolded and as teen music became more and more a pot of gold for the enterprising, this location would become known by wry wits as "Teen Pan Alley," a derivative of the Tin Pan Alley of an earlier era. It would become for a few years Phil Spector's Mecca.

According to one version of the legend—recounted in Tom Wolfe's 1963 essay on Phil, "The First Tycoon of Teen," there was no airfare to New York sent by Leiber and Stoller at all. Instead, according to the Wolfe version of the legend, Phil had gone to New York that spring to take a job as a stenographer with the United Nations, but fell in with some musicians instead, and never made it to the U.N. Another version of the story leaves out the U.N., but has Phil arriving at night in New York with no place to stay, and deciding to go to the offices of Leiber and Stoller at 40 West 57th Street, where he climbed up on a desk and went to sleep.

Later, in cooperating with Williams in *Out of His Head*,

---

[26] Ribowsky quotes Sill as placing the Brill Building at 1650 Broadway, while Williams in *Out of His Head* puts it at 1619 Broadway. Williams was correct.

Phil confirmed this version. "It's a silly story, but it's true," Phil told Williams.

But Williams asked Stoller himself about Phil's arrival in New York, and was told that Sill *had* called the songwriters and asked them to find a place for Phil. And Ribowsky, writing almost two decades after Williams, says Sill told him that he'd called Leiber and Stoller, and that the songwriters had sent Phil's plane fare. Rather than sleeping on a desk, Ribowsky has Spector curling up on a couch in the songwriters' offices, not because he had no money, but because he wanted to lurk in the writers' milieu. Nowhere is there any mention of the proposed job at the U.N. In fact, in Ribowsky's version, Phil arrived at the Leiber and Stoller offices only to find that the pair had no idea who he was—that is, they didn't recognize him despite the few earlier trips he'd made to New York as Sill's acolyte.

The point of these various incongruities in the legend is not their petty differences, but rather their potency when it comes to assessing Phil's credibility—an important issue, at least for a jury, if one eventually is to be charged with a crime such as murder.

Williams, for his part, notes in *Out of His Head*, "The discrepancy between stories is not surprising. This period of Spector's life, from late '59 through mid '62, is riddled with unknowns . . . Spector himself has either forgotten or prefers not to remember." Or, in some cases, simply made up. For example, "I was writing songs for Elvis Presley," Phil told Williams, "and I wasn't getting any credit, but I didn't care." Leiber and Stoller would dispute Phil's claims of authorship, however. Still later, Phil would claim he had produced some of Elvis' records, but that didn't appear to be true either—at least, Phil was never credited for his supposed Elvis Presley efforts by either ASCAP or BMI.

Ribowsky, on the other hand, fills in plenty of details about Phil's life in New York, many of them derived from his extensive interviewing of people who were there at the time. In Ribowsky's version, Phil hung around the Leiber and Stoller offices, soaking up the atmosphere, and spent a great deal of time frequenting restaurants and night spots favored by songwriters and music business wannabes.

If anything, however, Phil considered himself a cut above the rest. After all, at least he had written a Number One hit. Not that anyone cared very much, however. In retrospect, it seems clear that for the first few months in New York, Leiber and Stoller considered their hiring of Phil to be more of a favor to Lester Sill than anything else. At the time, they were at the top, with the Drifters and the Coasters, Elvis—Leiber and Stoller had written "Hound Dog," only to be sued for a piece of the action by Johnny Otis—and other front-line rock-and-roll acts. Phil was, if anything, simply excess baggage to Leiber and Stoller. "With Phil, I just think they were trying to be nice to Lester, patronizing Lester by letting this who-is-this-kid hang around," New York songwriter Beverly Ross later told Ribowsky.

But hanging around was something that Phil turned out to be very good at. Just being in the mix of popular music business personalities gave Phil the tools necessary to talk the talk, to pick up on the trends. Not quite sure what to do with Sill's export, Leiber and Stoller occasionally let him work as a $41-an-hour union session guitarist at a number of their recording sessions. Phil didn't like it much; perhaps worse, the union musicians, a rather crusty lot, didn't think much of Phil's musicianship. That was about the time that Phil focused on the control room as his future. His idea was that he would make his mark as a writer and as a producer, just like Leiber and Stoller.

Not long after arriving in New York, Phil made the acquaintance of Beverly Ross, who at the time was working as a songwriter for Hill and Range, the rock-and-roll publishing arm of Chappell Music. As publishers, both firms acquired the copyrights of songs and licensed them to performers. Ross was only a year older than Phil, but she'd also had a big hit: "Lollipop," a Number One for the Chordettes in 1958. By 1960, Ross, with Carole King, was one of the two top female writers in the rock-and-roll field, and was earning a salary of $250 a week. More importantly, Ross had *carte blanche* at Hill and Range for the recording of demos.

Phil soon hooked up with Ross, according to Ross' version of the events, which she would later impart to Ribowsky. Ross thought Phil was very smart, although somewhat diffident in manner. But Ross was particularly struck by Phil's wry sense of humor, which by this point had been rather substantially influenced by Lenny Bruce. Ross thought Phil was charming; besides, she said, he was the best guitarist she had ever heard.

Soon Ross and Phil were trying out song parts in one of the eleven small piano cubicles at Hill and Range's office in the Brill Building. Ross was most proficient at forming a melody, she told Ribowsky; what she really needed was a lyricist to fill the song out. Phil wasn't much of a lyricist, it turned out. But Phil had some strange instinct for the sound: "He could find interesting chord changes in raw material," Ross told Ribowsky, "or an interesting hook." It was "To Know Him Is to Love Him" all over again. Phil could take a piece of music and tweak a portion of it—sometimes relying on the classical riffs he had monkeyed around with on Michael Spencer's piano—and come up with the center of a song. "He was great at directing a song a certain way or shortening phrases to make it better," Ross said. "What he was was a great editor." Indeed, this seems to have been Phil's major contribution to the writing of all of the hits he was later to claim credit for.

Siding Ross like a shadow, Phil penetrated the music scene almost surreptitiously. With Ross in front, no one asked any questions. At one point, Ross took Phil to a recording session in a nearby studio. The producer had rattled the performer, according to Ross, and the session was bogging down. Suddenly Phil stood up and took over, altering all the arrangements, giving new instructions to the guitarist, the drummer. The producer, nonplused to say the least, walked out in a huff. Later, people in the music business repeated the story, marveling at Phil's chutzpah. "He had the nerve and confidence to do something like that," Ross told Ribowsky, "and it was where he first showed me his incredible lack of conscience and lack of concern for others."

By the late spring of 1960, Phil had so insinuated himself inside the Broadway music-business crowd that he had become something of a fixture. Where, when he had first arrived, he had worn a suit and tie, by the early summer he had begun to dress rather idiosyncratically: trousers with mismatched legs, a long, Zorro-like cape, and—galoshes. But others dressed weirdly, too—it was a sign of the times. Doc Pomus—a writer of songs for Elvis and the Coasters, among others—became fast friends with Phil. Part of his attraction, Pomus said, was that you never knew when Phil was putting you on, and his costuming was a case in point.

Meanwhile, Phil continued to see Beverly Ross, and in time, Ross began to feel emotionally attached to Phil. As Ross explained to Ribowsky, she had a developmentally disabled brother, and when Phil told her that his sister had gone to pieces after he'd left Los Angeles and had been placed in an institution, Ross felt they were kindred spirits. Phil told Ross that his father had killed himself, and Ross realized that this was a pain that was at the center of Phil's existence. But Phil would drive away any sharing of confidences with an abrupt, often sarcastic remark. "It seemed to me that his nature was not to have any conscience," she told Ribowsky. "He didn't want to feel anything for anybody."

Throughout the rest of the spring and summer of 1960, Phil continued to try to write songs, while working as a guitarist at various recording sessions. Leiber and Stoller introduced him to another songwriter, Terry Phillips. Unlike Phil, Phillips had ability as a lyricist, and Leiber and Stoller hoped the pair would generate some catchy tunes. Together the two wrote several songs that were recorded by various artists, but none lit up the charts the way "To Know Him" had. Again, Phil's primary contribution seemed to be finding the nut of a song, a portion of music that could be built upon.

Even while Phil was taking home his $150 a week from Leiber and Stoller, he was busy making what appears to have been a side deal with the publishers Hill and Range, Beverly Ross' employer. Singer Ray Peterson, who had had a big hit in 1959 with the saccharine "Tell Laura I Love Her," had started a new label with his manager, and arranged to be distributed by Hill and Range. When Peterson and his manager, Stan Shulman, discovered that Leiber and Stoller couldn't produce Peterson because of scheduling conflicts, Phil assured Shulman and the Hill and Range people that they didn't need Leiber and Stoller, that he could produce the record himself. As it happened, Peterson and Shulman did not get along. Later, Peterson would tell Ribowsky that Shulman, a former Marine, had terrorized him, even to the point of beating him up. Peterson also thought Shulman didn't have a clue about what made rock-and-roll work; that made him much more loyal to Spector when troubles later erupted.

That fall, Phil produced a Peterson cover of an old Joe Turner tune, "Corinna, Corinna." For the flip side, Phil resurrected the song he had written with his sister Shirley, "Be My Girl." It was on "Corinna" that Phil used violins for the first time, foreshadowing his eventual addiction to orchestral instrumentation in rock-and-roll. The original song by Turner had always been considered earthy, but Peterson sang it as if he were addressing a little girl. Although Phil had told Beverly Ross that Peterson would use one of her songs at the session, it didn't happen. Later, according to Ross, Phil implored her not to give up on him, that they could still find a way to work together.

"He didn't want to burn down any bridges," Ross told Ribowsky, "but I later felt this was the beginning of his terrible two-facedness. I was just too naive and trusting, and I believed him."

But only a week or so later, Ross discovered that she'd been too trusting by far. Earlier that summer, Phil had been at Ross' apartment while Ross was tinkering with a melody she'd been thinking of, a sort of triptych that suggested a small fountain. According to Ross, Phil jumped to his feet and told her he had to go see Leiber right away. This was the moment, according to Ribowsky, that the song "Spanish Harlem" came into being; if Ross can be believed, Phil swiped it from her to give to Leiber.

Again, there are multiple versions of the gestation of "Spanish Harlem." Williams, in *Out of His Head*, gives credit to Phil for the melody, Leiber for the lyrics, and Stoller for the arrangement. But Ribowsky says the real germ of the song came out of Ross' piano, and that Phil, rushing over to Leiber's townhouse, played the triptych that Stoller then used to form the song, keeping this all a secret from Ross.

In the fall of 1960, a month or so before Peterson cut "Corinna," when Phil was telling Ross to stick with him, Leiber and Stoller arranged for the former lead singer for the Drifters, Ben E. King, to record "Spanish Harlem." The song skyrocketed upward, a deft marriage between Leiber's wistful words and the slightly Latin arrangement by Stoller. When Ross first heard the song in November of that year, just as it started its climb, "[s]he knew she'd been had," Ribowsky would later report. The heart of the song was the three-note triptych she'd played for Phil that night at her apartment.

There would soon be more to the story: according to Ribowsky, Phil began claiming that he had been the hit record's producer, but had declined producer's credit because of deference to Leiber and Stoller. Those who had been at the session where the record was cut thought this claim was ludicrous. King, for one, told Ribowsky that "I seem to recall him [Phil] leaning against a wall or something." And this was when Doc Pomus delivered his famous verdict: "Phil always told a lot of stories," he told Ribowsky, "but here's the reality: what actually happened, what Phil wished could have happened, and what he *says* happened."

But talk was one thing, performance another. By the early

part of 1961, Phil would have four different songs on the pop charts: "Corinna, Corinna," "Spanish Harlem," "Some of Your Loving" by Johnny Nash (an assignment from Leiber and Stoller), and Curtis Lee's "Pretty Little Angel Eyes," a job for Shulman. The last song Phil produced in a new studio, Mira Sound, located in the back of an old hotel on West 47th Street. The place was overrun with rats, but Phil liked the way the sound bounced off the thick walls, giving a "fat" sound that reminded him of Gold Star. Using his reverb and delay tricks, he actually made Lee sound good, no small accomplishment, according to Ribowsky.

16

A FAST SHUFFLE

Just before Christmas in 1960, Phil returned to Southern California, filled with confidence after his successes that fall. He came back in part because of Lester Sill, who was having a crisis. For one thing, Hazlewood and Duane Eddy had parted company—that meant no more twangy guitar hits for Sill and Hazlewood. Lipsius and Finfer, the bosses at Universal Distributing, had possession of some master tapes of Eddy that Sill and Hazlewood wanted back in order to produce more Eddy songs, now that he was out the door. Lipsius and Finfer refused to turn the tapes over, and Sill and Hazlewood knew that they could not afford to alienate the big shots of distribution and survive as a label. They needed a new act, a new hit. Sill, at least, hoped that Phil had one in him.

At that time, Sill had a three-sister group act that hadn't done much. Priscilla, Albeth and Sherrell Paris were blond, McGuire Sister sound-alikes. Sill wanted Phil to see if he couldn't find a hit somewhere for the trio. Phil had heard the Paris Sisters before, and thought that Priscilla might be transformed into an Annette Kleinbard–style lead vocalist. He would use some of the same approaches that he'd used for the Teddy Bears, Phil decided. He also decided to use the old standby, "Be My Girl," as the A side of the new Paris Sisters record, again providing an opportunity for songwriting income for himself and Shirley. Naturally the gender was flipped, so that the song became "Be My Boy."

Shortly after cutting the track, Phil rushed back to New York. Sill took the master to several outlets, but nobody wanted to buy it. Eventually, Sill and Hazlewood decided to sell the record themselves using the Gregmark label. No one had any idea of how it would do.

Back in New York, however, Phil had had a brainstorm. It appears that, having slipped in ahead of Leiber and Stoller with Ray Peterson and "Corinna, Corinna," Phil now decided there was nothing to prevent him from writing and producing all the songs for Elvis Presley's film, *Blue Hawaii*. This really was taking food out of Leiber and Stoller's mouths, because Elvis was the duo's bread and butter.

Not only that, Phil told his writing partner Terry Phillips that they also had a chance to write songs for Bobby Darin and Connie Francis!

Phillips was overjoyed to hear about this monumental break in his still-budding career. In short order, he moved into Phil's apartment on East 82nd Street, and threw himself into all three projects. At one point, Phil took him to the Copacabana nightclub to meet Connie Francis and Bobby Darin, and when he and Phil played them some of the songs, both Darin and Francis were enthusiastic. Then came the word that Hal Wallis, who was producing *Blue Hawaii*, loved the songs Phillips and Phil had written for the movie.

In retrospect, it appears that Phillips was naive, to say the least. Or overly ambitious, to say the most. The plain fact was, neither Phil nor his new roommate were at liberty to write anything without the approval of Leiber and Stoller, who were, after all, their employers.

Phillips couldn't, or wouldn't, parse out what was going on. It appeared, from the little that Phil would let slip, that Phil had made some sort of side deal with Hill and Range, and specifically, with Paul Case, who was Hill and Range's manager. Phil implied that Case had worked out some sort of arrangement with Leiber and Stoller, but it appears that Hill and Range were actually trying to use Phil to cut

Leiber and Stoller out of the Elvis pie. Soon, the telephone at Phil's apartment was ringing, and Phil would begin whispering to whoever was on the other end of the line. When Phillips would press for details, Phil turned secret agent on him.

In truth, the relationship between Phil and Phillips was reminiscent of the earlier relationship between Phil and Marshall Lieb. Terry Phillips, like Marshall, was a large, powerfully built young man, and good looking. Yet Phil tended to run Phillips, the same way he had directed Marshall; in a sense, Phillips was Phil's second bodyguard.

This peculiar relationship extended to dating, Phillips was later to tell Ribowsky. Phil had so many hang-ups about his looks, particularly his diminutive stature, that it was difficult if not impossible for him to simply be himself when it came to women, according to Phillips.

"Phil wanted a love, he wanted to love and be loved," Phillips told Ribowsky. "But every woman he ever met used him. The women he was screwing were doing it because of what he might do for them. And he was very well aware that these women would hurt and use him."

This has to be seen as an unwitting commentary on Phil's inability to have intimacy with anyone, let alone a woman. As such attitudes go, it tended to be self-fulfilling. Believing that women were out to take advantage of him, Phil began to look for it; once he began to look for it, he began to find it. This would become apparent again and again over the next four decades, as Phil's relationships with women would eventually founder and then sink. Along with its self-fulfilling nature, it would stand as a significant observation as to Phil's fundamental attitude toward women—formed by his intense relationship with his mother and sister—even when an actress named Lana Clarkson wound up shot dead in his house in Alhambra, California, more than forty years later.

The double game Phil was playing with Hill and Range and Leiber and Stoller finally went bust in February of 1961, when the telephone at the 82nd Street apartment rang. Phil, after talking for a few minutes, hung up and told Phillips that all deals were dead: Leiber and Stoller had finally stumbled onto what was going on and put an end to it. Phil said Leiber and Stoller had told Hill and Range that they wanted half of the earnings for every song Phil and Phillips had prepared for the company. In effect, that would make Leiber and Stoller equal partners with Hill and Range if the deals went through. Hill and Range had said no.

Phillips, who had nearly killed himself churning out so much material in a matter of a few weeks, was flabbergasted. He told Phil that he thought that Leiber and Stoller had blessed the deal from the beginning. Now Phil had to tell him it wasn't so. In other words, Phil had lied to Phillips.

Phillips wondered why they couldn't go forward anyway—why Hill and Range just didn't agree to give Leiber and Stoller their 50 percent cut. He still didn't understand—the whole thing had been about snatching Elvis away from Leiber and Stoller. And at a deeper, double level, it also had the appearance of a ruse by Phil to get out from under his contract with his employers by interposing Hill and Range as musical "bodyguards" of a sort.

Afterward, Phillips tried to make amends with Leiber and Stoller, saying he hadn't known what was going on. For his part, Phil didn't care a whit about Leiber and Stoller. He soon had a lawyer inform them that he intended to break the contract he had with them on the grounds that he'd been a minor when he'd made the deal (based on his December 26, 1939, birth date, Phil would have been 20 years old when he'd signed). The fact was, Phil, after his four hits in the fall of 1960, realized that he didn't need Leiber and Stoller anymore.

Leiber and Stoller were angry at Phil's ingratitude. They felt they'd put him through the learning curve, had underwritten his care and feeding, only to have him sell them out when the payoff was just around the corner. Nevertheless, Leiber and Stoller didn't want to alienate Phil—not when it looked like he was about to get hot. So the three men continued to see each other, and even work together, acting like nothing untoward had happened. And when Phil took a new job—this one at Atlantic Records—Leiber and Stoller, potential vendors to the record giant, escorted Phil to his new digs.

During that winter of 1960–61, Phil's ego inflated again. After the deflation that occurred after the demise of the Teddy Bears, it had taken Phil two years to work his way back to the top. Now, with four hit records on the charts, Phil was again convinced that he was The Man. The huffy departure from Leiber and Stoller was a case in point. Newly installed at Atlantic Records, Phil soon began to throw his weight around.

Atlantic Records had become a record industry leader in the 1950s, cashing in primarily on the transition by African-American musicians into the mainstream, and the growing popularity of the soul sound. Its primary producer was Jerry Wexler, who had shepherded such talents as Big Joe Turner, Ray Charles, the Drifters, and Wilson Pickett to stardom. Later, Wexler would be behind Aretha Franklin's rise. But when Phil arrived at Atlantic, Wexler had to take a back seat.

"He came in as an instant sore winner," Wexler later told Ribowsky. When Wexler suggested something, Phil would shoot it down. Wexler was offended by the upstart, and almost immediately started talking about firing him. Worse, Phil seemed to have no set duties—he had the power to bounce around from act to act, kibitzing at will, seemingly sniping at everyone. But Wexler knew Phil had the imprimatur of Atlantic founder Ahmet Ertegun, a legend in the music business. Phil, in fact, had even taken to imitating some of Ertegun's mannerisms.

But off on his new high, Phil wasn't controllable by anyone, even Ertegun. Phil had the power to audition new acts, would make arrangements for the new talent to meet him at a studio, but then never show up. The same went for session musicians; at times there would be twenty or thirty people waiting around a studio for Phil to make his appearance.

When he did come in, Phil had a tendency to go over the top in his criticism of the talent. Sometimes he'd rush into the studio and jerk a guitar out of a player's hands, telling him to pay attention, that he wanted something done *this* way, not that. When he got into one of his moods, nobody could bring him back to reality.

Part of the problem was Phil's unfamiliarity with the more technically sophisticated eight-track recording equipment in use at Atlantic. Phil was used to mixing three or four tracks, not eight. Some at Atlantic thought Phil was intimidated by the equipment he didn't understand, and compensated for it by becoming nastier than he had to be. For all of his life, Phil would be far more comfortable with monaural recording—he never quite got the hang of stereo.

After several attempts to collaborate with Phil, Wexler finally gave it up as a lost cause. Phil, too, decided he'd come to the wrong address. Late in the spring, Phil abandoned his post at Atlantic, but not before walking off with advances totaling about $10,000, according to Wexler.

While this behavior might be characterized as merely boorish, there is every reason to conjecture that it may actually have been pathological, that is, the results of a recognized form of mental illness: bipolar disorder. Years later, when Phil told Mick Brown that he suffered from it, there is every reason to believe that he was telling the truth. Indeed, Phil's history throughout the decades since his days as a Fairfax High School student seems to show episode after episode of manic highs followed by depressive lows.

As early as 1960, in fact, Phil had begun to see a highly respected psychiatrist in New York, Dr. Harold Kaplan. Phil would later say that he began to see Dr. Kaplan as part of a campaign to avoid being drafted for military service. For some reason, Phil had an obsessive fear of being drafted, even though he had reached draft-eligible age at a time when the United States wasn't at war. But it appears that Phil's psychological problems were far deeper than a mere phobia about being in uniform.

Significantly, Phillips later told Ribowsky that Phil had difficulty sleeping—a classic symptom of bipolar disorder. "He never went to sleep," Phillips told Ribowsky. "I'd go to sleep and Phil would sit on his bed and listen to the radio until 6 or 7 A.M. and he'd have his guitar in his hands, playing riffs. . . . He was afraid of the night, afraid to sleep . . ."

Bipolar disorder remains one of the least understood of the more common forms of mental illness, in part because of the difficulty of its diagnosis. Some estimates are that somewhere between 3 and 9 percent of all Americans suffer from some form of the disorder—if true, that would mean that somewhere between ten and thirty million Americans have it.[27] The disorder is thought to have a genetic component, that is, it can be inherited from the parents. The exact neuromechanism that causes the disorder isn't clear. The manifestations, however, include significant swings in mood from elation to despair, sometimes taking place over months, even years, or alternatively, quite rapidly. Since most people seek medical attention for the disorder when they are in the depressed phase, it is often misdiagnosed by physicians as unipolar depression. A misdiagnosis may result in a patient being prescribed antidepressants, which can be extremely dangerous, not only for the patient, but for those around him, because antidepressants make the manic phase much, much worse. Suicide and occasionally homicide can result if the disorder is left untreated.

The main symptoms of bipolar disorder—previously known as manic depression—vary depending on the type,

---

[27] The 3 to 8.8 percent figure is cited in Dr. William R. Marchand's article for *Hospital Physician* magazine, December 2003. Other estimates, however, put the incidence at between .8 and 1.5 percent.

but the manic phase often includes "an abnormally elevated, expansive, or irritable mood. Associated symptoms are grandiosity, decreased need for sleep, increased speech, flight of ideas or racing thoughts, distractibility, increased activity and excessive involvement in pleasurable activities."[28] Over time, these symptoms can result in delusions, paranoia, irresponsible spending, car accidents, promiscuity or excessive reliance on drugs or alcohol. In 90 percent of the reported cases, bipolar disorder results in psychotic behavior at one point or another during the sufferer's lifetime. This illustrates part of the problem with bipolar disorder: while there are effective drug treatments available, notably lithium, they require the cooperation of the patient in self-medication. Failing that, sometimes the only thing that can be done is temporary institutionalization.

Phil's documented behavior from the Fairfax years all the way up to the night at his castle tends to strongly support the assertion that he indeed suffered from bipolar disorder. This organic pathology would likely have been inherited from either or both of his parents. Ribowsky's description of Phil's father—being a light-hearted, popular fellow, then taking his own life in an apparent suicide—suggests that Ben Spector may have suffered from undiagnosed bipolar disorder, and that the condition may have been passed down to his offspring.

But Phil also appears to have had other, perhaps non-organic psychological problems, among them a severe reaction to his father's death. Here, the long repression of the facts concerning the death would create an internal complex, a fusion of secrecy and puzzlement inside unexpressible anger, cloaked with constant feelings of inferiority that could only be brought to bay by proving to anyone and everyone that he was better than they were, which inevitably manifested itself in Phil's ever-growing need to have more and more control. The anger toward his father for his suicide, his

---

[28] Marchand, ibid.

abandonment, could never be expressed in a healthy way without tarnishing the icon of the beloved father. So the pressure would build up, year after suppressed year, until it became the hardened shell holding the withered soul within.

The details of Dr. Kaplan's treatment of Phil, of course, are the subject of confidential doctor–patient privilege—that is, unless such a privilege is waived by Phil—so one can only speculate as to the role Phil's psychological problems may have played in the death of Lana Clarkson. Under certain legal defenses, of course, the records of Kaplan's treatment could become known to prosecutors.[29]

That Phil relied heavily on Kaplan's treatment for years seems beyond dispute. Many of those interviewed by Ribowsky, for instance, told him that Phil often telephoned Kaplan, who had his offices in New York, from various studio gigs in Los Angeles over the ensuing decade, spending thousands of dollars in long distance charges while Kaplan endeavored to get him back on an even keel. Phil would later tell people that at times he had *two* psychiatrists at work on his case, and that his bill for such services was staggering. Phil liked to imply that his psychological suffering was the price he paid for being "a genius."

Despite the uncertainty about details of Kaplan's method of treatment of Phil, Ribowsky was able to isolate several interesting insights about the doctor's relationship with his famous client. In one, Ribowsky found a witness who asserted that Kaplan had attempted to treat Phil with LSD as a means of inducing Phil to confront the demon posed by his father's suicide.

Ribowsky heard the story from Danny Davis, who would later become Phil's most loyal executive.

"He put himself under the influence of LSD prescribed by Dr. Kaplan," Davis told Ribowsky, "and he told me that when he was under he saw his father commit suicide. Phil

---

[29] Kaplan himself cannot be a witness; he died in 1998.

always said he hated his father for what he did, for taking the easy way out. The acid [LSD] went right to the heart of that hatred, to the pain, and it horrified him. . . . it made him confront what he didn't want to."[30]

---

[30] *He's a Rebel*, Ribowsky, p. 233. In the early 1960s, the use of LSD to assist patients in coming to grips with deeply repressed psychological trauma was on the cutting edge of clinical psychiatric theory, largely as a result of the views of Dr. Humphrey Osmond. Osmond was a respected Canadian psychiatrist who had provided the substance to Aldous Huxley, and contended it offered great promise to the study of schizophrenia and the treatment of chronic alcoholism. Dr. Osmond died in early February of 2004.

17

THE DEAL OF THE ART

After leaving Atlantic Records, Phil participated (with about a dozen other songwriters, arrangers and producers) in the production of a new song, "Every Breath I Take," by Gene Pitney. Pitney had become acquainted with Phil back in his Los Angeles days, and liked him. Pitney told Ribowsky that the two had once had a meal at a Chinese restaurant together, and that Phil had impressed him as someone with clear ideas about rock-and-roll, and how to put them into practice, even before his sojourn in New York. Phil also made allusions about his own insanity to Pitney: "He said, 'My sister's in an asylum—and she's the sane one in my family,' " Pitney told Ribowsky.[31]

Unexpectedly, the Paris Sisters' recording of "Be My Boy" became a modest hit in the spring of 1961. Encouraged, Sill flew to New York in an attempt to induce Phil to return to Los Angeles to produce more Paris Sisters records. Phil agreed, and late that spring returned to Los Angeles with a new song for the Sisters, "I Love How You Love Me." Phil's idea was to take some of the yearning tone of "To Know Him Is to Love Him" and try to replicate it with the Sisters.

By all accounts the recording session was laborious, in part because of Phil's continued dissatisfaction with the

---

[31] Pitney would repeat this story in a news interview in 2003 just after Phil was arrested.

results. He knew what he wanted to hear, but just couldn't explain how to get there. So the studio musicians played the song, or its parts, over and over again, waiting for inspiration to strike Phil. He thought the lower ceiling at Gold Star would flatten the violins he wanted to use, so he put the violinists in another, regulation-sized studio, taped their contribution, then tried to blend the strings with the rest of the package. His idea was to somehow make the whole thing flow together, so that the parts were almost subliminal. He kept readjusting the volume of the violins so they were ever-present, just not dominant, and in fact, almost an extension of the singers' voices, as if they had stopped forming words and had started sounding like strings. At length, Phil took the package to Lester Sill's house in the valley, where he stayed up all night, listening to it over and over, trying to get the balance just right. Somehow, when he was done, the song emerged as a unified whole.

Sill's partner Lee Hazlewood began to chafe at Sill's indulgence of Phil. He began to feel that Sill preferred to work with Phil, rather than him, and the situation grew worse when Phil treated him dismissively, as if Hazlewood were yesterday's news. Finally Hazlewood told Sill he had to choose between him or Phil.

"I'll never forget it," Sill told Ribowsky years later. "I was there with Phil cutting the Paris Sisters and Lee walked in all pissed. He said, 'Look, I can't handle it. I'm doin' work, too, but you're spending all your time with Phil.'" Hazlewood told Sill that he was going to try to reunite with Duane Eddy. If Sill liked Phil so much, he could have him, Hazlewood said.

Sill said that was fine with him, and with that, the Sill—Hazlewood partnership broke up.

Shortly thereafter, Phil approached Sill with a proposition. Now that Hazlewood was gone, why didn't they form their own partnership?

This made sense to Sill. Rather than hiring Phil on a project-by-project basis, he would now have access to Phil as a partner. And if Phil continued to produce hits, that would more

than make up for the loss of Hazlewood. That summer, Sill and
Phil formed a new label, Philles Records, from both of their
first names. The pair also formed a publishing company—
"Mother Bertha Records"—which eventually would hold the
copyrights to many of the Spector songs, including, at one
point, "To Know Him Is to Love Him."

By that spring, the payola scandal had already burst open,
and was in fact even beginning to recede into the industry's
darkest don't-ask, don't-tell corners, something considered
extremely odiferous. By late 1959, investigators from the
U.S. House of Representatives' Special Subcommittee on
Legislative Oversight, having just finished a publicity-
garnering probe of television quiz shows like *The $64,000
Question*, decided to go after the broadcast music business.[32]
Soon committee investigators were quizzing deejays. Representatives of composers complained that deejays were
rigging the ratings of pop songs for cash. The Federal Com-
munications Commission weighed in with a threat to jerk
the licenses of stations whose deejays were engaging in payola. The Federal Trade Commission weighed in with charges
that some labels and distributors, including Finfer's and
Lipsius' Universal, were engaged in deceptive trading prac-
tices. Stories soon circulated that some deejays were pulling
in anywhere from $25,000 to $50,000 extra every year
from play-for-pay. There was also talk about organized
crime—that people who rocked the boat might "wake up in
an alley."[33]

Late in 1959 and early in 1960, a number of disk jockeys

---

[32] In some ways, the payola probe was a reaction to the rise of rock-
and-roll, and the penetration into mainstream radio by African-
American musicians. Unable to account for the rising popularity of
black artists, or performers who blurred the line like Elvis or Jerry Lee
Lewis, conservative congressmen came to believe that much of the music broadcast could only have been aired because of payoffs.

[33] *Payola in the Music Industry*, Segrave, p.103.

were fired by their stations after they admitted taking money from record promoters. As far as the House investigators could tell, the practice seemed endemic across the country. It wasn't long before they arrived in Philadelphia, where they questioned Dick Clark. The investigators were provided with information that Clark held a number of interests in music production firms. After being questioned, Clark said he would get rid of all his outside ties, and ABC said it would impose a new policy to forbid anyone who selected on-air entertainment from having such personal financial interests. Rather than comply with the edict, Clark's producer resigned. Alan Freed, meanwhile, was fired from his post in New York when he refused to sign a statement saying he had never taken money to boost a record.

Sensing blood, the House subcommittee decided to hold hearings in Washington early in 1960. By March, the investigators had zeroed in on Clark. One subcommittee member demanded that Clark be called as a witness by the subcommittee, saying, "This man is obviously seriously involved in payola." The subcommittee chairman, Oren Harris, an Arkansas Democrat, wasn't enthusiastic about calling Clark as a witness; some thought that Harris had decided to protect Clark because he rarely played songs by African-American artists, that few black teenagers were shown dancing on his show, and because he tended to moderate the pelvis-pushing of the entertainers who did appear.[34]

By this point, the subcommittee's staff investigators had determined that Clark held financial interests in some seventeen different companies involved with the popular music business.

Clark was called to testify in late April of 1960. By then, a data-processing company had analyzed all of the records played on *American Bandstand* between August of 1957 and the end of November 1959—a period that included the meteoric rise of "To Know Him Is to Love Him"—and determined

---

[34] Ibid, p. 109.

that the 1,885 records were played a total of 15,662 times. Records that Clark held a financial interest in were twice as likely to be played as those he didn't, the firm concluded, even while it asserted that there was no difference in favoritism between the two types of records! The firm admitted that it had been hired to conduct the study by Clark himself, and that it had counted the twice-daily plays of the *American Bandstand* theme song, in which Clark had no financial interest, which tended to make the "interest" songs even more likely to be played on the air. Subcommittee members were incredulous that someone would try to sell them such a bill of goods.[35]

Among those who also testified before Clark did was Harry Finfer, the mogul of Universal Distributing. Finfer admitted that he and his partners had sold a quarter-interest in a record label, Jamie, to Clark for $125, and that, when Clark decided to get rid of his outside businesses to keep his ABC job in November of 1959, he had sold the share back to them for $15,000. It also turned out that Finfer and his partners had paid Clark a salary of $200 a week, retroactive to May of 1958. Altogether, Clark had earned $31,700 from Finfer and his partners between June of 1957 and November of 1959—a very nice return on his initial $125 investment.

When it was his turn to testify, however, Clark told the subcommittee that he had never taken payola. "I have not done anything that I think I should be ashamed of," Clark said, "or that is illegal or immoral, and I hope to eventually convince you of this. I believe in my heart that I have never taken payola." Whereupon the subcommittee staff demonstrated that while Clark had earned $167,750 in salary over the prior three years, he'd also earned $409,020 in stock gains on investments of $53,773, a return of better than eight-to-one.

In fact, Clark said, he had interests in thirty-three different businesses, almost all of them tied in some way to his role as the leading teen music popularizer in the country. He

---

[35] Ibid, p. 144.

never intended to favor any records in which he held an interest, he said. "The truth, gentlemen," Clark said, "is that I did not consciously favor such records. Maybe I did so without realizing it." Besides, Clark added, until the subcommittee started poking around, no one had ever said there was any conflict between playing records that one had a financial interest in.

The subcommittee went on to detail many other instances of apparent conflict, including Clark's obtaining the copyright on many records that were played on the show. In all, Clark or companies he had an interest in held the copyright on 160 songs; 143 of these copyrights came to Clark as "gifts." The subcommittee cited an example: before Clark or his nominee obtained the copyright to "16 Candles" by the Crests, the song was played four times in ten weeks on *American Bandstand*. After acquiring the copyright, the song was played twenty-seven times in the next twelve weeks, and it soon shot up the charts.[36]

At least one of the companies that Clark held an interest in was one "which managed and recorded Duane Eddy."[37] This was Jamie Records, jointly owned by Finfer, Lipsius and Clark, which, through Universal, distributed the Eddy records produced by Sill and Hazlewood. Eventually, Hazlewood and Eddy left Jamie and signed a new deal with RCA Victor, after Hazlewood's breakup with Sill, but the incestuous relationship was marked as suspected payola by the congressional subcommittee.

Although both Clark and Finfer had been seriously embarrassed by the 1960 hearings, neither had been damaged beyond repair. Indeed, Clark was generally described as having done a persuasive enough job with his testimony to have saved his reputation. Not a word about the suspect rise of "To Know Him Is to Love Him" had come out at the hearing, and by the summer of 1961 Sill hoped that Finfer was still

---

[36] Ibid, p. 147.
[37] Ibid, p. 147.

willing to do business. He wanted Finfer and Universal to agree to distribute Philles Records. Finfer and Lipsius agreed to this. In return, Sill and Phil granted Jamie Records an interest in future Philles product, which had the effect of making Finfer and Lipsius shareholders in Philles.[38]

Even with a major distributor cut in on the action, Phil decided that Philles' working capital was still too small. He decided to lasso Helen Noga, a wealthy Beverly Hills woman who had "discovered" Johnny Mathis, and who was Mathis' manager. Noga had been born to a ranching family in the San Joaquin Valley, and had been intimately involved in the San Francisco nightclub scene in the early 1940s. Noga promised to provide the new label with working capital to pay for studio time; in return, she thought she would also get a piece of the action. In the end, however, she would be disappointed—just like Lester Sill.[39]

---

[38] *He's a Rebel*, Ribowsky. p. 96.
[39] Helen Noga died in April of 2002.

18

CRYSTAL CLEAR

After finishing the Paris Sisters' latest record, Phil returned to New York in early June of 1961. By this time, Phil's roommate, Terry Phillips, realized that his interests and Phil's had diverged substantially. Phillips wanted to write songs; Phil wanted to create a business. That same month, Phillips moved out. Eventually he would go on to write songs for a group called Jay and the Americans.

Not long after Phillips left, Phil's old friend Michael Spencer moved in. With his upper-class upbringing and his classical music training, Spencer tended to look on Phil as something of a curious novelty. He was interested to see what people made of Phil, not the momma's boy of the old Fairfax days, but this new, improved model, the one people believed was eccentric and flamboyant; by this time, Phil had begun to grow his hair long (unheard of in 1961), and habitually wore a long cape. People laughed at him sometimes, in his high-heeled boots, and even his best friends called him "D'Artagnan," after the character from *The Three Musketeers.* "Making it in New York fed his ego and his personality," Spencer told Ribowsky years later.

Spencer was sensitive enough to realize the core of Phil's problem: his personality had never had to mature, and then had gotten locked in, owing to his success in the music business. In short, Phil was a teenager, and would always be a teenager, even when he got to be an old man. He was incapable of growing, at least emotionally. Spencer tried to get his old friend to broaden his interests to matters other than music, with limited success. Sometimes they would prowl the city like tourists. But Phil resolutely refused to go back to the old Soundview neighborhood, possibly because the memories of his father still cut too deep.

During that summer, Phil continued to drop by Hill and Range, still the crossroads of auditioning acts. Here Phil seemed to be filling two roles: first as a contract producer for Hill and Range and its various labels, including Big Top Records, and second, surreptitiously, as an executive for his own label, Philles. As usual with Phil, the lines blurred; he hoped to pick up something that his inner ear told him might be worked into a hit, and if he could filch it for Philles, so much the better. Over a few weeks he heard the auditioning efforts of three different groups, the Ducanes, the Creations and the Crystals. The first two sang doo-wop; it was a style that Phil had never really had an affinity for. The Crystals, though, were a different story.

For the past several years, "girl groups" had been making advances in the largely male rock-and-roll field. The Shirelles, the Chantels, and other imitators featured a chorus-like rock harmony that seemed to sell, particularly when the subject was light romance. The Crystals—five African-American teenagers from Brooklyn—wanted to follow their lead.

The five Crystals were the creation of Benny Wells, the uncle of their lead singer, Barbara Alston, then 17 years old. Wells had fashioned the group after hearing them perform gospel songs in church. He took them to Hill and Range, where Phil first heard them perform a song called "There's No Other (Like My Baby)," an uptempo R & B composition by Leroy Bates. Phil convinced the group to slow the tempo down, then turned out all the lights in the studio. He wanted to see if the song might sell as a romantic concoction.

After two weeks of listening to the reworked song, Phil realized that Hill and Range hadn't yet signed the Crystals to a contract. On June 28, the same day that the five Crystals graduated from high school in Brooklyn, he brought them into the ratty confines of Mira Sound in Manhattan and signed them to a "personal services" contract. The fine print of the agreement gave ownership of all master recordings made by the group to Philles, promised royalties to the performers from future record sales, and provided a modest advance. The five high school girls, dazzled with the prospect of stardom, agreed to the deal without benefit of any legal advice; even so, it wasn't as if they had much bargaining power. As soon as they were on the dotted line, Phil put them to work, recording "There's No Other."

The agreement gave Phil virtually complete control over the group's output for Philles, forever and ever, and left them completely dependent on Philles for an honest accounting of the royalties, which would turn out to be much less than one might have otherwise expected, given the six hits that the Crystals would eventually produce. Years later, the agreement would still be the subject of litigation, as three of the Crystals tried to sue Phil for back royalties on Crystals hits that were eventually included in at least two movies, including *GoodFellas*.

But in the summer of 1962, Phil and Sill were anxious to get a product on the market. After finishing the cut of "There's No Other," Phil sent the master tape to Sill in Los Angeles, who decided it would be the first Philles release. That fall, Phil slapped another song, "Oh Yeah, Maybe Baby" onto the B side of the Crystals' first effort, and took credit with Leroy Bates for the songwriting. After this, Sill rushed the package off to Universal for its distribution services. Philles was in business.

Two months later, when Big Top and Hill and Range discovered that Phil had signed the Crystals to a contract with Philles, they were furious. They thought Phil had betrayed them—that he was only supposed to rehearse and produce the group on contract for Big Top, not swipe them for his own company.

"We were just incensed," Big Top co-owner John Bienstock later told Ribowsky, "because that was a terrific group, and for him to do that shows the type of character he was. We felt he was less than ethical, and, obviously, he was then shown the door." Big Top accused Phil of breaching his contract; Phil said that wasn't so, that Big Top hadn't made any effort to sign the Crystals, so as far as he was concerned, they were up for grabs. But now that he was *persona non grata* at Hill and Range, Phil had to make it on his own— there would be no more freebies he could swipe from his long-time pals in the Brill Building.

By that point, however, Phil had to realize what a crazy racket the record business was. What seemed like a hit in the studio sometimes did a swan dive, and what everyone thought would be a sure loser might suddenly ignite. There was no accounting for the public's taste. The Gene Pitney song Phil had worked on the year before made a modest move, then sank like a stone. Just when Phil began to despair, suddenly the Paris Sisters' "I Love How You Love Me" shot skyward, finally topping out at number 5. That made the Sisters the hot new act, so even as Sill was urging Jamie Records to distribute Philles' first record, the Crystals' "There's No Other," Phil found himself back on a plane to Los Angeles to make another song for the Paris Sisters. This was "He Knows I Love Him Too Much," written by Gerry Goffin and Carole King, a domestic tandem who had already reached the top with the Shirelles' "Will You Love Me Tomorrow," and "Chains," sung by the Cookies. Both songs tended to explore the borderline between love and abuse, a recurrent theme in Goffin–King collaborations. "He Knows I Love Him Too Much" was more of this same vein.

The new song made it to number 34, a modest success, and the Paris Sisters began to hope that their best days were still ahead of them. By this time, they had recorded enough material for an album (*The Paris Sisters Sing*), but somehow most of the material was inadvertently erased! Sill took the blame for the fiasco, saying that an underling had accidentally wiped the masters clean. It was his fault, Sill said, because he'd filed them in the wrong place. Then things got worse, when the Paris Sisters discovered that rather than the large pot of money they were expecting from "I Love How You Love Me" and "He Knows I Love Him Too Much," *they* actually owed *Philles*. Sill told the Sisters that the expenses on making the lost album had devoured the royalties from the two hits. Needless to say, the sisters were furious with Sill, as well as Phil. According to Ribowsky, "they staged a series of nasty scenes in the office," and alienated both Sill and Phil. Phil went back to New York.

The Paris Sisters faded into oblivion.

Even before he returned to New York, Phil heard from one of his partners—Helen Noga. After having given Phil some front money for producing the Crystals and the two doo-wop groups, Noga wanted her piece—50 percent—in writing. She made Phil sign a contract in October of 1961 outlining the terms and conditions of more sessions with the three groups. Now Phil was in the same position as someone who had sold more than 100 percent of an enterprise, as in the Broadway play *The Producers*. There was Noga in for 50 percent, Finfer and Lipsius were in for a third, and Sill and himself had two-thirds, which added up to 150 percent. Something had to give, and it would be Noga, the most expendable.

Looking for a way out of his predicament, Phil made yet another deal, this one with Liberty Records, the creation of—Lew Bedell's cousin, Si Waronker! Truly, nothing was ever wasted in the music business. In this deal, Phil would become head of Liberty's East Coast talent development and production for a salary of $25,000 a year. Liberty pre-paid the salary, and threw in a bonus of $5,000. Besides this, he would be able to independently produce the Crystals and the two doo-wop groups. Now that he had a slug of cash, Phil could deal Noga out of the over-subscribed Philles picture. He reached a new agreement with her in which he paid her back for money she'd advanced, and then cut her in for a share of the proceeds of the first three Philles records.

Phil moved into Liberty's East Coast offices on 57th Street in Manhattan. According to Ribowsky, he didn't like the desk the office came with, so he had the label replace it with a large conference table. There he sat, Mr. Big, behind the largest desk in New York. Phil spent most of his first few weeks on the job playing an air hockey game atop the giant desk, Ribowsky reported.

19

DANCING THE SCREW

In January of 1962, Phil again returned to Los Angeles. Now in the full flush of his sudden success, Phil began to focus all of his charm on Annette Merar—the "Spector's Three" front singer who had been the girlfriend of Phil's one-time friend, Russ Titelman. Phil had first started dating Annette—another tall blond—in the summer, when he was recording the Paris Sisters. Then, after he'd returned to New York, he telephoned her incessantly. According to what Annette later told Ribowsky, her family wasn't very excited about Phil's attentions; they thought he was just too weird.[40]

Now, after spending two weeks rushing Annette Merar off her feet, Phil wanted to return to New York. He pleaded with Annette to come with him and, throwing all caution to the wind, she agreed.

Later Annette would evince a sort of bitter wistfulness about her relationship with Phil. On one hand, she was very attracted to his quick mind, and what she saw as his artistic sensitivity and vulnerability; but on the other, she felt she could never really get close to him, a problem that grew worse after they married a year later, in February of 1963. Phil, she thought, was too driven to get to the top of the pile in

---

[40] Williams, in *Out of His Head*, never did get the Annettes, Kleinbard and Merar, straight. "It seems hard to believe," he wrote, "but none of Phil's closest friends . . . know whether or not both Annettes were in fact the same girl."

the music business to ever really be interested in someone for herself. "He was an emotional tease," Annette later told Ribowsky. "He would appear to be the sensitive, lovely genius, but the minute you expected it to bloom, it would fly off."

Immersed in his drive to dominate the record industry, Phil kept Annette on ice in their New York apartment—always there for him, but for no one else. Within a year of the marriage, Annette thought she would go crazy with frustration.

After a few months playing air hockey on his big desk at Liberty, Phil decided to make another record with the Crystals. This would be "Uptown," and for the first time, Phil began to move his music-making slightly away from teenage love angst, embedding a social message between the lines. Written by Barry Mann and Cynthia Weil, the song plugged into the aspirations of those on the bottom of the socioeconomic heap, and explored the yearning feelings of those who were looked down upon by the better-off. Ribowsky later reported that when writer Gerry Goffin, watching the takes from inside the control booth, asked Phil who had written the song, Phil said he had. Later, Goffin would wonder: why would Phil tell a lie that could so easily be exposed? He came to believe that Phil wanted to be seen as a creative person so badly, if even for a passing moment, that he didn't care what people later concluded about his veracity.

"Uptown" was released in March of 1962, and headed straight for the top. Suddenly the Crystals were hotter than the Paris Sisters had ever been. Phil decided to strike while the iron was still smouldering. He bought another seemingly sado-masochistic song from Gerry Goffin and Carole King, "He Hit Me (And It Felt Like a Kiss)," and put this through the Mira Sound studio machine. The Crystals hated the song for its abusive theme, and so did Sill. Phil didn't care. He thought it reflected the dark side of teen yearning that seemed to play well. He slapped a similar song onto the B side, "No One Ever Tells You," and shipped the masters off to Sill. Sill was convinced that Phil was out of his mind if he thought "He Hit Me" would sell.

"He Hit Me" came out in June of 1962, and almost immediately ran into controversy because of its lyrics. Major radio stations and their networks began receiving piles of mail protesting the violent imagery of the song, and soon Sill and Phil decided to pull it. They had thousands of copies recalled from record stores across the nation before the song could permanently demolish the label's image.

But even before this happened, Phil had decided to end his charade with Liberty Records. Less than a year after taking up his position behind his big desk, Phil in May told the label he was quitting. The label, after having paid Phil $30,000 upfront, realized they'd been conned. At the time, they didn't realize how badly, however. In June, just after the initial release of "He Hit Me," Phil walked out of Liberty for the last time and flew back to Los Angeles. He left Annette, not yet his wife, alone in New York.

A week later, now working exclusively for Philles, Phil almost feverishly began making the song that would later provide the title for Ribowsky's book: "He's a Rebel." The first problem was, he had no Crystals to make it with, since they refused to fly out to California. Sill told him it was no big deal: they could make the record with anyone, since they owned the name of the group. That was when Phil realized he didn't really need the actual Crystals to make the record. He figured no one would know—except the real Crystals—and he was right.

The genesis of "He's a Rebel" had some other interesting aspects as well. For one thing, Phil first heard the song, written by Gene Pitney, when he was still at Liberty—ostensibly reviewing Pitney material for that label. The virtue of his one-sided agreement with Liberty, however, was that while Phil could seem as though he was working for his employers, he could also be working for himself and Lester Sill. It was shortly after obtaining the rights to Pitney's song that Phil informed Liberty he was quitting.

But if Phil was playing both ends against the middle, so was Pitney's management. They suggested to Phil that if he bought the song (either for Liberty or Philles, it didn't matter to them), he could have it exclusively. But that wasn't possible under the Copyright Act. No sooner had Phil walked out the door with Pitney's song under his arm, than did Pitney's people sell it to another label—Liberty! Truly, in the record business there was little honor, only money. It seems possible that Phil knew that Liberty would soon be making its own cut of "He's a Rebel," and wanted to beat his old employer out of the box. That may have been why he decided to record the song immediately, with or without the real Crystals.

To make the record, Phil assembled a crew of six veteran West Coast musicians—two guitarists, a pianist, a drummer (Hal Blaine), and two bass players. *Two* bass players? This had never been done before, and some people thought it was ridiculous.

But by this point Phil had finally begun to grasp the sort of sound he wanted to make in a studio—a sound that was peculiar to Gold Star's pygmy ceiling. And here, if anything, stands Phil's most original contribution to rock-and-roll— the so-called "Wall of Sound." It was a concept born of necessity, not just because of the Gold Star ceilings, but mostly because of the advent of the transistor radio.

These days, with home sound systems that can fill up an entire wall and cost as much as a trip around the world, an era of sophistication in sound processing that would make Edison blush for his lack of foresight, people tend to forget how limited the delivery system was in the early days of rock-and-roll. By 1962, the cost of the transistor radio had fallen to the point where almost anyone could afford one. That was good, because it ramped up the growth and segmentation of the teen market that had begun seven years earlier. But the fact was, the single speaker of the transistor radio, or even of its larger cousin, the car radio, was both cheap and dinky—often no larger than three inches across. Stereo, of course, was unheard of as yet in radio—everything was monaural. For most teen songs, the noise that came out of the puny little speaker was flat and tinny, and often even scratchy. The sound quality made many of the songs hard to

take seriously, and if there was one thing Phil wanted, it was
for people to take his songs seriously.

How to get around this technical problem? By trial and
error, Phil realized that doubling the instrumentation tended
to make the music sound fuller—larger, more complete.
Paired with the low ceiling of Gold Star and tweaked again
with subsequent electronic manipulation, the sound simply
sounded more majestic despite its Achilles' heel delivery
mechanism. And the market seemed to respond to this bigger sound, which, if done well, tended to fold back in on itself as a harmonious whole. Phil even had a term for it:
"little symphonies for kids," he called it. Instead of a
scratchy, tinny, often thin sound that left the listener vaguely
dissatisfied, the Spector sound moved people in some primal, centering way.

Having rushed around assembling his musicians, now
Phil had to find some pseudo-Crystals. Sill directed him to-
ward a session group called the Blossoms, who had done
background vocals for Sam Cooke and Duane Eddy. The
Blossoms—originally managed by none other than Johnny
Otis—were comprised of Darlene Wright (later Darlene
Love), Gloria Jones, and Fanita James. They would be the
Crystals for the purpose of making the hurry-up-and-get-it-
to-the-stores-first version of "He's a Rebel," along with a
male singer who specialized in singing in a high voice,
Bobby Sheen.

Recording began in mid-July. As usual, Phil forced everyone to work-work-work until the sound was what he kept
hearing in his mind, even if no one else could tell the difference. Soon, the guitarists' wrists and fingers were in severe
pain. Still, Phil made the band play on, cranking the sound
up to full volume in the control room, trying to make all the
noises work together. This was how he intended to overcome
the limitations of the puny speakers that brought his product
to market.

For Darlene Wright, standing (or singing) in for the real
Crystals was just another day's work, one of many gigs that
the talented singer had as a backup vocalist. After getting

$3,000 from Philles—she split this with Fanita—Darlene guessed that she'd never see Phil again. Jones and Sheen got the standard session fee.

But Darlene was wrong: a few weeks later, Phil had her sign another one of his "personal services" contracts with Philles. This agreement, too, would later become a focal point of bitter litigation.

With the sounds recorded at Gold Star, Phil and Sill next hurried over to a better-equipped sound studio to mix the final master. Just as they were finishing, several musicians came into the control room. They were astounded to hear that Phil and Sill were mixing the same song that they'd been playing in their own recording session down the hall!

According to Ribowsky, this was when Phil and Sill heard for the first time that Pitney's people had sold "He's a Rebel" to Liberty as well as Phil. Liberty's version would feature Vicki Carr.

Both records would be released at about the same time that summer, in August. Phil put out the word: Philles had the song first, with the Crystals, and then Liberty came along with Vicki Carr to "cover" the five African-American Crystals—actually the four African-American pseudo-Crystals. The Liberty people tried to bill their version as the "original," and "the hit," but the pseudo-Crystals flattened them over the airwaves and in the stores. "He's a Rebel" shot to the top and remained at Number One for weeks as 1962 came to a close.

About the only people surprised at the Crystals' mega-hit were the Crystals—the real Crystals, that is. Driving in a car someplace in Ohio in late August of 1962, the real Crystals were stunned to hear the disk jockey over the car radio announce their new hit. "We were in the car late at night," original Crystal Mary Thomas told Ribowsky, "when all of a sudden we hear: 'Here's the new Crystals song'—and our mouths fell open." Worse, they soon had to sing the song on their tour, and they didn't even know the words! Luckily, Pitney was also touring just ahead of them, and was able to teach them the song. But Darlene Love's hearty Gospel-like rendition was so different from Barbara Alston's softer voice that the original Crystals had to promote La La Brooks, herself a stand-in for an original Crystal, to singing lead. She was barely 16. Privately, the Crystals fumed over the way Phil had used their fame, but because of the contract they'd signed, there was nothing they could do about it.

Now Phil was in his glory days. With the Crystals—both real and substitute—having become the hottest group on the radio, his ego swelled yet again. This time it would devour Sill himself.

Even as "He's a Rebel" shot upward, Phil began maneuvers that would have the effect of leaving him in total control of Philles. Sill suddenly realized that his partner was making himself hard to reach. He discovered that certain deals had been done without his knowledge. It was as if Phil considered himself the record company, with Sill just along for the ride. Sill soon got the message.

By September, Phil was ready for a showdown. Finfer got caught up in the collision, which appears to have been engineered by Phil with Lipsius' help. By then Finfer and Lipsius had already reached a parting of their interests in Universal Distributing, with Finfer selling his share to Lipsius. That left only their joint minority interest in Philles through Jamie Records. It appears that Finfer thought he could take Philles over for himself, forcing out Lipsius and Sill, thereby getting control of Phil and by extension, the Crystals. But Phil had other ideas. He offered to buy out Lipsius' and Finfer's one-third interest in Philles, and once Lipsius agreed to the deal, Finfer, apparently a minority stakeholder to Lipsius in the one-third Philles interest, had no choice but to agree to the sale. That left only Sill, holding his own one-third of the stock. Both Sill and Finfer, already suspicious of each other, also thought that Lipsius had already cut his own back-room deal with Phil to sell them out, since Phil had agreed to keep Philles' arrangement with Lipsius' now wholly controlled Universal Distributing. With Finfer out of the way, Lipsius told Sill he had little choice but to agree to Phil's proposed buyout. At first, Sill wouldn't deal, but eventually, under more pressure from Lipsius—who began acting as Phil's attorney—he agreed to dicker with his estranged protégé.

Phil asked Sill what he wanted for his third of the label. Sill, irritated by a cocky, condescending Phil, finally told Phil he'd have to pay him a full year's worth of Philles master recording royalties to see his back. With the Crystals' hits, that would be a considerable sum. It appears that Phil balked at this demand, because Sill soon brought in a lawyer and brought suit against Phil. In the end, though, Sill gave up the fight; according to Ribowsky, he sold his interest in Philles and Mother Bertha Music, the copyright owner, for around $60,000—"a pittance," he called it. But by then he was sick of Phil and just "wanted the fuck out of there," he told Ribowsky. "If I wouldn't have, I would've killed him. It wasn't worth the aggravation."

The bitterness went both ways, apparently. In January of 1963, Phil had the Crystals—apparently the originals—go into the Mira Sound studios in Manhattan, where they recorded an unbroadcastable record, "(Let's Dance) The Screw—Part 1 and 2." According to Ribowsky, the only person who got a copy of the record was Lester Sill.

20

UP AGAINST THE WALL

"Is it live or is it Memorex?" That was the question years ago when Ella Fitzgerald sang high enough to shatter a crystal goblet. The point of the commercial, of course, was that a listener—or a goblet—couldn't tell the difference between live performance or the recording on the magnetic tape Memorex wanted consumers to buy.

Much the same could be said about the rock-and-roll that now began to permeate the early 1960s, and Phil Spector was by far its leading practitioner, as well as innovator.

The "Wall of Sound" was less a performance than it was a painstaking pastiche of recorded and re-recorded song elements, woven together after the fact like some laboratory concoction. Long gone were the days when the likes of the Soggy Bottom Boys could sing into Pappy O'Daniel's microphone, and what they sang was what you got. It was just like the difference between theater and film: an actor on stage has to work without a net, but in the movie business, a performer can foul up a hundred times or more and the audience will never know about it if the director and the film editor know what they're doing. In essence, that's what Phil had become: a director.

The resonance and the possibilities of the layered recording method excited Phil's imagination; best of all, it liberated him from the stars. Hadn't he just proved that a big-name performer was unnecessary? In Phil's mind, the singers were, while not quite superfluous, merely another instrument to be mixed and matched.

In late August of 1962, just after making the ersatz Crystals' "He's a Rebel" and before reaching the split with Sill, Phil returned to Gold Star with a new idea: he wanted to make a layered "Wall of Sound" version of "Zip-A-Dee-Doo-Dah," a venerable tune from Walt Disney's 1946 animated classic, *Song of the South*. For some reason, Phil had a predilection for Disney—the movie may have reminded him of the innocent, happier days back in the Bronx before his father's death. After all, Phil would have been 6 years old in 1946, just the right age to be enraptured by Disney's classic when it first came out.

The recording to "Zip-A-Dee-Doo-Dah" brought the Wall of Sound approach into full form. At Gold Star, Phil had assembled a mob scene: an acoustic guitar, an electric guitar, three different basses, two pianists on one piano, two saxophones, Hal Blaine on drums, and a percussionist. The "Phil-harmonic," as some began to waggishly call it, played the song over and over for nearly three hours. Something wasn't right, but Phil couldn't say what it was. By now the players were used to this hit-and-miss approach to making music, however aggravating and fatiguing it was. The recording engineer, Larry Levine, realized that over time, all the recording needles had gone into the red. It was a mishmash. He thought the sound would be far too distorted. He turned all the microphones off, one by one.

Phil was infuriated. Three hours of making noise, he said, and he'd just about gotten things exactly where he wanted them, and then Levine had turned everything off! Phil very nearly collapsed in depression. Shrugging, Levine turned the microphones back on, one by one, trying to replicate what Phil had ordered over the prior three hours. Just as Levine began to dial in the last instrument, the electric guitar played by Billy Strange, Phil leaped to his feet. That was it! He told Levine to start the tape. Levine said he still had to turn on Strange's microphone, but Phil told him not to do it—the sound was just right without it. Unmiked and unregulated, Strange's solo was picked up by the other microphones and filtered back from the session speaker to be picked up yet again. The guitar emerged as a snatch of strangled, tinny noise. Williams, in *Out of His Head*, wrote that it sounded "as if he were playing next door with the door shut." Phil was ecstatic.

A bit later, Phil mixed in a lead by Bobby Sheen, backed by Darlene Love and Fanita James. He was convinced he had invented a new sound, and that the "sharpies" in New York would bid the moon for the right to sell the record. Levine asked Phil what the name of the song was. "Zip-A-Dee-Doo-Dah," Phil said. Levine couldn't believe his ears: they'd made this deafening mishmash, and Phil had named it after a cartoon ditty?

But some would later point to the day that "Zip-A-Dee-Doo-Dah" was cut as the day heavy metal was born.

Over the next year, even as Lester Sill was being forced out of the company he'd helped start, the Spector-directed hits kept piling up: more Crystals ("He's Sure the Boy I Love," "Da Doo Ron Ron," "Then He Kissed Me"), along with more by Sheen, Love and James (calling themselves "Bob B. Soxx and the Blue Jeans"), and three by Darlene Love as a soloist of sorts. Some of these were recorded at Gold Star in Hollywood, and others at Mira Sound in Manhattan. Phil was the talk of the business, taking an independent label like Philles (with help from Lipsius) and leaving all the big corporate labels in the dust. And by August, he'd added yet another group: the Ronettes. Again the legend gets muddled with contradictory facts, however.

Phil had actually had the Ronettes on ice for the better part of a year before recording them, it appears. According to Ribowsky's version of the legend, Phil had seen the Ronettes for the first time in late 1961 while they were dancing at the Peppermint Lounge in Manhattan. They'd been under contract with another label, Dimension, but hadn't had much success as recording artists.

The Peppermint Lounge was at 128 West 45th Street, just east of Times Square. It first became famous in the fall of 1961 as a club frequented by New Jersey teenagers, sort of the valley girls of their day, where the twist was almost a religious rite. At one point that fall—not long after President John F. Kennedy was filmed for newsreels dancing the twist with Jackie—the Peppermint Lounge became a sort of epi-center for Manhattan's rich and famous. Among the profes-sionals booked at the club were the Ronettes, a trio of young, lithe, mixed-race girls who had been raised on Manhattan's upper west side. The trio included sisters Veronica and Es-telle Bennett and their cousin, Nedra Talley. In the spring of 1962, heading nowhere with their contract with Dimension, the girls were surprised to get a mysterious telephone call, suggesting that they call a certain number if they wanted a new booking. Or so said Ribowsky.

Williams, in *Out of His Head*, acknowledges that the truth of how Phil first crossed paths with the Ronettes "re-mains a point of some dispute." In Williams' book, he quotes Veronica Bennett—"Ronnie"—as saying that she'd acciden-tally dialed the wrong number one night, and got Phil. After learning that they were a singing group, Phil invited them in for an audition. "It's all passed into legend now," Williams observed. Of course, Williams was writing in 1972; he pub-lished just before Ronnie and Phil had their nasty divorce.

Ribowsky's version of the legend differs somewhat. He quoted Nedra Talley as saying that the Ronettes were given a number to call for more work, and when they called the number, Phil came to the telephone, having worked out a subterfuge to prevent anyone from Dimension knowing that he was cozying up to their talent. He told the three girls to come over to Mira Sound to record for him, much as he had done with the Crystals the year before.

Ribowsky added a fillip (a Phillip?) to the tale, however. He contended that Phil, still working at Liberty Records at the time, told the Ronettes to tell Dimension that they were "quitting the business," a story he used himself in abandon-ing Liberty that spring. Ribowsky also notes that by May 26, 1962, the Ronettes were in Los Angeles recording for Phil at Gold Star—this was even before the (ersatz) Crystals had recorded "He's a Rebel," and before Sill had been forced out, so it seems to indicate that Phil had a long-term plan in mind even at that early stage of Philles.

For her part, in her own autobiography, *Be My Baby*, published in 1990, Ronnie said her group had no contact with Phil until 1963, when they decided to get rid of their existing producer and hook up with Phil, who was then at the top of the musical heap. Ronnie said Estelle got the Philles New York number from information, then dialed it. She asked to be put through to Phil Spector, and was. According to Ronnie, Estelle said she was one of the Ronettes, and with that, Phil invited them to Mira Sound. "We couldn't believe our luck," Ronnie wrote, "that a busy man like Phil Spector would agree to audition us, sight unseen."[41]

Great luck, indeed, as it would turn out—especially for Ronnie, at least until it all came apart. As Ronnie later put it in her book, "Of course, we knew that Phil was rich. We couldn't stop talking about it . . . so all we did that whole day was joke about which one of us was going to marry this millionaire."

To her later sorrow, it turned out to be her.

However they first met—Phil later admitted that he'd known all along who they were, Ronnie wrote—Phil's plans for the trio meant they would soon supplant the sometimes troublesome Crystals as Philles' main act. The Crystals might have been high school girls when they first started with Phil, but they learned fast. In addition to the festering resentment over the psuedo-Crystals, they began to have aggravating disputes with Phil over money. It was as if Phil had already lost interest in the group. The Crystals told Ribowsky that all they'd received in royalties from Philles was a total of $6,000, despite the fact that they'd had a string of hit records.

What the Crystals probably didn't know was that Phil

---

[41] Ronnie Spector wrote that Phil signed the Ronettes to a contract in March of 1963. In later litigation in New York over the contract, the year 1963 is also reported as a fact by the court.

himself was having a hard time getting money—apparently Lipsius at Universal Distributing was being slow to pay up.[42] The record distributor kept withholding payments on the grounds that the retailers might send him back huge numbers of unsold records, so-called "returns," which would have to be deducted from the amount Universal owed Philles. Phil grew increasingly distressed at the way the distributing company was treating him, and by 1963 was already thinking of ending the agreement with Lipsius—that meant finding a way to manufacture the records himself, and doing all the distribution and promotion as well. This would turn out to be a fateful decision, however.

By the summer of 1963, the music was up for the Crystals, and they suddenly discovered that their chair had been taken—one day they met Ronnie, her sister and her cousin as they arrived at the Philles offices on the mezzanine of the Upper East Side building where Phil had moved into a penthouse with Annette. La La Brooks, only 16 years old, who had taken over as the Crystals' lead singer from Barbara Alston, realized that Phil was enamored of the Ronettes, and especially Ronnie. The Crystals stopped getting rehearsal time, which went to the Ronettes instead. The Crystals thought that Ronnie had seduced Phil, according to Ribowsky. And they were right: by the summer of 1963, Ronnie was involved in a clandestine affair with Phil.

Or seemingly clandestine: it appears that Annette, upstairs in the penthouse, knew pretty much what was going on. And didn't like it. Ribowsky recounts La La Brooks meeting Annette on the street, walking her dog: "She was very, very unhappy," La La told Ribowsky. "She said she couldn't deal with Phil. She said he was crazy."

---

[42] See, for example, *Cabot* v. *Jamie Record Co.*, No. 96-4672, in U.S. District Ct. for the Eastern District of Pennsylvania, in which Cabot collected substantial unpaid royalties from Jamie.

21

IN FLIGHT

Crazy. Coming from the woman who had married him—who was at the time studying psychology at Hunter College in New York, and who had attended joint therapy sessions with Phil and Dr. Kaplan—this assessment has to be given considerable weight, particularly in light of the events of February 3, 2003.

Once again, Ribowsky provides the template, in prophetic words he memorialized fourteen years *before* the fatal event: "I think the man doesn't really know how to love," Annette told Ribowsky. "I think he loves his music and that's it . . . Phil is so charming and sophisticated and talented. But he has a shadow side, as everybody does. And his shadow side is violent, and it came out; he has no control over the beast inside of him. That's the trouble. He's a victim of his own mind. He doesn't control it . . ."

Ominous words. But reading the portions of Annette's interviews that Ribowsky published in *He's a Rebel*, one begins to get something of a glimpse of the "demons" that Phil was later to tell Mick Brown about.

Indeed, strewn throughout Williams' *Out of His Head* and Ribowsky's *He's a Rebel* are numerous anecdotes and observations, which, taken together, reveal a significant pattern in Phil's mental processes. Assembled by both writers long before the events of February 3, 2003, when they merely seemed like examples of Phil's eccentric "genius," they nevertheless disclosed many troubling predilections. When

Ronnie Spector's reminiscences in *Be My Baby* are added—although some of these stories might be discounted because of her bitter divorce from Phil—the combined imagery is disturbing.

There was, for example, Phil's incessant arguing with Annette—not over important things, but over empty intellectual concepts, like the difference between a demagogue and a dictator (Annette said they were different, Phil said they weren't). Annette formed the impression that Phil wanted to dominate her with his verbosity, that he took satisfaction in trying to prove that he was smarter than she was.

Annette believed that Phil had a compulsion to control everything and everyone around him, that he believed everyone was his tool in some way, to be used and manipulated for whatever advantage might accrue to Phil. "He wants everybody to be a moth around his flame," Annette told Ribowsky. He could also be snide and sarcastic with people simply for the pleasure it gave him. "Phil is definitely a sadist," Annette said, "but of the mind, not the body."

The songwriter Gerry Goffin, on the other hand, thought Phil had masochistic tendencies—that there was something peculiar in Phil's personality that took satisfaction from feeling that he was being threatened or persecuted (or, maybe, even prosecuted?). At the same time, Phil took great pleasure in outwitting people, all of whom he saw as real or potential adversaries bent on his destruction. Just as he'd smuggled in extra Monopoly money to win the game as a kid, Phil instinctively felt that playing by the rules was for suckers—that if the situation were reversed, his opponents would take advantage of him, so why not do it first?

Of these traits, by far the most evident was Phil's ravenous desire for control, which in time would become something of an obsession. It certainly is no accident that when he began to make his mark in the pop music business, it was not as a writer or an arranger or a performer, but as the director of the control room, often telling others what to do, sometimes yelling. Those who got with the program stayed around to enjoy the largesse, even if they had to swallow the excrement Phil enjoyed dishing up; those who balked were soon shown the door.

Most observant people around Phil recognized that these urges to dominate grew out of an internal mindset in which Phil secretly believed—or at least feared—that he was inferior to everyone else.

Tony Orlando, for example, told Williams that he thought Phil suffered from "inferiority complexes." Orlando, then beginning his career as a singer in the New York "canyons of Broadway," saw the real Phil as a shy and sensitive person so uncomfortable with being in the public eye that he overcompensated by being boastful, and often combative. But because Phil was so small—"he looks like he could break in half if you just blew on him," Orlando said—he surrounded himself with big, beefy bodyguards to do his bidding. With his hired muscle, he had control, or at least its illusion.

On the other hand, there were those who believed that Phil exploited his vulnerabilities, that he used them to create an image of himself as soft, sensitive and creative, the better to gain advantage. This was particularly his wont with women, some thought—a sort of residue from being the surviving male in a household of dominant females, Bertha and Shirley.

Both Michael Spencer and Marshall Lieb came to believe that Phil's early success and its accompanying lionization brought with it a sycophantic entourage of people who enabled—in fact, required—Phil to remain frozen in his personality: since everything was going so well, why change it? Whatever pressures Phil brought upon himself to grow and mature in his dealings with others were stifled by his need to appear as the icon others were saying that he was. He was a public person and hated it, he was a private person and hated it, not least because of the loneliness. The conflict over time would become almost unbearable, and lead to Phil's withdrawal from the rest of society, his famous reclusiveness, interrupted sporadically by his attempted forays back into the music business over the years. The two sides would remain at war all the way up to the fateful night he decided to go out on the town, the excursion that ended with a woman shot dead in his house.

By the middle of 1963, the lionizing entourage surrounding Phil had grown to significant proportions. After all, here was the kid who seemingly had the golden ear—he knew what the teenagers would buy, and the charts proved it. Flitting back and forth from coast to coast, from Gold Star to Mira Sound, Phil's ego just got bigger and bigger, and stories about his eccentric "genius" grew apace.

One such story was the airplane saga. Later, the tale would be reprised again and again, first by Tom Wolfe in his "Tycoon of Teen" essay, then later by Williams and Ribowsky. Each time it was recounted, it grew new details.

Wolfe, using the "new journalism" novelizing techniques for which he would later be celebrated, re-creates the incident as if he had actually been present, using word-for-word dialogue in quotation marks; since it was unlikely that anyone taped the event, this has to be seen for what it was, an attempt to lure readers into an intimate relationship with the subject, and obviously not to be taken literally. But there were other problems with Wolfe's essay, as we shall see.

In the essay, first published in the *New York Herald Tribune* on January 3, 1965, Wolfe thrusts the reader into the cabin of an airliner about to take off from Los Angeles on a flight to New York. Outside, it's raining. Phil is on the plane, and decides, with the rain, he wants to get off. The plane is taxiing toward its take-off point at the time. Phil calls the stewardess over and tells her he wants to get off, right away. The stewardess explains this isn't possible, but Phil insists. He thinks there's something "wiggy" about the plane, that it's doomed to crash. Now Phil's entourage chimes in—if Phil thinks the plane is wiggy, it must *be* wiggy. The pilot pulls out of the lineup, returns to the gate. Everyone—not just Phil and his entourage—is removed from the plane. Phil's baggage is searched for bombs. So, presumably, is everyone else's.

"So," Phil tells Wolfe, "they grounded me. They took away my credit cards, they suspended the pilot, I don't know."

Seven years later, the story is repeated in Williams' book, *Out of His Head*. Williams attributes his version of the incident to songwriters Barry Mann and Ellie Greenwich, who were providing material for Spector, and claimed to be on the plane. As in Wolfe, the plane is on its way to New York, but rain isn't mentioned. And in Williams' version, Phil looks around the aircraft cabin and decides that the plane is filling up with . . . "losers." The karmic status of his fellow passengers are what convinces him to get off the plane. The pilot turns the plane around, returns to the gate. But now, fifty other passengers want to get off, because they thought Phil knew something they didn't. In Mann's version, "the captain was grounded on the spot."

Once they were off the plane, Mann told Williams, they tried to get another flight. But the airline people wouldn't let them take any other planes, not until Mann explained that they had no idea who Phil was. They were simply innocent bystanders, Mann indicated. When they boarded the next plane, though, they were soon removed. At that point the airline began searching *Mann's* and *Greenwich's* baggage for bombs.

"He [Phil] probably wasn't getting enough attention," Mann told Williams. "He would know all the time what he was doing. I'm sure he believes he's too divine ever to crash."

And finally there is Ribowsky's version of the plane incident. Ribowsky attributes his version of the events to Sonny Bono—yes, *that* Sonny Bono,[43] who at the time was serving as Phil's main gofer, while his girlfriend, Cher Sarkisian—yes, *that* Cher—hung around Gold Star hoping to pick up a few bucks as one of Phil's session singers.

In Sonny Bono's version, he had taken Phil to the airport, but not before having fed him sleeping pills to allay his anxiety about flying. Phil was so tanked on the sleeping pills he fell down on the way to the gate.

---

[43] Sonny Bono later made his own records with Cher, then became mayor of Palm Springs, California, and was elected to Congress as a Republican. He died in a skiing accident in January of 1998.

"[Y]ou can't laugh at Phil," Bono told Ribowsky, "so I pick him up and somehow get him on the plane and I go home and got in bed with Cher. And it's like, oh man, finally he's gone, I can rest for a while."

Then the phone rings. It's Phil. He tells Bono he made the pilot turn the plane around and go back to the gate. "Phil freaked out," Bono told Ribowsky. "He was screaming, 'I'm not flyin' on this plane! These people are losers and the plane's not gonna make it!' " In Bono's version, the pilot might have gotten fired, but Phil was banned from ever flying on the airline in the future. Nowhere was there any mention of either the rain or Mann and Greenwich, let alone luggage being searched for bombs. According to Ribowsky, Sonny sent Cher to the airport in his place to deal with Phil. She gave Phil a St. Christopher's medal to wear, telling him it was blessed, and that if Phil wore it, there was no way the plane would crash. Phil got on another plane and returned to New York, praying to a Christian saint the whole way back.

The three versions are similar in their basic details, but grow more exaggerated as time recedes from the actual event. This is, in fact, how legends are made—germinating from facts, they evolve into taller tales by the retelling.

Is it likely that the pilot turned the plane around and debarked all the passengers? Probably, although being actually in the taxi line may be an exaggeration. It certainly was unlikely that the pilot was "suspended" or "fired on the spot." Standard operating procedure in such a situation would call for the pilot to do exactly what he did. Today, of course, Phil would have been arrested and charged with a federal crime, and at the least would have been referred for psychiatric observation. The fact that Phil could later tell it as a funny story to Wolfe and Williams, without a care to all the other people who had been inconvenienced, only illustrates the depth of Phil's apparent narcissism.

22

CHANGES

Throughout the rest of 1963 and into early 1964, Phil continued to make new records at Gold Star and Mira Sound, including some compilation albums for the Crystals and Bob B. Soxx and the Blue Jeans. One of these new records was another flight of fancy on Phil's part: *A Christmas Gift for You*, an album in which Darlene Love, the Crystals, the Ronettes, and Bob B. Soxx and the Blue Jeans performed various Christmas songs. The final cut was "Silent Night," which the singers crooned in the background while Phil recited a maudlin thank you to "his" fans, which soon verged into boastfulness. Larry Levine, the engineer, cringed at Phil's desire to insert himself into the performance. "It got past funny," Levine told Ribowsky, "after five minutes it wasn't funny at all." The album took six weeks to make, and when it was done, Levine decided that he'd had enough of Phil for a while.

Meanwhile, Phil pressed ahead with his affair with Ronnie. Ronnie's cousin Nedra told her it was wrong, according to Ribowsky. Nedra told Ronnie that Phil was "weird," that he was showing signs of insanity—particularly Phil's calls to the Bennett household in the middle of the night, demanding to know where Ronnie was. Here again was the fear and jealousy that would mark Phil's relationships with women—sort of the B side of the calls Bertha and Shirley used to make when Phil was a teenager. According to Ribowsky, Nedra told her cousin that Phil was already married. "If a man cheats on his wife," she said, "he'll cheat on you."

Not surprisingly, given the generally hagiographic nature of his book, Williams doesn't discuss any of the Phil–Ronnie affair in *Out of His Head*. But Ronnie, in her memoirs, recalls the events somewhat differently from the version recounted by Ribowsky.

In her version, Ronnie said that she didn't become physically intimate with Phil until June of 1964—much later than Ribowsky asserted. Of course, Ronnie said she and Phil began kissing almost the first time they met. But at the same time, Ronnie wrote that they had been lovers for some time when, in the spring of 1964, she discovered that Phil was married.

It happened at Gold Star one afternoon, Ronnie wrote. She was standing with Darlene Love, watching Phil, when she told Darlene that she thought Phil was "cute."

"Cute?" Darlene asked. "You really think Phil is cute?"

When Ronnie said she did, Darlene told her she was "hung up" on Phil. Ronnie said she was going to marry him one day.

Darlene said she didn't think so. Ronnie demanded to know why not. Darlene ushered her into the women's room and told her, "Honey, this guy is married."

Until that moment, Ronnie said, she hadn't known that. She said she was physically sick to discover this inconvenient fact, and demanded to know who Phil's wife was. Darlene told her about Annette, and Ronnie remembered seeing a row of women's shoes in a closet at Phil's apartment during one of the few visits he had allowed her to make there. But then, Ronnie said, she thought things over.

"The way I saw it," she wrote, "my choice was simple. I could keep my mouth shut and hold onto my career, my relationship, and my family [since Ronnie was vital to Estelle and Nedra's continued recording success]. Or I could confront Phil and throw it all away. And I was no fool. So I pretended I never heard of Phil's wife."

For her part, Annette told Ribowsky that she was oblivious to the affair between her husband and Ronnie—at least until a friend who frequented music people circles tipped her off. The friend told Annette—Ribowsky doesn't make clear exactly when—that Phil was having an affair with one of the Ronettes. Annette thought it was with Nedra. She called Mira Sound to confront Phil about the tale, and people there told her Phil wasn't in, although he'd told her he'd be rehearsing that night at the studio. Annette realized that Phil was probably downstairs in the Philles office. She took the elevator down to the office and banged on the door. No one answered. She returned to the penthouse, to find the intercom between the two locations buzzing. Answering it, Annette told Phil to "Get your whore out of my building." Phil told her he was rehearsing. He invited her to come downstairs so she could see it wasn't Nedra. Then she took the elevator down to the lobby of the building, and there saw Phil and Ronnie standing close together.

A few minutes later, Phil returned to the penthouse and screamed at Annette for spying on him. But he did not admit that he was having an affair with Ronnie. A week later, Annette told him to move out. He did.

By late 1963, the Ronettes had eclipsed the Crystals. Their first song, "Be My Baby," written by Ellie Greenwich and Jeff Barry (Phil claimed a writing credit, too), went off like a rocket, reaching number 2 in December. But this would be Philles' high-water mark for more than a year, and certainly the apogee for the Ronettes. A month after the assassination of John Kennedy, the popular music business would undergo a powerful, if at first subtle change. For one thing, the Baby Boomers were starting to grow up, a maturation that began with the killing of the President, and which would soon bring wrenching changes in the form of a seemingly interminable war 12,000 miles away. Teenage angst would be out, protest would soon be in.

The protest movement was at first inchoate, barely perceptible. It began with the vague sense that something was wrong, something was unnatural, about the way things were. The abrupt, bloody removal of a President had somehow catapulted the country into an orbit that had never been intended.

There was a growing, uneasy sense that things were not what they had seemed to be, that there were hidden, sinister forces at work. Innocence had been lost, at least among the Boomers, who had lived their entire short lives surrounded by the notion that things were always getting better. Now it appeared that they weren't, and to think otherwise would be to succumb to an illusion. Teen love began to seem shallow, even passé.

At first, the changes seemed benign, if odd. A year before the assassination, the Beatles had begun making hits in the U.S. market. Their mop-like moddish hair and funny accents divided the popular music world between traditionalists who favored a middle-American sound, and the avant garde, and it would be a split that would continue for years afterward. The division was even more sharply illustrated by the anti-Beatles, the Rolling Stones, cast from the rocker mold. While the Beatles sang of love, the Stones sang of rebellion. By 1965, the driving beat of "Satisfaction" electrified Boomers, and told them that all truisms were up for grabs. While the likes of Duane Eddy, the Four Lads, the Four Preps, Eddie Cochran, and the rockabillies stood for American values, the Brits seemed to show that maybe things were not all that hot over here, *ectually*. And as the war in Vietnam heated up in 1964 and then 1965, the split would grow wider, until a new theme would emerge: not war, not peace, just leave me alone, a trend that would culminate in the largely apolitical "Me Decade" of the 1970s, and the Disco Denouement.

The Beatles' success in America in 1963 left many in the South cold. The hair—it was un-American. It was rebellious. It was gender-bending, and this at a time when real men were being called up to fight the heathen Reds. But the girls seemed to love them. The boys, with their rolled-up tee-shirt sleeves holding packs of cigarettes, with their hair oil, were left to puzzle it out for themselves.

By early 1964, the Ronettes' success resulted in an invitation to Phil and his girls to go to England, where it turned out that the Ronettes' record was selling like crazy. The idea was to have the Ronettes tour with the Rolling

Stones. Sex would meet rock-and-roll, and drugs were not far behind.

For some time, Phil's Wall of Sound notions had been gaining appreciation in the United Kingdom. Sometimes, in fact, Phil felt much more appreciated in the U.K. than he did in the United States. Arriving in England, Phil pontificated.

"The records are built like a Wagnerian opera," he told the London *Evening Standard*. "They start simply and they end with dynamite force, meaning and purpose." It was as if the words, "Be my baby now" had assumed oracular significance.

The Stones' manager was Andrew Oldham. Oldham was an admirer of Phil, and especially his Wall of Sound. He arranged for Phil (the Ronettes had preceded him by two weeks) to be met by a gaggle of press people, among them Maureen Cleave of the *Evening Standard*. Phil took refuge in false modesty. "I've been told I'm a genius," he said. "What do you think?"

As the tour progressed, the Stones began to hit on the Ronettes, apparently competing with each other to see which of them would be the first to hustle a Ronette into the sack. Ronnie, however, was tacitly declared off-limits because of Phil. The Ronettes, it appears, were unimpressed by the Stones. Being teetotalers, they were disgusted by the band's incessant drinking and pill-dropping and also found them dirty and malodorous. But according to Ribowsky, Phil himself got into the swing of things—he availed himself of marijuana and pills "from Oldham's pockets."

According to Ribowsky, drugs were a new experience for Phil—until coming to England he'd eschewed them, afraid that they'd make him lose his self-control. But Oldham, himself an oddball even for Britain, saw in Phil a kindred spirit, and Phil apparently reciprocated. Soon he and Phil were great pals.

As it happened, Gene Pitney was in England at the same time, on his own tour. One night—his birthday, actually— Pitney went to the studio where the Stones were recording, armed with a large amount of duty-free cognac. Phil was there, too. Everyone drank the cognac, and when the band began to cover Buddy Holly's original, "Not Fade Away," Phil helped produce it from the control room. According to the legend, Phil showed Mick Jagger how to play the maracas. At another point, according to the legend, Phil began tapping the cognac bottle rhythmically with a coin. Supposedly, one can hear this on the record, which soon became the Stones' biggest hit in America up to that time. It was first released in Britain in February of 1964.

While in London, Phil began to affect the appearance that would later become his trademark—the long frizzy hair (by now, Phil's real hair was so thin, he'd taken to wearing a wig, one that, according to Ronnie, he had to glue on), and his funky Ben Franklin dark glasses. Otherwise he dressed as a dandy, almost foppishly. It was the In style, he believed—never mind what those rubes back in the States thought about it.

Whether it was Oldham's supposed drugs, or Phil feeling he was far enough away from home that it didn't matter, Phil began to show something of his wild side during the trip. At one point, while riding around in the back of a Rolls-Royce with a Decca Records promotion man, Tony Hall, Phil asked the driver to pull over to get some milk. As soon as the driver was gone, Phil jammed on the driver's cap, jumped behind the wheel, and took off. The wrong-way system of British streets apparently confused Phil; according to Hall, pretty soon the car was careening down the sidewalk.

At another point Phil and the Ronettes supposedly met the Beatles at Hall's house in Mayfair. According to Hall's description of the event, recounted by Ribowsky, the Beatles wanted to meet the Ronettes; they had no interest in Phil. The Ronettes came to Hall's house, and Phil showed up a bit later, with Oldham. According to Hall, the encounter was strained—not only because the Ronettes "weren't exactly overflowing of personality," as Hall put it, but because Phil was on some sort of trip. Oldham seemed to be egging Phil on. Soon they were aping people, Phil began speaking and giggling in a high voice, and the atmosphere turned even cooler. Oldham realized things were going wrong, so he managed to get Phil away from the party to help sober him up, according to Hall. A bit later, both returned, now seeming normal, and the party proceeded in a warmer fashion.

Ronnie Spector, in *Be My Baby*, provided an altogether different version of the first meeting between Phil and the Beatles. In fact, according to Ronnie, it never happened at all. In Ronnie's memoir, she asserted that the girls met the Beatles the first night they were in England, which was two weeks before Phil even arrived. This is not to fault Ribowsky: he accurately put down what people told him. But it is a reminder that when one is dealing with legends, there is always the possibility that something may not be true, no matter how vividly described.

In Ronnie's version, there was a party at Tony Hall's, all right. "George, John and Ringo had already arrived when we got to the party," Ronnie wrote. "The Beatles hadn't been to America at that time, so we didn't know their music."

This isn't very likely, however, since by early 1964, the Beatles had already had a number of hits in America, including "Please Please Me" in February of 1963, "From Me to You" in May, "She Loves You" in September, and "I Want to Hold Your Hand" in December. So maybe Ronnie's memory is at fault, not Hall's.

The three Beatles introduced themselves, according to Ronnie. "Naturally we hit it off right away," she wrote.

By this time, one has to wonder whether Phil, the Beatles and the Ronettes had doppelgangers—Hall said Phil was there, Ronnie said Phil was still in the United States; Hall said that things weren't going well because the Ronettes weren't "overflowing of personality," while Ronnie said they'd really "hit it off." And then in *Be My Baby*, Ronnie proceeded, to tell exactly how. First, the Ronettes taught the Beatles the latest dances: "the Pony, the Jerk and the Nitty Gritty," Ronnie wrote. Soon John was putting the moves on her, Ronnie said, while George started after Estelle. In Ronnie's version, John soon began to explore Hall's house with her, in search of an open and unoccupied room. Eventually they found one—or one they thought was empty. George and

Estelle had found it first, Ronnie said, and were sitting on the bed when they came in. Ronnie began asking John what it was like to suddenly be famous, and John told her what it was like. Soon, however, according to Ronnie, they began kissing. And just when John was getting somewhere, Ronnie decided it was time to get back to the party. Or at least, that's Ronnie's version of the first meeting between the Beatles and the Ronettes.

So, who has the truth of this event, Tony Hall or Ronnie Spector? Let's consult Williams' *Out of His Head* for a third opinion:

"Hall organised the party at which Spector and the Ronettes first met the Beatles," he wrote. So, in Williams' version, Phil *was* present. "The atmosphere was a little strained to start with—Spector went out for a while, then came back at three o'clock in the morning . . . After that they all got on fine."

So—Williams, admirer of Phil that he is, sides with Tony Hall in this matter. Unfortunately, since Williams' version reflects Tony Hall's version almost exactly, it appears that Hall himself was Williams' source. That makes it a tie game.

The importance of this isn't what actually happened at Hall's house—whether Phil was there or not—but what it might show about Ronnie's credibility, particularly when other issues related to Phil's behavior are described by his former wife, as they are, in great and often vivid detail, in *Be My Baby*. The point is, given that there are sometimes contradictory stories, Ronnie's version of what happened in her marriage with Phil ought to be taken with a certain degree of skepticism. But even so, it would turn out to be a harrowing account, indeed.

23

THE RIGHTEOUS TRUTH

At the end of the British tour, Phil and the Ronettes climbed onto an airliner for the trip back to the United States. Among their fellow passengers were John Lennon, George Harrison, Paul McCartney and Ringo Starr, about to begin their first live tour in America.

The Beatles were worried about their reception in the United States, a little over two months after Kennedy' assassination. Was it likely, they asked Phil, that someone would take a shot at *them*? After all, the Beatles reasoned, there were some in the United States who disapproved of their hair, their music, their role in upsetting traditions. They asked Phil what to expect, which was a bit like asking Chicken Little if they had anything to fear from the sky. But Phil assured them that they would be safe.

"It's really funny," he later told Jann Wenner of *Rolling Stone*, in an interview published in 1969, "but they were terribly frightened to get off the plane. They were really frightened of America. They said, 'You go first.' 'Cause the whole thing about Kennedy scared them very, very much. They really thought it was possible for somebody to be there and want to kill them."

That was Phil's take on the Beatles' 1964 arrival in America, five years after the fact. At the time, no one had any idea that eleven years after that, in late 1980, someone *would* shoot a Beatle to death. In those days it seemed so unthinkable as to be ludicrous, even to Phil Spector.

• • •

With one notable exception, the year 1964 marked the beginning of the end of the first phase of Phil's career. In contrast to 1963, when Philles released ten singles, all but one
making the charts—including number 3 for the Crystals'
"Da Doo Ron Ron" and number 2 for the Ronettes' "Be My
Baby"—in 1964 Phil released fourteen singles. With two exceptions, most of them flopped—six of them never made it
to the top-selling charts at all.

In retrospect, there seem to be several reasons for this
sudden plunge in the popularity of Spector-produced records. First was the so-called "British Invasion," which reflected changing market tastes, augmented by the emergence
of the Motown sound as a mainstream American answer to
the Brits. Bubblegum yearning was suddenly out; a more
mature and emotive lyric was in. Second, the aftermath of
the Kennedy assassination and the run-up to the War in Vietnam provided fertile ground for music with more of a message. And lastly, it appears that a decision by Phil to end
Philles' lucrative relationship with Lipsius' Universal Distributing was determinative. Phil wanted Universal to take a
fixed fee for its distribution services, but Lipsius balked. As
a result, Phil began negotiating separate deals with local distributors, in effect removing the middle man, Lipsius. Phil
believed that his product was so hot that he could make the
local distributors pay up front to get it, rather than wait for
Universal to calculate the returns. Phil was hard-nosed with
the local distributors—either they paid or they had to do
without his records. Some simply decided to give Spector
records a pass. At the same time, Phil made arrangements to
manufacture the records himself, now that Universal was
gone. Eventually he had his records pressed in Mexico, and
the physical quality of the product began to suffer. Phil's
back-office operations became disorganized, what with Phil
making deals on the fly, and soon the enterprise's paper files
were in a complete mess. Phil didn't seem to care.

In the meantime, however, Phil took the slumping interest
in his product personally—it was as if the music business
had insulted him. In his mind, "they"—the "cigar-smoking
sharpies," he would call them—were ganging up on him, because they resented his success.

That fall, he produced another Ronettes record, "Walking
in the Rain," on the Philles label. The record featured unmu-
sical sound effects like thunder and the patter of rain, a first
for Phil, but it seemed to work. The record rolled up to number 23 soon after its release in October of 1964, then faded
away. Today, many consider it a very good record, among
them Ronnie Spector, who sang the lead and considered it
the Ronettes' best. But by that time, Phil had come to the
conclusion that the girl groups' day had come and gone. Perhaps in keeping with the changing times, the maturing of his
market, Phil decided to go in a different direction entirely.

In October of 1964, just as "Walking in the Rain" was
stalling, Phil made a deal with a mid-tier label called Moonglow Records. For some time he'd been thinking that what
rock-and-roll needed was a return to the blues fork of the
tradition of R & B—some way to move beyond the empty
lyrics encompassed in bubblegum music. He'd had his eye
on a pair of singers he thought would be a perfect crossover
between black and white—the Righteous Brothers, they
were called, two young white singers who embodied the
ragged, raw edge of the blues that Phil had favored so much
while listening to the radio back in the fifties.

The Righteous Brothers—tall, lanky Bill Medley and his
shorter blond partner Bobby Hatfield—had had one mid-
chart hit, "Little Latin Lupe Lu," for Moonglow the year before, and had mainly been playing club dates around the Los
Angeles area. The "brothers'" grasp of the blues was such
that many of their live audiences, often comprised of
African-American listeners who knew the blues when they
heard them, began to call them "righteous," slang for truth-
ful reality. With the Righteous Brothers, Phil believed he
could bridge the growing gap between music consumers who

were white and those who were African-American, a gap that was becoming increasingly evident as the 1960s unfolded. In a sense, Phil wanted the Righteous Brothers to do what Elvis had done almost ten years earlier, only better.

This time, Phil made the effort to reach a formal agreement with a competing label, rather than simply engineer some sleight-of-hand, as he had done with the Crystals (lifted from under the unalert noses of Big Top) or the Ronettes (nominally under contract with Dimension). The deal with Moonglow gave Phil the right to produce Righteous Brothers records for sale in the U.S., the U.K. and Canada, with other foreign rights—e.g., Australia, New Zealand—being retained by Moonglow. More significantly, the labels' share of the copyright royalties—where the big money was—would be split between Mother Bertha Music and Moonglow's owners. Medley and Hatfield approved the deal in October.

For their first effort, Phil selected a song by Barry Mann and Cynthia Weil, "You've Lost That Lovin' Feelin'." It would be Medley's deep voice that dominated the song, singing the lyrics, while Hatfield would chime in on cue with his high-pitched affirmation of the feelings of the lead. Most significantly, the song's words and tempo moved through three phases—accusation, anger, then an emotional, almost primal plea for reconciliation. Just as Phil had suggested earlier in the year in his London interview, it started slow, began to build, and finally erupted in a driving finish that fused rock, blues and gospel. Again Phil laid in the instrumentation first, two basses, three guitars, three pianos, a harpsichord, twelve violins, and four percussionists—the quintessential Wall of Sound approach—and again he mixed (or had Larry Levine mix) the sounds so that it was impossible to pick out any one instrument. Then he laid in Medley's lead and Hatfield's affirmations.

Almost from the start, people knew that this was Phil Spector's best effort, ever. "To my mind, Spector's defining moment," *The Daily Telegraph*'s Mick Brown was to write almost four decades later. But Phil couldn't resist, in his interview with Brown, gilding his own leaf:

"I worked for six months on that fucking record," he told Brown, "overdubbing and re-overdubbing . . . finally I had it down to where I thought it was pretty good."

Six months? Actually, only a little more than a month. (It may have seemed like six months to Levine and to Phil's studio musicians, however). After all, Phil had only signed the Righteous Brothers in early October. By December of the same year, "You've Lost That Lovin' Feeling'" was already on the charts, where it would eventually have an extended stay at Number One. But telling Brown it took six months to make the record sounded a lot more serious than six weeks.

The penchant for exaggeration and even outright deception—seemingly present all the way back to the days of the Monopoly money—reached an early landmark of sorts the following month, in January of 1965. This was when Tom Wolfe published his famous—indeed seminal, if one wants to find the origin of the legend—essay on Phil, "The Tycoon of Teen," in the *New York Herald Tribune*'s Sunday magazine. The essay would be larded with errors of fact that would go down in history as the truth, forming the foundation of legend later disseminated by Williams, and even Ribowsky and Brown. Like a ship steering slightly off course, almost four decades later the destination arrived at would be far, far away from the land of reality.

In fairness to Wolfe, he wasn't much interested in investigating the truth of assertions by or about Phil. He was much more interested in using language to describe the changing culture of the era—in Wolfe's view, "the proles" (the proletariat) had taken over the drive wheels of culture in America, unceremoniously shoving the stuffy old elites to the sidelines, and teenage tastes were the main fuel in the combustion chamber. It didn't much matter to Wolfe that the facts he reported were wrong; what was important was the image, conveyed in Wolfe's free-floating language. Or, as Marshall McLuhan was saying at the time, the *medium* was the message.

Wolfe began his essay with his cinematic version of the

fabled plane ride, the one where Phil had demanded to be let off the aircraft. But soon Wolfe was enmeshed in the thorny thicket of factual error.

"Spector is the one record producer who wouldn't go near Broadway," Wolfe recorded. Well, that wasn't exactly true—Phil had cut his producing teeth with Leiber and Stoller in "the canyons of Broadway," as Ribowsky would later point out, and indeed had been banned from the Brill Building's Hill and Range for his filching of the Crystals.

"He *likes* the music he produces," Wolfe continued. "He writes it himself." Actually, no—virtually all of Phil's songs were written by professional songwriters like Ellie Greenwich, Barry Mann, Jeff Barry, Cynthia Weil, Gerry Goffin and Carole King. It was true that Phil had himself listed as a co-writer, but the words and melodies belonged to the hired help. The only song he could claim sole credit for writing was "To Know Him Is to Love Him," and that was largely lifted from his father's tombstone, and supposedly from one of Wagner's operas, as Phil himself admitted.

"In point of fact, he had turned twenty-one when he made his first clear million," Wolfe wrote. Of course, Phil, having been born on December 26, 1939, would have turned 21 in December 1960. That was just when Phil was claiming credit for writing "Spanish Harlem," and it wasn't at all likely that he had made "his first million" by *that* birthday.

"[S]tarting at the age of seventeen . . . Phil Spector developed into a great American business man," Wolfe continued. When Phil was 17, of course, it was a year before he'd made any records—unless someone in the audience at Fairfax High School (Prelutsky, maybe?) had secretly taped his rendition of "Rock Island Line" for unnoticed sale to the multitudes, and later covertly gave Phil all the imaginary money.

Wolfe gave a version of the back story of "To Know Him Is to Love Him," the 1958 hit, and then observed, "He made $20,000 on that record, but somebody ran off with $17,000 of it, and, well, no use going into that."

This seems to have been the origin of the part of the legend about Phil's Teddy Bears payout, and one that seems to be contradicted by the facts, if one believes what Ribowsky reported about the actual sums earned by Phil for the record, whether $38,000 or $200,000. Wolfe likewise missed the evidence about possible payola in connection with the record's rise, and the roles played by Finfer, Lipsius and Dick Clark in its success.

"Then he was going to UCLA . . ." Wolfe continued. Actually, Los Angeles City College, although Wolfe may have meant that Phil *wanted* to go to UCLA. "[C]ouldn't afford it . . ." Wolfe said of Phil's college intentions. "[B]ecame a court reporter." Not so—he may have taken classes to become a court reporter, but there's no evidence he ever worked as one.

"[D]ecided to come to New York and get a job as an interpreter at the UN," Wolfe wrote. This tale is completely at variance with what Lester Sill, Jerry Leiber and Mike Stoller told Ribowsky and Williams. In their version, Phil came to New York specifically to work for the songwriters, and in fact, they even sent him the air fare.

"[T]he night before the [U.N.] interview, he fell in with some musicians and never got there," Wolfe wrote, and this was certainly inconsistent with everyone else's recollection, especially since there apparently never was an "interview" scheduled at the U.N.

"He wrote another hit that year, 'Spanish Harlem,' " Wolfe continued. Actually, Jerry Leiber wrote the lyrics, Mike Stoller the arrangement, and, if Beverly Ross is to be believed, she wrote the key part of the song, which Phil immediately ran off with.

"And then—only nineteen—he became head of A & R, artists and repertoire, for Atlantic Records." Actually, by the time Phil became head of A & R at Atlantic, in the winter or early spring of 1961, he would have been 21 years old, not 19. Wolfe never did get Phil's age right.

"Working with . . . Elvis Presley," Wolfe wrote of Phil. Here was another easy-to-check fact that was not true. While Phil claimed to have written for Elvis while with Leiber and Stoller, but just never having received credit for it, there is no evidence to support this, unless one counts the songs that Terry Phillips wrote, then had to junk, for *Blue Hawaii*.

"Spector formed a partnership with two other people in 1961, then bought them out and went on his own as Philles Records in October of 1962," Wolfe continued. Not even close, as we have seen. He formed a partnership with Lester Sill, Harold Lipsius and Harry Finfer, in the summer of 1961 as Philles Records, and later inveigled the unwitting Helen Noga to contribute, then aced her out using some of his front-loaded payment from Liberty Records in early 1962. The buyout of Finfer, Lipsius and later Lester Sill didn't take place until October 1962, and even with that, Lester Sill sued, and wasn't completely out of the deal until well into 1963 or possibly even 1964. Without understanding any of this background—it appears that he took Phil's word for the history—Wolfe wrote that Phil's first big hit as an independent producer was "He's a Rebel" by the Crystals. Of course, that skips over "There's No Other" and "Uptown," and in any case was what Phil and Sill were squabbling over in the summer and fall of 1962—who owned the Crystals, or even the pseudo-Crystals, which, after all, were Sill's idea.

"Spector does the whole thing," Wolfe reiterated. "He writes the words and the music." No and no.

"He handles the control dials like an electronic maestro . . ." Well, actually, Levine turned the knobs, even if Phil told him what to do.

None of this is meant to pick on Wolfe, who after all wasn't embarked on a major investigation of Phil's veracity. But almost forty years later it would become germane, particularly when the credibility of the subject of the assertions was at issue—not only in the public prints, but in a court of law.

24

LOST

As 1965 began, the legend of Phil had already taken shape, fueled considerably by Wolfe's admiring essay. Phil had already made several appearances on television, including one appearance on a show hosted by David Susskind, where Phil's musical taste was ridiculed. Susskind read the lyrics of one song, using a deadpan inflection that seemed to render it—well, inane. Phil reacted with anger, telling Susskind what he was missing was the beat. He later told Wolfe in their interview that it upset him when people condemned rock-and-roll. "It has limited chord changes," he admitted, "and people are always saying the words are banal and why doesn't anyone write lyrics like Cole Porter anymore, but we don't have any Presidents like Lincoln anymore, either. You know?" Rock-and-roll, he told Wolfe, was "very American. It's very *today*."

At another point Phil was guest on *The Tonight Show*, hosted by Johnny Carson. Another guest—Ella Fitzgerald, she of Memorex fame—asked Phil about his biggest act. The Righteous Brothers, he said. Ms. Fitzgerald said she'd never heard of them. Phil shot back that it was okay, because they'd never heard of *her*.

In mid-February, Phil was profiled in *Time*—"A Giant Stands 5 Ft. 7 In." the headline read. The piece took off from the Righteous Brothers' smash, and the legend got another workout. Significant of the era still dawning, the magazine's cover featured a drawing of a confident-appearing General William Westmoreland in front of a skirmish line of combat-helmeted G.I.'s, fighting 12,000 miles away from the cares of love-sick teenagers.

Asserting that Phil was the "songwriter, arranger, producer and distributor"—two out of four wasn't bad—*Time* said that Phil had "sold a fantastic total of 20 million copies" of Philles records since 1962. *Fantastic* was probably the right word: that meant that Phil's performers, assuming a standard "mechanical royalty" rate of 5 percent of the average record price of $1, should have received an aggregate total of about $1 million on record sales alone. The fact was, none of the performers—not the Crystals, not the pseudo-Crystals, not the Ronettes, and not even the Righteous Brothers received anything like that amount, even added together. So the total sales figure was probably a fantastic exaggeration.

Following in Wolfe's tracks, *Time* asserted that Phil had first made the charts at the tender age of 17—like Wolfe, they never did get Phil's age correct. The magazine said that Phil had moved to New York to try "to crash 'Teen Pan Alley.'"

It was only after arriving in New York, the magazine said, that Phil realized how much smarter he was than everyone else, when it came to picking songs teenagers would like.

"Ninety-five percent of the music business is heavily infiltrated by morons," Phil told the magazine, doubtless endearing himself to Leiber, Stoller, Wexler, Ross, Sill, Hazlewood, and the people at Liberty Records who'd paid him $30,000 for almost no work. "If they hadn't been so greedy and vicious, I wouldn't have tried to control them. . . . I function well in a world of hostility."

But whose hostility? *Time* offered its readers a clue: "His maladjustment [that was a popular term back in the early 1960s] seems to stem from a feeling of non-acceptance by the adult world." Phil said the adult world didn't understand him, and it didn't understand teenagers. His music brought meaning into teenagers' lives, Phil said. "If we're not what's happening today, then what is? Maybe I'm living in an America that doesn't exist?"

Time made some hay with Phil's appearance, unconventional as it was for the mid-1960s. After noting that Phil said that he liked "to stay in the background," the magazine pointed out that his dress nevertheless seemed calculated to attract attention: "Standard costume: stiletto-pointed boots with three-inch Cuban heels, tight pants, cloth cap, Davy Crockett pullover" (what the heck was a Davy Crockett pullover?).

"He ignores the rude hoots that greet his progress down the street," *Time* reported, and "confides that 'in case of real trouble, I could literally kill a guy. I've studied karate for years.'"

Here it is again, the projection of the tough guy, reminiscent of the mobster-dressed band, the hiring of a posse of bodyguards to intimidate. Why was it important for Phil to have people believe he could crush them if he chose to do it? This would become an increasingly relevant question, all the way up until the early morning hours of February 3, 2003, when police arrested Phil and charged him with shooting a woman to death in his house.

There was one more fragment from the *Time* profile that would be worth recalling: "Entrepreneur Spector has co-founded a new company to make TV documentary films. The first production, starring Spector, will be called *A Giant Stands 5 Ft. 7 In.*" Here, it appears, was the genesis of Phil's desire to have a movie made of his life, still a goal even as Lana Clarkson's life ebbed away in his Alhambra castle, nearly forty years later.

In the real world, though, things were not going quite so well as Phil would have had Wolfe and *Time* believe. The slump in Crystals and Ronettes hits was only lifted by the Righteous Brothers, and by the spring of 1965, Phil's associates—principally Danny Davis, whom Phil had hired to manage his business—were pressing Phil to find more new acts. Associates took him to see a band called the Rascals, who were overjoyed that the famous Phil would consider producing them, but Phil turned them down. The Rascals went on to record as the Young Rascals, and charted ten hits in the Top Twenty over the next few years. Phil went to see another group called the Lovin' Spoonful, but passed on them, too. That group recorded five top hits over the next three years.

Why didn't Phil pick up on these opportunities? The main reason seems to have been that the Rascals, like the Lovin' Spoonful, were a "self-contained band." That is, like the Beatles and the Stones, they wrote, played and sang their own material. To some of Phil's associates, that meant that Phil had too little control over the groups' work, and almost no opportunity to punch up the product with the session musicians he used in his Wall of Sound. In short, there was no place for Phil to be the star.

The advent of the "self-contained band" was actually the inevitable outgrowth in the popularity of rock-and-roll. As the market segmented and grew broader in the late 1950s and early 1960s, it was natural for young people to learn to play and sing themselves, just as Phil had in 1958. As these new groups proliferated, the rock music business underwent a profound if subtle change: from the mid-sixties forward, the performers would have the whip hand. Phil wasn't able to make the adjustment to this new reality. It wasn't that he couldn't, some of his associates thought; it was just that he didn't want to, because there was no ego payoff in it for him.

And things weren't going very well on the domestic front, either. For the better part of a year-and-a-half, Phil and Annette had been in a cold war, mostly over Phil's affair with Ronnie. When "You've Lost That Lovin' Feelin' " went to Number One, Phil told Annette that he had written the song for her. Take that! Phil and Annette made several attempts to reconcile, but it never worked out—not as long as Ronnie was in the picture. Eventually Annette told Phil that she wanted a divorce. Late in 1965, Phil flew to Mexico and obtained one there; Phil and Annette Merar Spector were history.

Divorce was what the Righteous Brothers were thinking about, too—not only from Phil, and Moonglow, but also from each other.

Flushed with their great success, the Righteous Brothers quickly made another record, "Just Once in My Life," again featuring Medley as the lead. The single was released in April of 1965 and reached number 9 in May before falling back. A second song, "Hung on You," came out in July, but got no higher than number 47. Nevertheless, by that time, people were so hungry for the Righteous Brothers that the deejays flipped it over and started playing the B side, a cover of "Unchained Melody," this time led by Bobby Hatfield. That went to number 4 by mid-September. Then things began to fly apart.

Part of the problem was the complex web of contractual relationships between Phil, Moonglow Records, and Medley and Hatfield. Larry Levine wanted to produce an album of Righteous Brothers hits even while "Lovin' Feelin' " was skyrocketing. Phil wasn't interested. Levine finally convinced Phil to let him produce the album, and in early 1965, *You've Lost That Lovin' Feelin'*, the album, was released. The longplay record featured ten songs chosen by Medley, and the record went to number 4 among long-play recordings. A few months later, Medley decided to make a second Righteous Brothers album, *Just Once in My Life*.

By the middle of the summer, Hatfield began to feel that Medley's star was outshining his own, despite his singles success on "Unchained Melody." Resentment set in, and soon Hatfield refused to sing anymore with his old partner.[44] Phil tried to get the Brothers back together, and finally hit on the idea of producing a third album, this one with the song leads evenly divided between the two singers.

---

[44] Bobby Hatfield died November 5, 2003, in Kalamazoo, Michigan. He and Medley had reunited and were touring together when the 63-year-old Hatfield was found dead in his hotel room just before a scheduled performance.

In September, Phil began work to produce this album, *Back to Back.*

But in early October, open warfare broke out, this time between Medley and Hatfield on one side, and Moonglow Records on the other. The two Brothers had hired an auditor to go over Moonglow's books, and discovered an alleged shortfall of $26,000 in royalties they were owed by the label. The Moonglow people, meanwhile, were peeved at Phil; they said Phil hadn't turned over the Brothers' record masters so Moonglow could sell the records in foreign countries, as per the original agreement. On September 15, 1965, Moonglow terminated its contract with Phil for alleged failure to perform.

Ow! After all the work to make the Righteous Brothers the hottest (non-British) act in the country, to Phil it suddenly seemed like the people at Moonglow were trying to rip him off. He'd done all the work to make the Righteous Brothers stars, and now Moonglow was going to claim the cream. Moonglow soon sent a letter to the Brothers instructing them to make no more recordings with Phil and Philles.

The Brothers now decided to get together with Phil to settle everyone's differences. But by now they suspected that Philles was holding out on royalties, too—they'd had their agent try to get Phil to fork the money over, but Phil wouldn't listen.

Because the *Back to Back* album wasn't finished, Medley and Hatfield thought they had Phil over a barrel. Phil by this point had rented a twenty-two-room mansion on La Collina Drive in Beverly Hills. In the wake of the cold war between Phil and Annette, Phil had decided to move all his operations to Los Angeles. He'd rented the Beverly Hills house from an aging British actor, Reginald Owen. At one time the mansion had been the main house of the Woolworth family. It was not in very good repair, it appears. In late September, Phil invited the Brothers over to his house to talk everything over.

When the Brothers got there, accompanied by Danny Davis, they were informed that Phil wasn't home. The Brothers knew it was a lie, because they could see Phil hiding behind the door. Phil apparently didn't realize that Medley and Hatfield could see him. They left in a huff.

The Brothers now sued Moonglow and Phil, contending that because Moonglow was in default on the royalties they owed to the Brothers, the agreement between Moonglow and Phil for the Brothers' services was invalid. Arghh! Phil wanted to get the Brothers back into the studio to finish the album in time for the Christmas market. But the Brothers wouldn't do it. Phil called on Moonglow to help him cajole the Brothers back into the studio, and Moonglow agreed, reasoning that if the album never got finished, everyone would be a loser. They could sort all the money out later. Still the Brothers wouldn't budge.

Exasperated, Phil returned to the studio by himself and finished the album, salvaging it by using some old tracks that Medley and Hatfield had left behind before they walked. Phil got the album out in time for Christmas, and now it was the Brothers' turn to be furious—they thought that Phil was trying to ruin them by releasing an inferior product. They asked the court to stop the release, but the judge wouldn't do it.

The Brothers retaliated when their agent began negotiations with MGM Records for a new contract with the Brothers, to be distributed on Verve's label. Now it was Moonglow and Phil's turn to rush to court. Phil argued that letting the Brothers go to MGM was tantamount to a death sentence for Philles. The case dragged on for the first few months of 1966, but not before the Righteous Brothers went to an MGM studio and cut a song by Barry Mann and Cynthia Weil, "You're My Soul and Inspiration." This was a double blow: Phil figured that Mann and Weil owed him as much as the Righteous Brothers did for their success. But Mann and Weil reasoned that since Phil had cut them out of new Righteous Brothers songs after the success of "Lovin' Feelin'," turnabout was fair play.

Phil tried to stop the recording session. He instructed Danny Davis to call anybody he could think of, including studio musicians who were scheduled to play, to induce them not to cooperate. Davis failed.

"The session was at noon," Davis later told Ribowsky, "and I'm tryin' at four o'clock to stop it. By then it's obvious we don't have a prayer, so now Phil is absolutely . . . I mean he's out of his mind, berserk."

Late that afternoon, Phil turned out all the lights in the Philles office, then pulled a chair over to an open window overlooking Sunset Boulevard. Davis was sure Phil was going to jump. He called Dr. Kaplan in New York, trying to get him to call the despondent Phil. Kaplan refused to make the call, telling Davis that he could only help if Phil called *him*. He told Davis to stay with Phil, no matter what. Phil did not jump, obviously, and Davis took him home with him for the weekend. After breakfast on Sunday, Davis diffidently suggested that Phil call Kaplan. Phil didn't want to do it, but finally did. The crisis passed, according to Davis.

Eventually, however, Phil prevailed in the litigation involving the Brothers and MGM—he won a $600,000 settlement from the record company for their subornation of the Righteous Brothers from Philles, according to Ribowsky. But by this time, Phil's ego had deflated to the point where he was afraid to try anything for fear something would go wrong.

25

INTO THE ABYSS

Depressed by the collapse of his ambitions, Phil spent most of the last part of 1965 and early 1966 in his rented Beverly Hills house, rarely going out. His few visitors saw him as glum, uninterested in music. He spent hours morosely playing pinball or pool, and nursing his grudges. He'd been at the top, and now the business had kicked him in the teeth. Thanks a lot!

The main problem was that Phil's way of making music was going the way of the dodo. The self-contained band had taken over; so too had individual performers, like Bob Dylan and Joan Baez, who provided their own accompaniment. Dylan wrote his own songs, played his guitar, sang and even blew his own harmonica, for crying out loud! The influence of folk music had begun to crest, soon morphing into something called "folk rock," epitomized by the Byrds' "Turn! Turn! Turn!" Protest was moving in, hormonal heartthrob was moving out. Phil didn't understand this music; he was from a different era.

It's a truism in the popular music business that rock-and-roll acts generally have a very short shelf life. In contrast to the pre-transistor era of popular music, when an act like the Ames Brothers or the McGuire Sisters or the big bands could hold sway for years, in the increasingly segmented market of the 1960s, performers rose and fell with dizzying rapidity. A sound that worked in January was passé by June. The pressure to create something new was enormous.

At least part of Phil's depression could probably be traced

to his relationship with his old iconoclastic idol, Lenny Bruce. Phil had always been something of a social chameleon—he tended to take on personality characteristics of others who were around him, especially those he admired or looked to for social cachet, such as his imitation of Ahmet Ertegun's stutter in the early 1960s, or his adoption of Andrew Oldham's drug-colored manic persona in 1964. It was as if Phil, realizing that he had no self-actualized personality of his own, looked for safety in his unconscious imitation of others who were out on the fringe.

By 1965, Bruce was in sorry shape. Addicted to heroin, the one-time comedian had lost his sense of humor, and had begun to feel the corroding psychosis of persecution. Having been prosecuted in the east on obscenity and drug charges, Bruce saw himself as a scapegoat, a pincushion for the establishment. His pain resonated with Phil. When Bruce relocated to Los Angeles, Phil became his acolyte as well as protector, soon providing significant sums of money to prop Bruce up. As Bruce's depression deepened, he retreated to a rented house in the Hollywood Hills, morosely blaming the straights for his problems, and passing the time by jabbing his arm full of heroin and Methedrine. Phil arranged for Bruce to make an album, *Lenny Bruce Is Out Again*, in late 1965, but the project flopped. By this time, Bruce's comedy monologue had degenerated to his reading of various legal briefs filed in connection with his interminable court cases. At one point Phil rented the Music Box theater in Hollywood for a ten-day run of Bruce's stand-up act, but hardly anyone bothered to show up. People had better things to do, or more pressing things to worry about, than a former-comedian-turned-junkie trying to make an art out of feeling sorry for himself and angry at the world.

As the relationship between Phil and Bruce deepened, Phil began to adopt some of the characteristics of Bruce's personality, much as he had done years earlier when he'd run through the Bruce repertoire while on the plane with Annette Kleinbard and Marshall Lieb. Only now, Phil posed as a heroin addict himself, an act which gave rise to rumors in

later years that Phil was a heroin user. It wasn't so, said
those who were close to him: Phil was too frightened of needles to get involved with smack.

By February of 1966, Phil had begun to shake off some of
the lethargy that had attended the aftermath of the loss of the
Righteous Brothers. Having lost the white R & B act that he
had shaped to cross-racial stardom, Phil conceived of a re-
entry—this time involving a black R & B act whose appeal
might cross over to white audiences. He settled on Ike and
Tina Turner, who had a number of R & B hits in the 1950s,
along with some rock-and-roll successes. But he wasn't interested in Ike, who, by that time, had become the personifi-
cation of the angry black male of the inner city. Phil was
interested instead in Tina, whose strong voice consistently
cut through the arrangements and made the audience sit up
and take notice.

In early February, Phil "leased" Ike and Tina from their
label for $20,000, and, presumably, a cut of the action. This
deal was in some ways similar to the one he had made with
Moonglow for the Righteous Brothers. According to Williams
in *Out of His Head*, the up-front money was advanced on the
condition that Ike vacate himself from the studio altogether.
According to Danny Davis, Phil promised Ike that if he
agreed to stay away for the song Phil wanted to produce,
then Ike could produce some future Ike and Tina records for
Philles. Taking the cash, Ike agreed—happily, according to
Davis. This relieved Phil, who didn't want Ike interfering
with his plans for Tina; besides, according to Davis, Phil was
afraid of Ike and his reputation as a hard-drinking, drug-
using, gun-toting angry black man in an era, just after riots
in Los Angeles, when racial animosity was becoming far
more commonplace.

Phil's idea was to meld Tina's driving R & B voice with
the Wall of Sound. The recording sessions began in late February. He recruited Ellie Greenwich and Jeff Barry to write a
song for Tina. Greenwich and Barry, who had been married,

had just finished their divorce, a factor which added to the emotional atmosphere behind the writing. Over a week of collaboration with Phil in Los Angeles, Greenwich and Barry fashioned "River Deep—Mountain High," with a lyric by Barry that bespoke of an adult woman's pain of love, backed by a melange of three different melody lines that the writers somehow mashed together, not unlike "Lovin' Feelin'." What emerged was something different: not exactly R & B, but not pop, either. In effect, this was Phil's attempt to strike out for a new direction in the world of music.

For the first two studio sessions, Phil assembled a virtual orchestra at Gold Star—nearly two dozen musicians, all crammed together in one room. Four guitars, four basses, three keyboardists, two percussionists, six horn players, and two drummers. Playing for hours and hours as Phil took the tapes and tinkered with the arrangement, the bill came to nearly $22,000—a huge amount for a single song.

Tina Turner came to the studio to record her vocal on March 7, and discovered that Phil had enlisted nearly two football teams of background singers. Tina was intimidated by the sheer numbers. Her first try didn't work, so Phil had her come back another day. That time, she sang the song without the backups, but over an engorged rhythm track that pulsated through her headphones. Still Phil wasn't satisfied, so the sessions went on and on and on, until finally around midnight, Tina, dripping with sweat, peeled off her blouse and sang her heart out. Perhaps recalling his experiment with the Crystals, Phil had ordered all the lights turned out.

The song still wasn't ready, Phil decreed. He spent the next week or so dubbing and re-dubbing, adding strings. Phil continued to fiddle with it; and finally, it appears, he overdid it: by the time he was satisfied, Tina's voice, stentorian though it was, had been overwhelmed by Phil's Wall.

Williams, in *Out of His Head*, nevertheless admired the result. "Immediately," the music critic wrote, "the listener is thrown into a crazy melange of emotions. This heavy thighed Earth Mother [he meant Tina, although his description of her as "heavy thighed" was way off], wailing like there's a hell-hound on her trail, is singing about rag dolls and puppies. It sounds silly, but it comes out just right.

"But the *SOUND* . . . God, what sound. Mountains, walls, valleys, caverns, chasms, cliffs—a world full of noise, it seems, only channeled into something approaching that 'rushing, mighty wind' the Bible talks about."[45]

The record flopped in the United States, and with that, Phil's first incarnation as a music mogul was over.

Later, people tried to find an explanation for why "River Deep—Mountain High" never made it in the United States (the song did fairly well in the United Kingdom). Ike Turner thought it was because it was too much of a tweener: it wasn't R & B, and it wasn't pop, he thought. The race factor played a role, Ike said. R & B radio stations wouldn't play it, because it wasn't R & B. Rock-and-roll stations wouldn't accept it as pop, either. The fact that an African-American performer was singing a song that was a hybrid threw the deejays off.

Barry, who wrote the lyric, concluded that the record flopped because Phil's ego needs—to make the Wall of Sound the star—overwhelmed his own better musical instincts. Phil, Barry told Williams, had "a self-destructive thing going for him, which is part of the reason that the mix on 'River Deep' is terrible, he buried the lead [Tina] and he knows he buried the lead and he *cannot stop* himself from doing that."

Barry thought that if you listened to all of Phil's records in the order in which they were produced, "the lead goes further and further in . . ." meaning that it progressively became harder and harder to distinguish from the Wall. Barry thought that this was because Phil was cursed with a ravening desire to be the star . . . that it was him, Phil, who was the main man, even though he was only the producer, not the performer. In effect, Barry indicated, over time Phil's songs had become more and more about Phil's ego, and his

---

[45] Williams, *Out of His Head*, p. 120.

need for control, and less and less about the hired players' performances.

From a psychological perspective, this trend has significance: following his ego deflation after the loss of the Righteous Brothers, and the anger that attended what he considered to be their betrayal, Phil's effort with "River Deep" might be seen as an attempt to reinflate his feelings about himself. But like most such self-aggrandizement, it went too far.

A second factor in the mix was Phil's relationship with the radio business, which had taken a turn for the worse in the fall of 1965 and continued on into 1966. Suddenly the deejays were saying Phil's records were passé, that they just didn't cut it anymore. Phil took this personally; when deejays asked him to make personal appearances on their shows, he refused. He wasn't about to answer their questions or endure their gibes— not when he was "the Tycoon of Teen," and thought he knew more about pop music than they did. Phil considered most deejays at best musically ignorant, and at worse, corrupt.

This was, it appears, a reaction on Phil's part to the old bugaboo of payola, which, according to Segrave, was back in full fettle by the mid-1960s.[46] Rather than taking straight cash, as had been the practice in the fifties, by the mid-1960s some deejays were leaning on producers and performers to make free appearances on their shows and at deejay-sponsored concerts in return for playing records. Other deejays were surreptitiously demanding complimentary resort trips, clothing, booze, and sometimes even women in return for playing the right records. By May of 1966, the federal government had finally bestirred itself to look into the new round of payola. The investigation dragged on into 1968 before finally petering out, having caught a few small fry in play-for-pay schemes. But by then, Phil had disappeared from the rock music scene—some thought, for good.

---

[46] *Payola in the Music* Industry, Segrave, pp. 159–165.

26

DO RON RONNING

The next two years of Phil's life are probably the least documented in his storied existence, in part because he essentially wound up his producing business. Although he produced three more records in 1966 after the flop of "River Deep"—including one single from some old Righteous Brothers tape he still held, another Ronettes song, and a third by Ike and Tina that was never released in the U.S., Philles had basically had it.

"That record ['River Deep'] really put Phil out of business," Danny Davis later told Williams. "He took it as a deep personal insult, and it was a great personal tragedy for him. In fact, I can't impress on you too greatly what a tragedy the whole thing was."

Faced with this commercial failure, Phil withdrew, according to Williams. "He retired from the business completely," Williams wrote, "did not make another record for two years, and disappeared into the California desert, apparently finished." Later, as the legend grew, it would have Phil riding off into the arid, trackless badlands on a motorcycle, Mad Max–style, a prophet cast out, the only honest man in a cultural wasteland.

That certainly was a dramatic description, but the truth was a bit more prosaic. For one thing, Phil was still around on August 2, 1966, when Lenny Bruce was found dead in his bathroom, a needle in his arm, a victim of his own excesses. Hearing the news on the radio, Phil grabbed Davis and raced over to Bruce's house. According to Ribowsky, Phil rushed

Phil Spector in his heyday—as a rock-and-roll record producer. *Getty Images.*

BELOW: Lana Clarkson. *Courtesy Clarkson family.*

The Bronx tenement that housed the Spector family when Phil was born in 1939. The family lived here until Phil was about thirteen, four years after his father's 1949 suicide. *Carlton Smith.*

The Teddy Bears in 1958. *Left to right*: Marshall Lieb, Carol Connors, Phil Spector. The trio had a number one hit, "To Know Him is to Love Him." *Courtesy Carol Connors.*

Lana Clarkson as a young girl in Northern California, riding her horse Breeze. *Courtesy Clarkson family.*

The Ronettes, Phil's smash "girl group" act from the early 1960s. He later married Ronnie Bennett, *left*. *Getty Images*.

The La Collina Drive mansion today, without the security "enhancements" erected by Phil in the 1960s. *Carlton Smith*.

Lana Clarkson in Argentina during the filming of *Barbarian Queen*.
Courtesy Clarkson family.

Lana Clarkson as Amethea, the Barbarian Queen.
Getty Images.

The House of Blues, showing the entrance to the VIP Foundations Rooms, where Lana Clarkson was working as hostess the night she met Phil. *Carlton Smith.*

Aerial view of Phil's Alhambra castle. Phil liked to have his guests approach the house by climbing the steps from the street below, although it was more convenient to ride up the driveway to the rear of the dwelling. *Carlton Smith.*

ABOVE: The concrete retaining wall, topped by a wrought-iron fence that surrounds the three-acre Spector property in Alhambra. Phil is said to have been obsessed with security. *Carlton Smith.*

Los Angeles County Sheriff's Department Detective Mark Lillienfeld talking to an Alhambra police officer outside Phil's mansion in the wake of the Clarkson shooting. *Getty Images.*

Phil Spector at a hearing at the Alhambra Courthouse in May 2004, more than a year after the
Clarkson shooting. *Carlton Smith.*

past all the cops, tore up to Bruce's bathroom, and threw himself to the floor next to Bruce's body.

"You killed him!" Phil yelled, meaning the police—referring to the collective law enforcement attempts to jail Bruce for obscenity and drug charges. Phil would maintain for decades afterward that Bruce had died because of police harassment, but finally came to accept the death of his hero, and in a way that the sardonic Bruce would have found funny, or at least witty: "Lenny Bruce," Phil would say, "died of an overdose of police."

The following day, according to Davis, a detective from the Los Angeles Police Department dropped by the Philles offices. The detective produced a proof sheet of photographs, most of them showing Bruce lying dead on the bathroom floor with the needle very visible in his arm. Davis said the cop wanted to sell Phil the pictures, saying he thought Phil might be able to use them for an album cover. Davis said he called Phil at home to tell him about the offer. The cop, he said, wanted $5,000 for the lot. Davis said he asked Phil what he wanted to do. Phil ordered him to buy the pictures, but Davis sent the cop up to Phil's house so he could make the deal himself. At the time Davis thought that Phil wanted the photographs to prevent anyone from exploiting them, but later he learned that Phil had sold the pictures to a movie company which was making a film about Lenny Bruce's life. Davis thought that Phil had made a substantial profit on the entire transaction.

By the time of Lenny Bruce's overdose, Phil had already begun eyeing the movie business as a possible new career direction. And why not? The music business seemed to be growing away from him, and by this time he had plenty of money, always a useful commodity when one is trying to get into—or even onto—celluloid.

Over the previous year Phil had made the acquaintance of a number of people in the movie business, including Peter Fonda and actor/photographer Dennis Hopper. Hopper was iconoclastic enough to suit Phil's taste, and by the spring of 1966 it appears that Hopper had convinced Phil to put up some money for an independent film. In mid-May of 1966, even before "River Deep" was released, Phil took an option on a treatment for a crypto-western called *The Last Movie*, described by Ribowsky as a story about an American film crew shooting a movie in a Mexican village. The option called for Phil to pay the writer, Steven Stern, $71,000 for the treatment and the script—ten grand up front, another $36,000 by the end of the year, and a further $25,000 or $12\frac{1}{2}$ percent of the proceeds once the thing was released. According to Ribowsky, Phil and Hopper took a junket to Mazatlán to scout locations for the shoot. Other deals were made with an award-winning cameraman, for the rental of a studio and for the construction of sets.

Over the next year, the costs for the movie kept mounting; pretty soon the tab ran over a million dollars, and Phil was on the hook for most of it, although he had yet to turn over any money at all to the writer, despite his agreement to pay $71,000. In the end Phil pulled out of the deal, precipitating a lawsuit by Hopper and Stern. Eventually the lawsuit was settled, with Phil agreeing to pay half the accumulated costs of the proposed movie, about $600,000, according to Davis.

For some reason this did not seem to sour Phil on Hopper. Two years later, when Hopper, Fonda and Jack Nicholson made *Easy Rider*, Phil was given a part. He played a wealthy drug dealer who financed the trio's ride into the dark side of American culture. The way the script was written, Phil did not have a single spoken line, although he did address several lines of white powdery substance while sitting in the rear seat of a white Rolls-Royce. Davis, for one, thought it was Hopper's joke on Phil—for once, Phil was speechless.

As this mostly unsatisfying period of Phil's professional life unfolded, Phil's personality began to take on some of the aspects that would later be most frequently associated with his eccentric lifestyle, most notably his penchant for hiring bodyguards, and having what appeared to be excessive concern over his personal security. Ribowsky noted that by 1966, Phil's house in Beverly Hills was already taking on the appearance of an up-country bunker, surrounded as it was with razor wire, alarms, guard dogs and bodyguards. And at another point, during an argument with engineer Larry Levine, Phil ordered his bodyguards to beat Levine up. The guards didn't know what to do, since Phil was paying them, but they weren't about to commit bodily mayhem on Phil's say-so. Eventually the squabble was patched up, but Phil's predilection for ordering his guards to whack people he got into disagreements with would continue over the years.

What was this behavior all about? Some thought it was just Phil's way of telling the world he was different—another plea for attention. Others thought the pathology ran deeper: that Phil had a deep streak of paranoia that only seemed to increase as the years went by, as he became more financially successful, but artistically more irrelevant. It was as if, by commanding beefy ex-cops and military types to do his bidding, he was reassuring himself that he was important. But a likely part of it was also a sign of the times—an era when violence was ever-present, on the news from Vietnam, in the inner cities, in the nightclubs and culture where drug-taking was making people do crazy things. Phil had always seen himself as a target, not only because of his diminutive stature, but also because he had what he thought everyone else wanted—money and power. The more the latter seemed to be slipping away, the more Phil flexed his surrogate muscles to show it wasn't really so.

By this time, Ronnie Bennett had moved in with Phil, even as her career as the lead for the Ronettes had gone into eclipse. Ronnie's cousin Nedra thought that Phil was simply using Ronnie. But she also thought that Ronnie was using Phil. As in many relationships, it appears that each saw in the other only the things they wanted to see, and ignored everything else.

As with his former wife Annette, Phil was extraordinarily jealous over Ronnie. He took great pains to make sure that she was never alone with another man, pains that would eventually reach the most absurd lengths. "To Phil, any man was a threat," Ronnie said later. Ronnie recalled going out for a hamburger one night with Sonny Bono, while Phil was busy late at night in the mixing room at Gold Star. When they returned to the studio, "It looked like an earthquake had struck," Ronnie wrote in *Be My Baby*. "There wasn't a soul in the studio, but all the music stands had been knocked over and there was broken glass everywhere." Someone had upset an entire pot of coffee all over the carpet. "And it must have been Phil," Ronnie concluded. "Who else could've caused this much damage in such a short period of time?"

That was when Phil confronted them, demanding to know where they had been. Sonny, trying to shield Ronnie, confessed that it was all his fault. Phil agreed that it *was* Sonny's fault, that he should have known better. And Ronnie, Phil said, should have known better than to leave without telling him. Phil sulked for several days afterward, Ronnie recalled.

Yet at the same time, Ronnie was convinced that Phil was madly in love with her, an assessment that was doubted by Danny Davis. Davis thought that Phil regretted paying so little attention to Annette, and so now tried to make up for it by paying almost obsessive attention to Ronnie. "He definitely threw himself at Ronnie," Davis told Ribowsky. "He romanced her pretty good." Yet with all of this, Davis still wasn't convinced that Phil was really in love with her. It was so difficult to tell when Phil was in love with anything or anyone other than himself.

But in wooing Ronnie, Phil was unable to separate himself from who he seemed to be, that is, his position as a music mogul. He promised to make Ronnie a star, which was what Ronnie wanted. But then Phil would think, once Ronnie is a star, she won't need me anymore. So Phil would talk about making her a star, but never really do much to make it happen.

Nedra Talley, Ronnie's cousin, picked up on this almost immediately. "It was the extreme jealousy," she told Ribowsky. "Phil knew that Ronnie was not in love with him as a man. She was in love with who he was." Nedra thought Phil feared that Ronnie would dump him once she didn't need him any longer. "So he would only do so much with her, he would give her an inch and take back two inches. And then he took back more than that."

27

TAKE THE MONEY, PLEASE

According to Ronnie's version of events, she'd first taken up residence with Phil in the fall of 1965, just about the time he was feuding with the Righteous Brothers and getting his Mexican divorce from Annette.

Almost as soon as they moved in together, Phil took steps to separate Ronnie from other musicians. When they went to Gold Star, Phil made her sit in the control room with him. He didn't want her interacting with the other talent, she thought. And Ronnie quickly became aware of Phil's cyclical moods. When "River Deep" tanked, Phil became extremely depressed, Ronnie recalled. "There was nothing I could do to cheer him up," she said.

For Ronnie, her only sanity (and income, as it would turn out) came from the touring she did with her sister and cousin. Phil grudgingly allowed the tours to take place, although he didn't like them. On several tours, he burned up the telephone lines, calling Ronnie every few hours to make sure she wasn't straying. Nedra and Estelle thought he was nuts. Then, on one tour, in Manhattan, Ronnie was told there was someone in the audience who wanted to speak to her, someone who had billed herself as "a good friend of Phil's."

When she went out into the audience, a waiter took her to a table where a young blond woman and a man were sitting. The woman stood up and shook Ronnie's hand. "I'm Annette Spector," Ronnie said she was told. "I've heard so much about you."

Ronnie was so tongue-tied at meeting the ex–Mrs. Spector,

she didn't know what to say. Annette told her that she had no hard feelings for Ronnie. Annette and her companion offered to buy her a drink, but Ronnie said she didn't drink; and she didn't, at least not in those days. Then she got up to go. She turned back to Annette. "Thanks," she told Annette, and she meant it.

Shortly thereafter, the Ronettes were invited to tour with the Beatles. But Phil discouraged Ronnie from going, telling her that she had to choose between doing a "freak show" with the Beatles, or making hit records with him. Ronnie feared that Phil had heard that John Lennon had put the moves on her, and was giving her a test: either it was the Beatles (Lennon) or it was the recording business (Phil). Ronnie decided not to go on the Beatles tour. Instead, her cousin Elaine took her place.

Then came Lenny Bruce's overdose, and things turned even more weird.

According to Ronnie, "nothing could have been worse than the month I spent with Phil in his mansion," in August of 1966. Phil was still depressed about "River Deep," and had taken to locking himself inside his study.

Ronnie was never entirely sure what Phil was up to when he was in his study, locked away from the world. Sometimes she would listen through the door, and it appeared that Phil was on the telephone, talking to someone; at other times, he simply played his old records, over and over. Phil, Ronnie realized, was extremely, pathologically depressed.

"But what really put Phil under," Ronnie wrote in *Be My Baby*, "was when he got the news that his old friend Lenny Bruce had died of a drug overdose."

To Ronnie, Phil's devotion to Bruce was aberrational. She said he'd stuck "a huge blow-up poster of Lenny right over our bed." Because Phil usually fell asleep before she did, Ronnie spent much of the night with Bruce's drug-addled mug staring down at her.

Ronnie said at first that Phil hadn't told her that Bruce had died, that she'd only found out about it one night when she encountered a red-eyed Phil when he opened the door to his study. She asked him what was wrong. Nothing, Phil said. Phil said he'd get a snack for Ronnie to eat, and headed off toward the kitchen. Ronnie, returning to the bedroom, noticed that Phil had left his study door open. This was Phil's inner sanctum, and "I wasn't really allowed in there," Ronnie wrote.

Obviously, the open door was more temptation than Ronnie could withstand, so she went in to look around. She said later that she thought she might find a magazine to read. She couldn't find one, so she pulled open the top drawer of Phil's desk. That was when she saw a small stack of photographs, and she recognized the naked body of Lenny Bruce, lying next to a toilet. There was a hypodermic needle next to the body. Even Ronnie could see that Lenny was dead.

Ronnie sat down in Phil's chair and studied the pictures. The next thing she knew Phil was sailing a grilled cheese sandwich past her head. He was so furious he could barely talk. Ronnie asked him what had happened to Bruce, but Phil exploded, cursing her for invading his privacy. She locked herself in the bathroom, and Phil locked himself in his study, and there the happy couple spent the rest of their respective nights.

That fall, the Ronettes went on a tour of U.S. military facilities in Germany. The trip was strange, not the least because the generally sex-starved G.I.'s went nuts for the seductively dancing Ronettes. At one point, there was a mini-riot when some soldiers couldn't get into the show; after a quick rendition of a few songs, the Ronettes beat a quick retreat, being transported away from the base in a large truck. "Don't worry," a military policeman told Ronnie, "it's bulletproof." He wasn't kidding, either, Ronnie said.

While the Ronettes were on this tour, Phil probably broke the record for transatlantic telephone charges, dialing Ronnie whenever he could. Sometimes Ronnie never hung up the telephone, drifting off to sleep while Phil talked to her. "In the morning, I'd pick it up and there would be Phil," she wrote, "yawning and saying, 'Good morning, baby. Did you sleep well?'"

After the Ronettes returned from Germany, Ronnie said, she began to miss her mother. Phil suggested that she simply call her. Ronnie said she couldn't do that, because her mother would realize she was sleeping with Phil, "and I can't lie to her anymore."

That was no problem, Phil said. Why didn't Ronnie just tell her mother that she and Phil had been married the week before? Ronnie said she couldn't do that. Phil said that if she wouldn't, he would. He placed the call. And then, according to Ronnie, he told Beatrice that he had great news, that Ronnie and he had been married the previous week. Beatrice, who was nobody's fool, started asking him questions. Phil began unwinding a long, increasingly fantastic tale. "The service was performed by two practicing rabbis," he told Beatrice, according to Ronnie. "There were no witnesses. That's right. It was an obscure Hebraic ceremony. Very ancient."

Finally Beatrice demanded to speak to Ronnie. Tremulously, Ronnie said it was true: they had been married. Beatrice didn't buy it. She said she would come to Beverly Hills right away to check this situation out, and if it turned out that Phil and Ronnie weren't married, she intended to bring Ronnie straight back to New York with her.

When Beatrice flew in a day or so later, her first question to Ronnie was, "Where's the ring?" All she had to do was look at Ronnie's face to know she'd lied.

After a few more questions, Beatrice accused Phil of using her daughter. Phil said they'd been "rehearsing." Beatrice said, "Rehearsing? For three months?" Then she told Phil she intended to take Ronnie directly back to New York. She called a taxi, and when it arrived, she took Ronnie by the arm and pulled her toward it.

Phil pleaded with Ronnie not to leave, but Ronnie insisted she had to go with her mother. "Besides," she added in *Be My Baby*, "I knew that no matter how hurt Phil acted, this kind of scene appealed to his sense of drama."

According to Ronnie, this was when Phil reached into his pocket and pulled out a roll of $500 bills. He threw them at

Beatrice's feet and begged her to take the money and leave Ronnie behind!

Beatrice and Ronnie got into the cab. Phil got down on his knee and begged: "Leave my wife! Take the money, just leave my wife!" It was almost a scene out of a Woody Allen movie, with a dash of Borscht Belt. As the cab drove off, Ronnie said, she looked through the rear window, and saw Phil carefully gathering up all his $500 bills before they blew away.

Beatrice and Ronnie returned to New York.

According to Ronnie, Phil began calling her in New York almost immediately, and threatened to come there to get her. Beatrice began moving Ronnie from relative to relative, as if she were an undercover informant going from safe house to safe house. "There was nothing to do," Ronnie complained, meaning that it was boring. Not that there'd been all that much to do at Phil's mansion, either. But, Ronnie observed, "having nothing to do in Beverly Hills is a far cry from having nothing to do in Spanish Harlem."

Soon, Ronnie started drinking gin to pass the time. It was a fateful decision.

Phil did come to New York to look for her. His rented limo took him to Spanish Harlem, where it parked out in front of Beatrice's place, at least until Phil found out that Beatrice was keeping Ronnie hidden by moving her around from relative to relative. So Phil had the limo take him to the relatives' neighborhood, where he encountered one of Ronnie's cousins, and asked him to take him to Ronnie. The cousin said he was under strict instructions not to tell Phil where Ronnie was. Phil said he was sure that Ronnie wanted to see him—he'd been hurt, Phil said, and he opened the door of the limo to show Ronnie's cousin that his leg was in a cast. The cousin finally gave in, and took Phil to the place where Ronnie was hiding out.

Phil clumped into the apartment and called out for Ronnie. By this time, she had learned to drink quite well; in fact, she looked like a mess. But Phil was overjoyed to see her, and so, it appears, was Ronnie overjoyed to see Phil. Then she noticed the cast on his leg. He'd been in an accident, Phil told Ronnie.

Phil took Ronnie to a hotel, where she cleaned up. The next day they made arrangements to fly back to Los Angeles. Before they left, Ronnie went to see her mother. Beatrice said that if Ronnie really wanted to live in sin with a man, that was her decision. But, she said, she sure hoped that Phil would marry her. Ronnie burst into tears, but left with Phil.

A few months after they returned to Los Angeles, Phil and Ronnie were married for real, for better and especially for worse.

28

LOCKED IN

On April 14, 1968, Phil married Ronnie in a private ceremony at the Beverly Hills City Hall. And while Ribowsky asserts that Phil "tried to give Ronnie a great deal of attention after the wedding," Ronnie tells it differently.

For one thing, no sooner were they married than Phil treated the entire wedding party to tickets to a Mahalia Jackson concert. It wasn't Ronnie's idea of wedding night entertainment. Sitting there in the audience with her mother, Phil's driver, and Phil's driver's family, Ronnie swallowed her disappointment. But then things began to get even more weird. Walking out of the concert, Ronnie recalled, Phil asked her if she wouldn't mind going home without him. Phil told her he needed to go see his mother, Bertha. When Ronnie protested, Phil told her that he hadn't yet told his mother that he and Ronnie had decided to get married.

Thus, an underling drove Phil off to see his mother so he could give her the happy news, while the driver took Ronnie back to the Beverly Hills house. There Ronnie prepared to spend her first night in officially wedded bliss.

Two hours later, according to Ronnie, Phil came storming in, slamming doors behind him. He cursed Ronnie, calling her a "bitch," and telling her, "I know your game, Veronica. You just want my money. That's it, isn't it?"

Ronnie got out of bed and ran into the hallway, thinking that Phil was so angry he might try to kill her. She managed to ask Phil what his mother had told him to set him off like that.

"The truth," he shot back. "That this whole marriage is about one thing—my money."

Ronnie fled downstairs to where her mother had recently been lodged in a small apartment as the wedding day approached. Beatrice thought that Phil was hopped up on cocaine. A few minutes later, Phil came downstairs and started pounding on the door.

"Open up, Mrs. Bennett!" he called out. Phil always called Ronnie's mother "Mrs. Bennett."

"Not until you start acting like a grown man, Phil," Beatrice replied.

"The hell with you," Phil shouted back. He disappeared. But then, according to Ronnie, he returned, this time with a set of keys to the apartment. Ronnie and her mother locked themselves inside the bathroom. Phil demanded that Beatrice open the door to the bathroom, but she refused. Phil began pounding on the door in a rhythmic fashion—literally, a wall of sound.

"I'd never seen him looking quite so mad," Ronnie said later in *Be My Baby*, "with saliva dripping down the side of his mouth and his eyes looking like a wild coyote's . . . And he was scaring the shit out of me."

The next morning, when Ronnie dared to go back to the bedroom upstairs, she found a dozen red roses on her pillow and a note from Phil:

> *Forever yours,*
> *Okay?*
> *—Phil*

Phil's second marriage was off to a rocky start.

Ronnie should have known what she was getting herself into—she had lived with Phil for a bit more than two years before they were married.

Even before the wedding, the walls had begun going up around Phil's "mansion" in Beverly Hills. And the walls weren't only physical; there were psychic walls, as well. Ronnie soon learned that Phil preferred that she stay at home; that meant she had almost no one to talk to. Soon Ronnie began conversations with the household staff, particularly the cook, George Johnson. Johnson was a congenial sort who had once worked for Humphrey Bogart, Ronnie recalled. He enjoyed telling stories about Bogart, Lauren Bacall and other film stars of the thirties, forties and fifties. And Ronnie loved to hear them. Until one day Phil overheard Johnson telling one to Ronnie. The next day, Johnson refused to tell her any more.

Ronnie asked him what was wrong, why he wouldn't tell her any more stories about famous movie stars. Johnson went over to the kitchen tap, and turned the water on so that it splashed loudly in the sink, apparently so he couldn't be overheard. "Some people," he said softly, "don't like other people to hear stories that have too much happiness in them."

The day after the wedding, just as she was discovering the roses on her pillow, Ronnie looked out the window and saw a construction crew installing a chain link fence around the property, one with barbed wire across the top. That was when she first began to suspect that she was trapped—and in a house with five bedrooms, a living room, dining room, breakfast room, library, game room, television room and swimming pool, not to mention a mother-in-law apartment for Beatrice Bennett.

The worst of it was the boredom: there simply wasn't anything for Ronnie to do. She'd accepted that her singing career was on permanent hold—in fact, she guessed that she was all washed up as a recording star. But there wasn't even anything for her to do in the house, because Phil's staff took care of everything—the cleaning, the cooking, answering the telephones, *everything*. Phil, meanwhile, had a decidedly nocturnal nature; according to Ronnie, he liked to stay up late, sometimes until 4 A.M., then sleep in late the following day, sometimes until 1 or 2 in the afternoon—an echo of the observations of his old roommate, Terry Phillips, from their days together in New York.

"My only household duty," she said, "was to get up in the morning and discuss with George [Johnson] what Phil and I wanted for dinner. After that, I'd go out to the pool and watch Phil do his laps."

After that, Phil would go off to his study or the office or the studio, and Ronnie would go to the television room, usually dialing up an old Bette Davis or Joan Crawford movie on the box. "Bette always seemed to be crying about something," Ronnie said. "Or getting drunk . . . after awhile I started doing the same thing."

So here it was again—the same thing that had unraveled Phil's marriage to Annette, only this time with Ronnie. He'd wooed and won the girl, then hardly knew what to do with her. Just as Annette went stir-crazy in their penthouse apartment in New York, now Ronnie was going nuts in their Beverly Hills mansion. Living with an eccentric millionaire was no bed of roses, florally decorated pillows notwithstanding. To Phil, the woman wasn't so much of a real person as she was physical proof to the rest of the world that he was a success.

Left to her own devices in the huge house—although always under the eye of the staff (the "manservants," Phil called them, according to Ronnie)—Ronnie soon began poking around. That was when she discovered Phil's hidden bar, in the game room, concealed in a wall near the fireplace. She noticed a button, and as curious as ever about the millionaire she'd married, she pushed it. An antique bar emerged from above.

Because she'd abstained from drinking most of her life—Ronnie said later that her father sometimes spent the night on the front porch, sleeping off a bottle of gin, which probably accounted for her mother's raising her daughters as teetotalers—Ronnie really didn't understand alcohol. She began drinking it "like soda pop," she said, and although she disliked the taste, it had the great attraction of making her numb and eventually putting her to sleep. So Ronnie began drinking, but taking care not to let Phil know about it.

As the first year of their marriage unfolded, Phil continued to exhibit his pattern of extreme jealousy. He took pride in introducing Ronnie to various people who came to the house to see him, but as soon as they'd had a chance to look her over, Ronnie said, he'd send her back upstairs, away from other men's eyes. This applied even to the "manservants." Once when Ronnie put on a bikini to swim in the pool, Phil was horrified. He demanded she get back inside and change into something more modest. Ronnie pooh-poohed Phil's reaction, asking him who was going to see her in their own back yard. "The manservants," he said. Ronnie went back into the house and changed.

At some point that fall, Phil apparently realized that Ronnie was tired of being cooped up in the house; this may have been after things blew up in August, as will shortly be seen. At that point Phil brought home a brand new Camaro, wrapped in a ribbon for Ronnie. She was overjoyed, Ronnie said; it looked like she might finally be allowed to get out of the house. But Phil said that wasn't all he had brought her. He opened the trunk and removed an inflatable plastic mannikin. It was Phil—or at least a life-sized doll made to look like him. Phil's idea was that Ronnie would put the pseudo-Phil in the passenger seat of the car, so it would look like he was always with her whenever she went out by herself. "Don't you get it?" Phil asked her. "Now nobody will fuck with you when you're driving alone."

The fence that Ronnie had noticed the day after the wedding was soon in place—ten feet tall, and electrified. Then came the dogs—German shepherds running loose, an Irish wolfhound that was Phil's pet, a pair of borzois—enough sets of fangs to tear an interloper to shreds. The fence was hung with signs warning that trespassers' lives would be in danger if they entered. Floodlamps mounted in the upstairs windows bathed the grounds as if it were the yard at Sing

Sing. Then there were the human watchdogs—principally, Phil's personal bodyguard, a man named George Brand who was always armed, and who soon came to serve as Phil's messenger when he wanted to tell Ronnie what she could not do.

As the fences and bars (the metal kind) went up, Ronnie soon realized that all the doors and windows of the house were locked—from the inside, too. If she wanted to go out, she had to get Brand or one of the staff to unlock the door, and before that could happen, they had to get Phil's permission. "When the last servant went home," Ronnie recalled, "you were in for the night."

Phil finally realized that Ronnie had become a secret drinker when he discovered that one of his Scotch bottles was half-empty. He accused a friend of George Johnson, the cook, of being the culprit. That was when Ronnie said she'd been the one. Phil was shocked, she said. The next day, she found that Phil had put a large padlock on the hidden bar.

But, as Ronnie later observed, locking up the booze isn't really a solution. When a person has an addiction for alcohol, they'll find a way to get it, however devious. Ronnie began inventing excuses to go to the supermarket. After gorging herself on all the magazines Phil wouldn't let her read at home, she said, she'd go to the liquor section of the store and pick up a bottle of Manischewitz wine—because its twist cap didn't require a corkscrew, which Ronnie didn't have. She'd smuggle the sweet wine home, then hide it in the toilet tank in her bathroom. After that, whenever she thought she'd scream if she couldn't blot things out, she'd go to the bathroom for a slug of relief.

The walls—of sound, of chain link, of barbed wire, of booze—soon began to close in on Ronnie. Only four months after the wedding, she sued for divorce.[47] She hired a Los Angeles attorney, P. F. Caruso, to initiate the action, asserting

---

[47] Los Angeles County Superior Court file D 734482.

that she and Phil had separated on August 20, 1968. Caruso contended that everything Phil owned—"my money," as Phil had put it to Ronnie—was community property. Caruso wanted the court to authorize the hiring of a certified public accountant to go over all of Phil's business records so Ronnie could see just how much she might be entitled to.

"Since the marriage of the plaintiff and defendant," the complaint for divorce read, "the defendant has treated plaintiff in an extremely cruel manner and has inflicted upon her great and grievous mental and physical suffering, and said conduct on the part of the defendant has defeated the object of matrimony.

"The defendant has a mean and ungovernable temper and has grabbed plaintiff violently and has threatened to stick his fingers in her eyes and he has stated to her that he could not permit her to get a divorce from him . . ."

Caruso asked that Phil be enjoined from "annoying, molesting, or harming plaintiff in any way whatsoever."

This was the last anyone heard of Caruso until a year later, when the litigation was formally dropped. But two days after Caruso had filed his paperwork in the proposed divorce, Phil hired his own lawyer, Jay H. Cooper, from Beverly Hills, who filed Phil's action for divorce.[48]

This lawsuit put the date of separation as August 21—one day after Caruso's earlier action. Phil signed a paper approving the complaint on August 22.

So it appears that during August of 1968, only four months after marrying Phil, there were *two* lawyers, each working on a separate divorce action. Where Caruso's complaint claimed that all of Phil's assets were community property, Cooper's asserted that "there exists no community property of the parties herein." And Cooper said Ronnie was cruel to Phil, although he chose not to specify how.

Parsing this out thirty-six years after the fact is difficult, in part because these preliminary filings stand as the entirety

---

[48] Los Angeles County Superior Court file D 734564.

of the official records on these two simultaneous divorce actions, which doubtless would have been consolidated by the court had they gone forward. Ronnie herself does not mention them in *Be My Baby*, nor does Williams in *Out of His Head*. Ribowsky had the facts, but his version has statements made in Caruso's pleading that weren't found in the microfilmed court file thirty-six years later, for some reason. Both of these divorce suits were initiated before the California legislature approved the state's no-fault divorce laws; thus they both required the claim of "cruelty" as a grounds for divorce.

Despite the dual—and dueling—filings, Phil talked Ronnie into remaining in the marriage. The lack of additional documents filed in connection with either case over the following year shows that Phil was successful in inducing Ronnie to stay. By April of 1969, both lawsuits had been dismissed by the lawyers who filed them.

That didn't mean the troubles between Ronnie and Phil were over. In August of 1969, Ronnie again filed for divorce.[49] A new brace of lawyers accused Phil of "extreme cruelty toward the plaintiff," and again asserted there was community property to be divided, including the ownership of the Hollywood office building where Phil's current business, Phil Spector Productions, was located; the business itself; the Beverly Hills "mansion"; furniture; automobiles, including Ronnie's new Camaro and Phil's Rolls-Royce; and various "bank accounts, the exact locations and amounts of which are unknown to the plaintiff."

This lawsuit, too, died for lack of prosecution on Ronnie's part.

Under these circumstances, and going only by the sketchy documents included in all three files, it's difficult to avoid wondering whether Phil might have been right all along—that Ronnie *had* only married him for his money, and that she had been prepared to put up with him only as

---

[49] Los Angeles Superior Court file D 752 577, filed August 5, 1969.

long as she had to in order to qualify for some significant property settlement. After all, these lawsuits weren't *Phil* talking—they were Ronnie's attempts to get out of the short-lived marriage with as much as she could, twice in a little over a year.

And by the time her third divorce suit was filed, she had something to help her with her claims—a bouncing baby boy.

29

NOT JUST ANY WHITE GUY

This was Donté Phillip Spector, who came into the world on March 23, 1969; and of his arrival, there is substantial comment from Ronnie.

According to Ronnie, she first saw her son on television. He was only a few days old. Cradling her glass of Manischewitz as she channel-surfed in the game room, she happened upon a program about "unwanted babies." And suddenly it struck Ronnie: if there was one thing she wanted, it was a baby.

So too, it appears, did Phil. This seemed to be the answer to all the emptiness: someone little, helpless, who needed them, who would fill their unhappy lives with meaning. Ronnie got into Phil's Rolls-Royce—she said Phil had her Camaro that day—and rolled down the freeway to the adoption agency mentioned on the program, and demanded to see the baby she'd seen on the tube.

Once the agency realized they were dealing with the wife of multi-millionaire Phil Spector, Ronnie said, the adoption, while time-consuming, was easy. It was always easier for wealthy people, she said.

And here is an interesting facet of the lives of Phil and Ronnie: while the agency checked them out to see if they would be fit to serve as parents, somehow they overlooked some rather salient points: Ronnie's alcohol addiction, Phil's obsessive behavior, his apparent bipolar disorder, the couple's frequent spats, and not least, the fact that the house was, for all practical purposes, a maximum security installation.

Later, when Donté Phillip Spector would tell the story of his own life, and observe that his adoptive father was "crazy," those omissions by the adoption agency would seem hard to countenance; they certainly didn't do much for Donté while he was growing up.

The craziness started almost immediately. As Ronnie was readying the baby's crib one day just before the adoption, Phil walked in and showed her a card. It depicted a baby. Underneath were the words: "Presenting the Smash-Hit Production of Donté Phillip Spector."

And then, in three acts, more craziness: first, Donté's "premature" birth—implying that the baby was the natural child of Phil and Ronnie; second, Donté spending weeks in the hospital because of the prematurity, thereby accounting for the time between the birth and the actual taking of possession of the infant; and third, the healthy baby going home from the hospital with Phil and Ronnie. The card's tag line: "The above is a Veronica and Phil Spector Production."

It seems clear that Phil thought this was clever—cute, even: comparing their new baby to a record. But the duplicity—it was reminiscent of Phil claiming to Gerry Goffin that he'd written the song "Uptown." Why did Phil think he could advance such a falsehood—that Donté had not been adopted—and no one would realize it? It was as if Phil were living in a fantasy world, where whatever he *said* was truth *was* truth. On the other hand, maybe Phil thought that so few people had seen Ronnie in recent months that no one would realize that she hadn't really been pregnant.

According to Ronnie, she protested the announcement. "But Phil," she said, "everyone's going to know I wasn't pregnant."

"If I say you were pregnant, who's going to say any different?" Ronnie said Phil told her.

Who, indeed, was going to say any different? Having surrounded himself with hired help to do his bidding, Phil's isolation could only grow. Dispenser of largesse to great and small, Phil had become the center of an adoring circle of sycophants: They said he was a genius, and Phil believed it. It had to be true—everyone around him, his reality mirror, kept telling him he was the fairest prince of all. The legend grew ever more divergent from the facts, and Phil, so quick to adopt others' perceptions of him as the truth, soon got psychically lost. The trouble was, Phil's mind was like a car with only two gears: either he was bumping along in low, or he was screaming down the highway in high. He never did have to find a gear for city driving, with its need for compromise and peripheral vision. In short, he had never had to mature as a human being.

Ronnie later attributed some of Phil's mental problems to the lionization that always seemed to surround him. "As time went on," she observed, "they started writing about him being a genius, and then he said, 'yeah, I'm a genius.' And then they would say he was a mad genius, so he became the mad genius." When people said Phil was a recluse, he became one. Phil adopted these personas, she thought, because he craved attention.

This picking and choosing of different personas as if they were costumes for the drama of life may have been because, as Ronnie said, Phil loved the limelight. But at the same time, they might be seen as evidence for the proposition that Phil had never really grown his own personality—that, flushed with all the early success, he had turned into a fragmented soul who kept trying to act in ways that would justify others' expectations.

Take Phil's hair—according to everyone who had ever known him, Phil's hair loss was one of his biggest internal bugaboos. Ronnie wrote of Phil sitting in front of mirrors for hours, trying to get his wigs just right. The loss of hair, in fact, was one of the main reasons why Phil believed he could never be a stage performer, along with his "adenoidal" voice. But the art of becoming a full person consists of finding a style that embraces what one has, not what one doesn't have. Had he attempted to be a singer—a bald-headed, adenoidal-voiced singer—and brought it off with panache, glorying in his own selfhood rather than trying to be something he wasn't with his wigs, who knows how successful he might have been? At first, Bob Dylan was considered by many to be an adenoidal-voiced geek. But he went with it and made it stand up, saying, in effect, This is who I am, so get used to it. And people soon appreciated the raw honesty of it—and by extension, the power of it.

The trying-on of personas in this period of Phil's life had its strange and sometimes even comical moments, and nowhere more than in Phil's attitudes about race. Ronnie came to believe that Phil wanted to be African-American more than anything. She recalled, after the assassination of Martin Luther King, that Phil locked himself inside his study, weeping and playing recordings of King's speeches, for days and nights on end. And it has to be true that Phil always felt a solidarity with black Americans, whose struggle against racial oppression, so much a part of the 1960s, resonated with his own deep-seated feelings of being an outsider. Yet the same Phil, by all accounts, took advantage of his African-American acts, signing them to onerous contracts and allegedly withholding royalties for years after they had made so many hits for him. As late as 1969, in his interview in *Rolling Stone*, Phil referred to African-Americans as "colored," a term that had long since been relegated to the ash-heap of racial patronizing.

One of the more vivid examples of Phil's desire to demonstrate his solidarity with black America was recounted by Ronnie in *Be My Baby*. At one point, after Ronnie's mother Beatrice—a very sharp lady—came to live with the couple following Donté's arrival, Phil asked her to drive to south central Los Angeles to find an Afro wig for Phil. Beatrice and Ronnie set off in search of such a wig, and eventually found three. They brought them back to the "mansion." Phil seemed delighted with his new hair, Ronnie wrote.

"I guess it made him feel like he had soul or something," she remarked. Not long after, Phil convinced Beatrice and Ronnie to go with him to hear gospel music at a black church in Watts. Ronnie wasn't enthusiastic—she had no interest in gospel music, and admitted that she didn't understand it. But

Phil insisted, so off they went—in the Rolls-Royce, accompanied by two bodyguards. Before they left, though, Beatrice and Ronnie noticed that Phil had armed himself with a pistol. When Beatrice asked him why he was bringing a gun to church, for God's sake, Phil explained that it was his "peacemaker . . . I brought it along in case there's trouble."

Arriving at the church—Phil was probably the only white man in attendance, and certainly the only white man wearing an Afro wig—the trio settled into a pew to enjoy the music. Phil really got into it, Ronnie wrote.

"They were wailing and moaning and singing out the way gospel people do," she wrote, "and Phil was moaning and wailing right along with them . . . here I was, this black girl, bored out of her mind at a gospel concert, sitting with a Jewish man in an Afro [wig] who looked like he was about to speak in tongues."

When the singing was over, Phil ran to the front of the church with a $100 bill in his hand for the collection plate, while Beatrice cringed. As he bobbed toward the front of the church, Ronnie could see Phil's .38 revolver jiggling in his jacket pocket. She was scared to death it was going to fall out.

As they left, according to Ronnie, Phil told his wife and mother-in-law, "I guess I showed them I'm not just *any* white guy."

"That you did, Phil," Beatrice said, with irony that seemed to go over Phil's head. "That you surely did."

30

NO EXIT

As 1969 headed toward "the Me Decade" of the 1970s, Phil decided it was time to go back to work. He didn't think much of the music he was hearing on the radio. That year had hits from the Fifth Dimension, "Aquarius," and "Wedding Bell Blues"; the Beatles, with "Get Back" and "Come Together"; the Rolling Stones, "Honky Tonk Women"; Peter, Paul and Mary, "Leaving on a Jet Plane"; the Temptations, "I Can't Get Next to You"; the Supremes, "Some Day We'll Be Together"; and Sly and the Family Stone, with "Everyday People." A family of siblings called the Jackson Five recorded "I Want You Back," Neil Diamond made "Sweet Caroline," Creedence Clearwater Revival had "Proud Mary," "Bad Moon Rising" and "Green River." A very popular tune was "Grazing in the Grass."

Looking back, it seems apparent that many of the songs recorded as the sixties came to a close were reflective of the growing disillusionment over the war, and a desire for the return of so many who were dying so far away. "Get back to where you once belonged," the Beatles sang, and its message worked on multiple levels. "Some day we'll be together," Diana Ross sang, in expectation of reuniting with someone lost.

At the same time, the edge of the music began to reflect the far wider dissemination of drugs in society, and increasing internalization, a turning away from the outside world in search of some sort of separate peace. "Grazing in the Grass" was groovy; so was "Come Together." The Doors were opening things up, especially eyes.

Phil couldn't get his brain around this kind of music. To him, it sounded unfinished—"an idea," as he put it to *Rolling Stone*, not a complete song. There was too little control, for his taste.

Phil still thought he could span the gap between white and black audiences, as he had done with the Crystals, the Ronettes and the Righteous Brothers, but had failed to do with Ike and Tina Turner. He located another lounge act, the Checkmates, who offered both an integrated group as well as blues technique. Phil thought he might be able to pump the group up with his Wall, and make them into the new Righteous Brothers. Early in 1969 he recorded the Check-mates' "Love Is All I Have to Give," and the song did not exactly set the charts afire. He tried again the following month with "Black Pearl," and this one seemed to work: it rolled up to number 13. Significantly, the Wall was far more muted on "Black Pearl," and the track allowed lead singer Sonny Charles' voice to carry the piece, a love song that cast off the heavy chains of racial depression. Ribowsky thought it was the best record of Phil's career. "Black Pearl," with its melange of strings, woodwinds and electric pianos, he said, presaged the coming style of the 1970s and 1980s, with "synthesizers and stringed hooks of soul."

Now that Phil had another hit, he began to enjoy himself again. Larry Levine recalled that Phil took pleasure in taking him down Sunset Boulevard, by 1969 jammed with con-glomerations of drug-soaked "hippies" morning, noon and night—and tormenting them. Levine said Phil put American flags on his car antenna and drove slowly enough so the hip-pies could yell at him and throw things at him. It wasn't be-cause Phil was an American chauvinist, Levine said; it was simply because he reveled in the attention.

But if Phil was inflating again, Ronnie was getting deeper into her own depression. Her drinking had become a very serious problem. Once Phil had discovered her addiction, Ronnie no longer bothered to hide it. She simply marched down to the bar and picked the lock with a screwdriver (the tool, not the drink). Phil responded by getting a bigger lock,

Ronnie said, so she simply got a bigger screwdriver. And so it went, escalation upon escalation. Phil was disgusted with her, and blamed Ronnie for what she was "putting me through." Phil induced Ronnie to see a psychiatrist, and when Ronnie told the shrink how unhappy she was, and how she was living her life, he suggested that Phil come to see him, too. The psychiatrist thought some group therapy might be just the ticket. But Phil flatly refused to go, according to Ronnie, and soon forbade Ronnie to see the psychiatrist anymore. All their problems, he told Ronnie, were her fault: she seemed to enjoy tormenting him, and defying him, he said.

But by then Ronnie had discovered another of alcohol's secrets: when she got drunk, she didn't care. And when she didn't care, Phil no longer frightened her. Not being frightened of Phil was good, Ronnie thought; so she drank and drank and drank.

Then one day, Beatrice, who had been in New York, returned to Beverly Hills. Ronnie was drunk. Phil made her get up to greet her mother as she arrived. Ronnie could barely get to her feet, and then passed out.

"Phil," Beatrice said, "what in the world's been happening around here?"

Phil didn't say anything, but walked away, disgusted.

Beatrice put Ronnie to bed in her small apartment. The following day, Ronnie said, when she awoke, her mother poured her a glass of orange juice. As she drank the juice, she said, she heard Phil outside, yelling. When Ronnie asked what was going on, Beatrice said that Phil was trying to train one of the German shepherds. The dog cowered at Phil's feet while Phil brandished a stick at him. Phil's eyes were glaring, Ronnie recalled.

" 'I will control you,' " Phil told the dog, according to Ronnie. "Suddenly it dawned on me that I was seeing Phil in a true light for the first time in years," Ronnie wrote. "He'd stared at me that exact same way at least a hundred times before."

With this insight, Ronnie turned to her mother. "I hate him," she said.

• • •

In retrospect, it's difficult not to have compassion for both Phil and Ronnie in this unhappy period in their lives. In a way they were like two motorists who arrived at the same intersection, ninety degrees apart, but both thinking they had the right-of-way. Phil wasn't able to liberate himself from his "demons," and neither was Ronnie. Instead each partner's demons fed on the other's, making everything worse, much worse. Ronnie was caught in her own conflict, between wanting to be the wife of the millionaire, and hating herself for putting up with him to get it, and feeling guilty about her deepest, largely hidden motives besides, trying all the while to make the story come out like the fairy tale she wanted. Phil was so insecure in his deepest awareness of himself that he could never let Ronnie go, to be the light-hearted and happy person she might otherwise be. The tighter he grabbed, the more Ronnie pulled back, soaking herself in her booze to escape. The storybook life in the "mansion" had become a nightmare for both, and all the exits always seemed to be locked.

Then, in 1970, Phil got a call from the Beatles.

31

GET BACK

By late 1969, the Beatles were coming apart. So much success over the previous five years had turned toxic, with squabbles over money, management and musical direction. John Lennon had already begun to pull away from the group, embarking on a solo career with Yoko Ono, which some saw as Lennon's riposte to Paul McCartney's vision for where the group should now head. Lennon had also become increasingly political, a development which made the more mainstream McCartney feel uncomfortable; he, too, began to record on his own. Months before, in early January, the group had recorded a number of songs intended for a documentary film, to be called *Get Back With the Beatles*, but which eventually became *Let It Be*. By the end of the unhappy session, the group had a mess of recorded tracks that had not been fully mixed; none of the members were happy with the product, and they were unable to agree on what should be done with it.

Then, early in 1970, the Beatles' new business manager, Allen Klein—called in to try to soothe the members' bitterness over music and money—suggested that the group call in Phil to see if anything might be done with the unmixed tracks, according to Williams in *Out of His Head*. It appears that the decision wasn't unanimous: while Lennon and George Harrison favored the idea, McCartney was less enthusiastic. By that time, McCartney wanted to take the group back to its roots as a rock-and-roll band, while Lennon and Harrison seemed to want to go in new directions.

Phil went to London, but not before moving Ronnie and Donté to a hotel in New York. To Ronnie it felt like she was home at last. Her drinking abated, and with Phil busy in London—he'd taken "The Eye" with him, as Ronnie called bodyguard George Brand—she had the opportunity to get out of the house. "Donté was just starting to walk," Ronnie recalled in *Be My Baby*, "and I loved being able to take him out to Central Park just like any other mom. That time I spent in New York was the happiest period in my marriage."

In London, Phil went over the unmixed tracks from the unnamed album, and also began producing singles for both John Lennon and George Harrison. The Wall had largely receded, or at least had been tamed; for some reason, Phil seemed content to take a back seat to the performers for the first time in more than a decade, working within his capabilities, not trying to shove the line with a blast of sound, as he had with "River Deep." It seemed to be working, and Phil for the first time in years began to relax—it was as if he'd finally reached that elusive middle ground between the highs and lows.

Every few weeks, Phil flew back to New York to be with Ronnie and Donté, often bringing tracks from the unnamed album with him. There, he'd play the songs on the apartment's piano, while Ronnie sang. Indeed, it seemed idyllic, or as much as it would ever be for Ronnie and Phil.

While in London—now working as a producer for Apple Records—Phil produced "Instant Karma" for Lennon and Ono. Released in February of 1970, it rolled up to number 3, a huge hit. The demon of failure, which had been riding Phil's back since the collapse of the Righteous Brothers, had flown away.

In producing "Instant Karma," Phil displayed a refined, far more controlled version of the Wall. Williams, for one, thought it was excellent. "But it was the sound which sold the record," Williams wrote. "No Beatles record had ever possessed such a unique sound; Spector had used echo to make the drums reverberate like someone slapping a wet fish on a marble slab . . ." (Ribowsky compared the same sound to "hands slapping a mattress.") Most distinctive, Phil monkeyed with the singers' voices (a chorus of people had been assembled at random from a nearby discotheque, according to Williams), making the singers sound "hollowed and decayed." He tweaked Lennon's voice, too, so that it sounded older and cracked, almost hoarse, to give the lyrics their punch. He'd wanted to add strings back in Hollywood, but Lennon called him off. He liked it the way it was.

Ribowsky's version of this part of the legend is slightly different. In *He's a Rebel*, Ribowsky indicates that Klein had arranged with Lennon to bring Phil in to produce "Instant Karma" first, and that only after the song became a hit did the Beatles decide to give Phil a shot at the unfinished album. "Phil had done so well that John and Allen Klein asked him to take a crack at the dormant *Let It Be* tapes," Ribowsky wrote. Phil went into the basement at Apple Records and began listening to the stuff; according to Ribowsky, the whole project was kept secret lest it turn out that not even Phil Spector could make it work.

Even as Phil was listening to the tapes, McCartney released his own solo album and simultaneously announced that he was quitting the Beatles—in effect, the Beatles were finished. That put pressure on Phil to make the album stand up—it would be the Beatles' final effort, even if it had been recorded a year before. If it flopped, that's what people would remember—that and the fact that it was Phil Spector who'd had his hands on the controls when this came to pass.

Working as fast as he could in the spring of 1970, Phil produced an odd package, *Let It Be*, the album, released in late April 1970. Some of the tracks he largely left alone, favoring the unadorned, unmixed recording that gave the songs the flavor of live performance, such as a cut of "Get Back," which ended with Lennon's quip: "I hope we passed the audition."

But for most of the others, Phil laid in huge overdubs of strings and back-up choirs that would goose the sentiment for what had been but would never be again. Then he sent a copy to each of the Beatles, who telegrammed their approval.

According to Ribowsky, Phil knew that no matter what he did to the tapes, some people were going to be unhappy with the album—that he'd be seen as an interloper, from the United States at that, treading on the holy ground of the Beatles. And Phil was right—almost as soon as the album was released, McCartney weighed in with a blast at Phil. He was horrified by all the strings and harps, the background singers that Phil had brought in to pump up "The Long and Winding Road." Originally, it had been just a wistful tune sung to an acoustic guitar accompaniment. With all the Spectorian gewgaws, it sounded sappy, McCartney thought. He wanted Klein to pull the song back so it could be recut without all the trimmings, but it was too late. The album was already being pressed. Months later, McCartney sued Klein and the other Beatles, contending that his former cohorts were trying to ruin his reputation as a musician by releasing the song. He also hated the puffery on the back of the album cover, which featured Phil's name prominently as the producer.

McCartney was soon joined by music critics, both in the United Kingdom and the United States. A writer for *Rolling Stone* said Phil had taken one of the best Beatle albums ever recorded and turned it into "costume jewelry . . . to Phil Spector, stinging slaps on both wrists." *Time* called the album "the Specter of the Beatles."

The controversy over the "Spectorized" version of *Let It Be* would rage for years, and would still be going on in February of 2003. Just a few weeks before Lana Clarkson died, in fact, it was announced that the "de-Spectorized" version of the album would be released, a triumph for McCartney. The new–old record would soon become known as *Let It Be (Naked)* in some circles.

Phil defended himself gamely: he'd taken on the album when it was in "deplorable condition," he told Williams in *Out of His Head*. Besides, he added, if any of the Beatles hadn't liked it, they could have stopped it. And, he noted, McCartney won a Grammy Award for "The Long and Winding Road," and if he'd hated it so much, why did he bother to pick up the trophy?

Interestingly, both Williams and Ribowsky were later to agree that the "Spectorized" version of *Let It Be* was a very good package. Williams thought that Phil had been unfairly savaged, and that he had actually made a number of the tracks much better. Ribowsky was even more admiring and pointed out that whatever the critics said, the public certainly liked it: nearly two million copies of the album were sold in the first two weeks it was out, and by the following year, the total had risen to three million and counting.

Lennon, for one, didn't really care all that much—he told Williams he was just glad the record had finally come out, and that the struggle over the end of the Beatles was finished. As for Phil, the verdict was even simpler.

"It was," he told Williams, "like being back again."

32

PRIMAL SCREAM

As 1958 had been, as 1963 had been, the year 1970 became another high-water mark for Phil's career and reputation. Producing for the Beatles gave him satisfaction that he hadn't had for a long time. Significantly, Phil was not listed as a writer on any of the records he produced that year for the individual Beatles, that is, for John Lennon and George Harrison. While that might have limited the future income from the sale and play of the recordings (since Phil would have no share in the copyright), it also relieved him of much of his ego burden—and its usual toxic inflation.

Still, it would later appear that Phil reached some sort of percentage arrangement with Apple Music, the Beatles' publisher, for his work as producer, since he would later report earning nearly $400,000 from Apple Records in just two years, 1970 and 1971. In any event, Phil seemed more relaxed than in the past, as the songwriting portion of his persona took a back seat to the producer side. Although Phil was to claim co-writing credit on seven more singles over the next decade, none of them would ever make it to the top-selling charts. Clearly, Phil's gift was as a musical director, not as a writer, and it appears that Phil was coming to accept that.

Almost immediately after the release of the "Spector-ized" version of *Let It Be*, Phil returned to the studio, this time with Harrison. Phil brought in an amazing array of talent to back the former Beatle, including Eric Clapton and Dave Mason on guitars, keyboardist Billy Preston,

horn player Bobby Keys, and Ringo Starr on drums. Together the group worked through twenty-three songs,
which were packaged in a three-record set, *All Things Must
Pass*. One single from the album, "My Sweet Lord," went
to Number One and stayed there for five weeks, and a second, "What Is Life" topped out at number 9. When the album was released in November, it too became a Number
One seller.

In contrast to Harrison's generally sweet and optimistic
melodies, Lennon's new musical direction took on a much
harder edge. Phil also spent much of the fall of 1970 working with Lennon, producing "John Lennon [and the] Plastic
Ono Band," described by Williams in *Out of His Head* as
"just too raw, too naked, too hard to take for anyone who still
clung to the notion that the ex-Moptops should *all* be making pretty music."

Williams and Ribowsky both ascribed the new, nastier
Lennon to extended psychotherapy that Lennon had received
from a California psychologist, Dr. Arthur Janov, whose the-
ories about the origins of neuroses were just then coming into
vogue, with the publication of his book, *The Primal Scream*.[50]
Janov believed that early childhood trauma led to unconscious psychic "wounds" that later expressed themselves in a
variety of psychological and physical manifestations. The
way to heal those wounds, Janov counseled, was to confront
the memory of the time they were inflicted, most particularly
the emotions at the time, which were often repressed as part
of the maturation process.

"Repressed pain divides the self in two and each side
wars with the other," Janov has written.[51] "One is the real
self, loaded with needs and pain that are submerged; the

---

[50] G. P. Putnam, 1970.

[51] Janov has established the Primal Treatment, Training and Research
Center in Venice, California, to treat patients and to train other psy-
chotherapists in what has become known as primal therapy. The quotes
above are from the Center's Web page, www.primaltherapy.com

other is the unreal self that attempts to deal with the outside world by trying to fulfill unmet needs with neurotic habits or behaviors such as obsessions or addictions. The split of the self is the essence of neurosis and neurosis can kill." This in fact sounds like a remarkably succinct description of Phil's "devils."

Primal pain, said Janov, is the result of needs that have been unmet in early life. "The Pain [Janov uppercases this] goes unfelt at the time because the body is not equipped to experience it fully and deal with it. When the Pain is too much, it is repressed and stored away. When enough unresolved Pain has occurred, you lose access to your feelings and become neurotic."

Treating the Pain, according to Janov, involves going backward in time to the moments in which the Pain was inflicted. But just identifying the origin of the Pain, the "unmet needs," isn't enough, "Because you must recall not only the scene but also its emotional content," Janov contends. "In traditional analysis patients discuss certain memories in detail, but in Primal Therapy they are put in contact with the emotional component of these same memories. That is an entirely different experience. Reliving opens the gates to emotional storage areas that are different from cognitive recall. The agony that was never felt is now experienced. The tears, never shed, are now flowing. The sadness or rage that has been held back is now all encompassing."

Getting the Pain or rage out leads to, if not a cure, at least a mitigation of the neurosis. Just talking about it isn't enough, says Janov. "You have to express your rage and your hurt in context, you can only heal where you were hurt. It doesn't really help you to understand why your parents acted the way they did. Understanding can only cover up the painful memory."

The confrontation has led some to call the therapy "primal scream therapy," but only out of ignorance, according to Janov. Actual screaming is not required, just as long as one confronts all the emotional contents associated with the Pain.

It appears that sometime around May, Lennon and Ono

came to Los Angeles, where Lennon began a three-month-long course of primal therapy with Janov.

Williams in *Out of His Head* suggests that Phil came with them, but offers little evidence of that, other than to quote *Rolling Stone* as reporting that Lennon and Ono had been staying at Phil's house in Beverly Hills that summer. A gaggle of private detectives from the notorious Pinkerton agency guarded the couple, even keeping the local police at bay, Williams asserted. But then, Williams also reported that the house was in Bel Air, not Beverly Hills.

"The treatment had a profound effect on John," Williams wrote. "For years he had found an alternative expression for his malice and his inner rage through the imagery of songs . . ." But under "the Primal Scream," as Williams called it, "Lennon felt he had found the handle at last—the answer was total honesty. No longer could his music be 'art'; his words must carry nothing but the most naked truth, the starkest and most direct expression possible."

Ribowsky in *He's a Rebel* was a bit more judgmental toward primal therapy. Noting that Lennon was searching for an explanation as to why he was the way he was, Ribowsky wrote, "His solution, temporarily, was the sneering program of 'new wave' California therapist Arthur Janov. . . . John was put through agonizing sessions in which he lay spread-eagled on the floor and cried and screamed in anger as he recalled his tragic childhood—his frightening apparitions not unlike those seen by Phil while on his LSD trip."

After undergoing primal therapy, it appears, John and Yoko returned to England and Phil, where they made the Lennon/Ono albums, which were heavily influenced by their experiences with Janov. Just what Phil, who had spent so much on psychiatrists like Dr. Kaplan over the years, thought about primal therapy was unrecorded by Williams or even Ribowsky, although it would seem that Phil might have been a prime candidate for primal therapy himself, what with his anger toward his dead father and his other insecurities. Ribowsky notes, however, that Lennon eventually "spurned" Janov and his ideas.

The Lennon/Ono album, however, stood as a testament to "primal rock," as it was then called, and based on its content, one would have to conclude that Phil had at least a basic grasp of Janov's ideas. The album, said Ribowsky, "is as compelling and important a work as any in rock . . ."

Whether Phil participated in primal therapy or not, or whether he had accompanied Lennon and Ono back to Los Angeles for the treatment, Ronnie would recall Phil commuting between London and New York for much of 1970. As noted, from time to time he brought back tapes of the songs he'd been working on with Harrison and Lennon. Sitting at the piano, Phil would play "My Sweet Lord" for Ronnie, and ask her to sing it. After running through the song multiple times, Ronnie got the idea that Phil was drilling her so she could go back to the studio and sing professionally. She was right.

Sometime just before the end of the year, as *All Things Must Pass* went to Number One on the album chart, and *Lennon/Plastic Ono* rose to number 6, Phil called from London and asked Ronnie if Beatrice could come with her to London to take care of Donté while Ronnie would be at the studio. Ronnie would be signed to a contract at Apple Records, where Phil was now acting as the de facto head of A & R. Ronnie was overjoyed that the Beatles—or Lennon and Harrison anyway—hadn't forgotten her.

In March of 1971, Ronnie, Beatrice and Donté flew to London. The day after they arrived, Phil escorted Ronnie to Abbey Road Studios to make the record he'd picked out for her, "Try Some, Buy Some."

"Try Some, Buy Some" was written by Harrison, and reflected his preoccupation with matters spiritual. When Ronnie arrived at the studio, Harrison sat at the piano and played the song for her. "Exactly what he was trying to try and buy wasn't exactly clear," Ronnie said later. "Religion? Drugs? Sex? I was mystified. And the more George sang, the more confused I got." There was a line about seeing gray sky and meeting "big fry." *What?* Ronnie said she wondered whether this was some sort of practical joke, but both Harrison and Phil seemed dead serious.

Ronnie gave it her best shot, though, laboring through lyrics she didn't get and trying to hit notes she thought were too high for her. Afterward she sat on a folding chair and listened to the playback. "The record stunk," she said later.

"Guys," Ronnie said she told Harrison and Phil, "I'm not sure that's my kind of song."

Ronnie was right—"Try Some, Buy Some" was a George Harrison song, written for and by someone on a spiritual quest. Ronnie Spector was a sexual motor scooter, not some sort of celestial harp. "[I]t was completely wrong for her," Ribowsky observed, "another of George's mystic chants, it forced Ronnie to try to appeal to the spirit instead of the flesh and it was ignored."

Williams didn't agree, though: "The record was nevertheless wholly magnificent," he wrote in *Out of His Head*. "One of these days somebody will call it a classic." Sometimes it's hard to believe that Williams and Ribowsky heard the same records.

One thing Phil called it was quits, at least as far as Ronnie's career was concerned. Shortly after "Try Some, Buy Some" was made, Phil bought plane tickets back to the United States for Ronnie, Donté and Beatrice. Beatrice's ticket was for New York, but Ronnie and Donté's were for Los Angeles.

The idyll was over; now it was time for Ronnie's own primal scream.

33

ROSEBUD

That summer, Phil produced another single for Harrison, "Bangla Desh," about the suffering in what had formerly been referred to as East Pakistan, recently devastated by war and horrific floods from a cyclone. This also reflected Harrison's commitment to spiritual values, evidence of a conscience that seems rare indeed in the music business. That the song made it to number 26 before stalling was more a testament to Harrison's huge popularity than to its message.

By the summer of 1971, in fact, the popular music marketplace was well-embarked on the introspective quest turn that would mark the Seventies. Almost all of *Billboard*'s top hits for 1971, in fact, reflected the "Me" trend, and the withdrawal from the activism of the Sixties, each reflecting a sense of inward-turning, away from the cultural preoccupation with protest, war, and social justice—"Joy to the World," by Three Dog Night; "It's Too Late" and "I Feel the Earth Move," a double-sided hit by Phil's former songwriter, Carole King; "Brand New Key," by Melanie; "Indian Reservation" by the Raiders; "Gypsys, Tramps and Thieves," by Phil's one-time session singer, Cher; and most evocatively, "Me and Bobby McGee," by Janis Joplin, singing the blues in a yearning ache for something intensely personal that had gone, and fatalistic acceptance of its loss. The tone in almost all the songs was about coping with an imperfect world, and accepting the fact that one had to compromise to survive— the focus of interest was the self, not the group or the country or the world.

That summer, Phil recorded Harrison's production of *The Concert for Bangla Desh*, probably the last gasp of altruism in rock for the next decade or more. The talent at the two benefits to help the people of Bangladesh, devastated by war and weather, was staggering: Harrison, Bob Dylan, Ringo Starr, Eric Clapton, Billy Preston, Leon Russell, Joe Cocker and Ravi Shankar, who had introduced the sitar and raga to American audiences.

Whether it was because of his return to America, or because of his failures to make any of the later songs he had co-written with Harrison and Lennon sell, Phil's ego was dangerously inflating again. As the evening concert got under way, Phil got into a beef with backstage security guards; it appeared that they did not know who he was, always a surefire trigger to Phil's temper when his ego was ballooning. Phil started shouting at the guards, who soon weighed in with their billy clubs, according to Ribowsky; Williams doesn't mention the incident in *Out of His Head*, nor does Ronnie in *Be My Baby*.

But according to Ribowsky, as the argument unfolded, Phil could be heard yelling, "I'm Phil Spector! Don't you know who I am?" Apparently they didn't, because they were about to eject him bodily from the backstage area. Phil probably wasn't wearing his backstage pass, thinking that of course he was instantly recognizable to anyone. The guards didn't get it; no pass, you're out. That was when Harrison saw what was happening, and yelled at Pete Bennett, a one-time Beatles promotion man, to save him. For some strange reason, Bennett later told Ribowsky, George "The Eye" Brand, the former federal marshal who was Phil's most trusted bodyguard, was doing nothing to intervene.

"George Brand was just sitting there, he didn't make a move to save Phil," Bennett told Ribowsky. Bennett ran over and grabbed Phil to get him away from the billy clubs, telling the guards that Phil was the producer.

"I don't care what he is, he's a nasty son of a bitch!" one of the guards shot back, according to Bennett's account to Ribowsky.

Later that night, Phil seemed on a manic high. A group of performers, including Keith Moon from the Who, Ringo, Keith Richards of the Stones and Billy Preston, went with Phil to a restaurant/nightclub after the show, and all of them climbed on stage and began an impromptu jam, with Phil on the piano. Not long after they started, according to Ribowsky, singer Andy Williams came in, apparently intending to dine. He had no idea who the maniacs on the bandstand were. Phil recognized him, though, and called out to him to come up on the stage and sing a song. Ribowsky quoted Preston:

"I mean Phil was really shouting at him. He was just in a good mood, but Phil is a wacko and Andy freaked out, man. He got scared, he didn't know who these weird rock-and-roll guys were and whether Phil was gonna go on like that. I looked up and Andy was running out the door. Phil could do that to you."

That was so true, as Ronnie was just about to demonstrate.

Throughout the rest of 1971, Phil continued to work with Harrison and Lennon, producing Lennon's post-primal single, "Imagine," which went to number 3 that fall. The *Imagine* album, released just before the single, went to Number One in long-play sales. Just after the record was finished, Lennon and Yoko Ono decided to move to New York. Phil soon obtained an apartment of his own in the city.

This was bad for Phil. Always prone to adopt the personality characteristics of popular iconoclasts—Doc Pomus, Lenny Bruce, Andrew Oldham and Dennis Hopper spring quickly to mind—Phil soon began aping Lennon's hard-drinking ways as he and Lennon tried to craft a new Plastic Ono record. According to Richard Williams, who recounted the story years later, after Phil was arrested, while all three were at the studio in New York, "there were plenty of bathroom breaks, after which he and the Lennons emerged refreshed," which seems to suggest that something more than liquor was being consumed. All of this took its toll on both Lennon and Phil.

By late 1971, Lennon in fact was a near wreck, his paranoia

mounting exponentially after the Nixon administration labeled him a security risk for his support for trendy left-wing causes in Manhattan. While Phil didn't support the causes, he was infected by the blow-by cast off from Lennon's paranoia, as well as other substances, perhaps. Already pretty paranoid himself, Phil became even weirder and more manic. At some level, Phil must have realized what was happening—he had to get away from Lennon before Lennon, now hell-bent on the immolation of his own career, took Phil down with him. Late in 1971, Phil returned to Los Angeles, his nearly forgotten wife Ronnie, son Donté, and the mansion in Beverly Hills.

Ronnie picks up the story in *Be My Baby*: Phil returned to the mansion as if nothing had happened, as if he hadn't spent most of the preceding two years out of the country, hobnobbing with Lennon and Harrison. Phil waltzed in, Ronnie said, and immediately told Ronnie to come downstairs with him, that he wanted to watch a movie.

"What movie, Phil?" Ronnie said she asked. But she already knew.

"*Citizen Kane*," Phil said.

Phil loved *Citizen Kane*, and had run it over and over again; Ronnie had probably seen it a hundred times during their marriage. Exactly why Phil loved it so much wasn't made clear by Ronnie, and Ribowsky never mentioned this obsession, so one can only conjecture. But some of the parallels between Charles Foster Kane and Harvey Phillip Spector would seem to be obvious—the little poor boy who became a rich man, who tried to change the world, and who was rejected, only to surround himself with everything that money could buy, except happiness. According to Ronnie, Phil always cried at the end, "Rosebud," the reminder of the innocence of childhood at the moment of death.

Ronnie was sick of *Citizen Kane*.

"No," she said.

Phil couldn't believe it. "*No*? What?"

Ronnie said she wasn't going to watch *Citizen Kane* anymore. Phil asked why not.

"Because I hate it," Ronnie said.

Phil said he didn't know what had come over Ronnie, for her to be so obstreperous. Ronnie said she'd had it with Phil, because he would never let her leave the house. Phil said she could leave the house when she'd learn to act like a grown-up. Phil went to the bedroom door and slammed it. Ronnie could hear him trying to lock it from the outside.

Quickly she ran into the bathroom, remembering that the bathroom led into another bedroom. She wanted to get out of the other bedroom before Phil remembered to lock that one too. Ronnie made it, and was going down the stairs before he saw her.

"Go ahead, try to leave!" Phil shouted, according to Ronnie. "See how far you get!"

Ronnie ran through the kitchen, where George Johnson was slicing tomatoes.

"Hi, George," she said as she ran through the room.

"Hello, Miss Veronica," Johnson called back.

Then Ronnie was out, and as she put it in *Be My Baby*, on her way to freedom.

34

BREAKING UP IS HARD TO DO

Ronnie kicked off her bedroom slippers as soon as she made it through the gate. She said she walked barefoot down to Sunset Boulevard, and as she walked, tears streamed down her face. She wasn't sure why she was crying—was it relief or regret? She headed east on Sunset, until she came to a small apartment complex. A woman watering the lawn in front suggested she come in for a cup of tea. Ronnie went in, and soon the two women were drinking more than tea.

Late that night, Ronnie's new friend drove her back to the mansion. Just how Ronnie got through the presumably locked gate wasn't clear. She said she crept up to the bedroom, hoping to pass out before Phil could realize that she was smashed. As she lay in bed, Ronnie said, she realized she was about to have a seizure from toxic alcohol overload. The next morning she woke up in a hospital.

Ribowsky didn't mention this development in *He's a Rebel*, but went straight to its denouement: Phil's decision to adopt two more children, 6-year-old twins, Gary and Louis. Ronnie, in *Be My Baby*, provided a vivid description of how this came to pass. In Ronnie's version, she'd already had several stays at the dry-out clinic before the end of the year. Each time things got to be too much for her at the mansion, she'd tie one on, and wind up back at the hospital. Phil began to complain about the expense, Ronnie said, and accused her of treating the mansion like "a halfway house."

After another stay at the hospital in December of 1971, Ronnie wrote, Phil came to pick her up. "I've got a little surprise for you," Ronnie said he told her. Phil had the driver take them to a playground. There he showed her the two little boys. The kids were available for adoption, Phil told her. He wanted her to see them before she made up her mind.

If this is what really happened, it seems as deplorable as it was typical of Phil's aberrational thinking. Here was a woman, still shaky from a stretch in an alcohol-detoxification facility, being asked to make up her mind on the spot on whether to add two new personalities, small children at that, to a domestic mix that was, to say the least, volatile. As if Ronnie could come to such a momentous decision by looking over strange children as if they were new cars or some sort of material object to be bought off the shelf! And in any case, Ronnie was hardly in a condition to be at her most assertive.

But Phil had everything organized. According to Ronnie, they took the long way back to the mansion, and when they arrived, the adoption people were waiting for them. So were Gary and Louis, happily running about in the mansion's courtyard. "Merry Christmas!" Ronnie said Phil told her.

"The worst part of adopting twins," Ronnie wrote, "was that I knew it was just another one of his schemes to keep me at home." She understood, if Phil didn't, that you couldn't put a family together as if it were a recording session. A Wall of Sound indeed! "I'd only been married three years and already I had three kids, five dogs and twenty-three rooms," Ronnie wrote, not mentioning the mansion's staff, including "The Eye," George Brand, Phil's bodyguard and enforcer.

The most striking aspect of the saga of the "instant family," as Ronnie termed it, is what it reveals about Phil's essentially chaotic personality. Here it's worth separating intentions from methods. The intentions are conflicting, as usual: on one hand, Phil wants Ronnie to be happy and fulfilled, and concludes that one way to realize that is to give Ronnie more of something she seems to enjoy, i.e., Donté. Now Gary and Louis are piled on, Wall of Sound–style. This is a good intent, but a lousy methodology, because it doesn't encompass Ronnie's feelings, to say nothing of her capacity at the time. The second, negative part of the intent is something Ronnie picks up on right away: that Phil is bringing the new players—like musicians?—on board as a means "to keep me at home."

Why? Why on earth did Phil want to keep Ronnie at home, where she was so obviously unhappy? Why did he want to keep first wife Annette segregated in the Manhattan penthouse? Why was it that Phil felt he had to have total control over every woman he'd been intimate with? Most pertinently, was this behavior meaningful in the context of Lana Clarkson's death so many years later? Had Lana Clarkson expressed a desire to leave, and had Phil attempted to stop her at the point of a gun? Was that what had happened that night at the castle?

The roots of this were deep in Phil's being, and likely formulated by his learning about controlling behavior from his mother Bertha and older sister Shirley. To Phil, it was normal to keep everyone in the family, indeed anyone he felt close to emotionally, under the tightest supervision. Who knew what might happen in the outside world? People might kill themselves, for one. They might abandon Phil—they might repudiate him. He couldn't stand that. That only would bring up those old feelings of self-worthlessness.

Ronnie never bonded with Gary and Louis, and why would she? In her mind, they were Phil's instruments of control, not her children. Within six months of the adoption, Ronnie was gone for good.

The split finally became permanent on June 12, 1972, Ronnie said, when she came home late from an Alcoholics Anonymous meeting—she'd begun attending them in January, and kept it up throughout the spring—and discovered that Phil had everything locked up. She went around to a window in the small downstairs apartment that Beatrice often stayed in and asked her mother to let her in the house.

Beatrice opened the kitchen door and told Ronnie that she wanted her to stay in her room because Phil was acting crazy that night, according to Ronnie. But as they made their way to the apartment, Phil appeared in the hallway. He was angry, and, Ronnie said she realized, also drunk. He wanted to know if Ronnie had a boyfriend in A.A. In her account, Ronnie stood up to Phil, telling him that if he didn't stop insulting her, she'd leave.

"That did it," Ronnie wrote. "He lunged at me and pulled me down to the floor." Phil tried to hold her down while Ronnie kicked to get loose. Phil grabbed one of Ronnie's shoes and pulled it off. Ronnie believed this was Phil's way of trying to keep her under his control—take away her shoes. (Doubtless Ronnie's mind flashed back for an instant to the row of Annette's shoes in the penthouse apartment in Manhattan—more evidence of control?) "Phil always hid my shoes when we fought," Ronnie noted. "It was one of his ways of making sure I didn't walk out."

Phil was yelling at Ronnie, telling her not to even think about divorcing him—she'd never make it through the trial, Ronnie said Phil told her. He said he'd "destroy" her on the witness stand—apparently a reference to Ronnie's alcoholism and her fitness to be a mother. He continued holding her on the floor and yelling at her, Ronnie said. At that point Beatrice, who had been watching, doubtless dumbfounded, suddenly sprang into action. She began hitting Phil's head and shoulders from behind, according to Ronnie. Between blows she told Phil to let Ronnie up or she'd kill him. Suddenly, said Ronnie, everyone was screaming at and hitting each other. Beatrice hauled Ronnie to her feet and shoved her into the mother-in-law unit, then stood in the doorway glaring at Phil, "daring him to cross," according to Ronnie.

"I'll tear that wig right off your skinny little head, I swear I will," declared Beatrice.

Phil was breathing hard. He wanted the last word, according to Ronnie.

"Who do you think you're dealing with?" he asked, in Ronnie's version. "If that bitch tries to walk out on me, I'll have her killed the minute she steps outside the gates. And I can do it, too."

Beatrice locked the door. Outside they could still hear

Phil raving, saying that he already had picked out Ronnie's coffin.

Ribowsky did not include any of these vivid details of the parting of Phil and Ronnie, but moved straight to the divorce itself. Filed on June 16, 1972,[52] four days after the fracas in the mansion, the lawsuit subsequently provided facts that Ronnie did not include in the version she recounted in *Be My Baby*. It appeared that Phil had seized the keys of Ronnie's Camaro on June 9, just as Ronnie was getting ready to drive someplace, and refused to give them back. That night, Phil locked Ronnie out of their bedroom, according to the court file. "My husband locked me out of our bedroom and told me to stay out," she said in her complaint for divorce. She spent the next two nights, June 10 and 11, in Beatrice's room. Then, on June 12, Ronnie said in her complaint, "My husband came to my mother's room, [and] told me I should get a lawyer to get a divorce." There was no mention of the wrestling match on the hall floor, threats to have her killed, or a coffin. But, said Ronnie, "he hit me in the face while I was sitting down . . . he then kicked me and yelled and screamed at me." When she tried to get away from Phil by going for the kitchen's rear entrance, Phil chased after her, grabbed her purse, then shoved her out the door. "When I left the house, I had no funds or assets of any kind," she said. She had been completely dependent on Phil to deposit money into a small checking account for her use, and after June 12, she said, the account was closed.

This, of course, is an entirely different take on the events—in Ronnie's *Be My Baby* version, Phil is threatening to kill her if she tries to divorce him or even leave the house. But when under oath, Ronnie contended that Phil actually *told* her to get a divorce, and threw her bodily out of the house. So one would have to conclude that Ronnie's version in *Be My Baby*, colorful though it might have been, wasn't

---

[52] Los Angeles County Superior Court case WED 20405.

necessarily the whole truth, especially if one takes the official court documents as more likely to have veracity. It also seems to illustrate that even Phil's infamous obsession to have control over women had limits.

After leaving the mansion, Ronnie decamped to a Beverly Hills hotel. She returned the following day, June 13, to the mansion, and stayed in her mother's room for the next few nights. At one point she tried to get into the bedroom to get her clothes, but the door was locked and Phil wouldn't let her in. On June 14, Ronnie hired lawyers Jay Stein and Daniel Jaffe to represent her in the divorce, and the next day, after the divorce was filed, returned with Beatrice to the hotel, the Beverly Crest. She sought custody of Donté, but not Gary and Louis, and still wanted her clothes, since all she had was what she'd been wearing on June 12, three days earlier. Phil told Ronnie's lawyers in a telephone call that he'd bundled up all of Ronnie's clothes in a garbage sack and abandoned the sack on La Cienega Boulevard.

The divorce action unfolded in the summer of 1972, with Ronnie and Beatrice staying in the hotel, virtually penniless. Relationships went from very bad to even worse. In a declaration Ronnie filed on June 26, she asserted that at some point while she was staying in Beatrice's room in the mansion, Phil had come to the door "and threatened to kill me (as he has done previously) and get the dogs on me." Phil had refused to let her have her driver's license, credit cards or car keys, she swore.

A month later, Ronnie filed a motion to obtain sole custody of Donté, then 3 years old. "My husband," she swore in a declaration obviously written for her by her lawyers, "has a very suspicious nature. There are chain link fences near the front door; there is barbed wire strung around the premises, with warning signs indicating the wire is electrified and of high voltage; there are signs in and about the front gate entrance and elsewhere warning persons not to enter, and there are sentry guard dogs on duty. There are in fact on the premises, more or less continuously, five dogs, including two German shepherd dogs, which are trained to attack on command, and one Irish wolfhound. In addition there are floodlights on or about the house which are turned on and which light up the exterior thereof. One George Brand is employed by my husband [or one of his companies]; he resides on the premises and acts as a bodyguard." It was apparently Ronnie's intent to suggest that the mansion was inherently dangerous for Donté; she wanted the court to give her custody of the child, and said she was willing to have a court-ordered psychiatric evaluation of everyone, including Phil, to see if that wasn't the best solution.

After initially being represented by Jay Cooper, Phil soon retained Godfrey Isaac, a prominent Los Angeles trial lawyer who had become well known for defending Sirhan Sirhan, when Sirhan was convicted of assassinating Robert Kennedy. Late in July of 1972, Isaac filed an opposition to the proposed psychiatric examinations. Evaluations were unnecessary, Isaac said, because everyone involved had already been seen by psychiatrists before all the trouble started, and especially since Gary and Louis had been enrolled in a private school, which required them. Moreover, said Isaac, he'd already taken a deposition from a psychiatrist who had "information" about Ronnie. Isaac asserted that Ronnie had had "repeated commitments to psychiatric wards," and that while in New York with Donté while Phil was apparently commuting between London and New York, she had "sustained an emotional breakdown." If the court really needed any more psychiatric evidence as to the fitness of the parties for Donté's custody, Phil was willing to pay Ronnie's lawyers' costs to go there to interview the psychiatrist who had treated her. Thus, it appeared that, just as he had threatened, Phil was moving to "destroy" Ronnie's reputation as a mother.

Ronnie's lawyers retaliated with a blast at Phil, claiming that since mid-July, Phil had been calling the Beverly Crest Hotel, sometimes as late as 3 A.M., demanding to speak to Ronnie "for purposes of annoying and harassing" her. In trying to reach Ronnie, Phil had "plagued" the hotel staff with "voluminous numbers of abusive and threatening phone

calls, and has succeeded in tying up the hotel's switch-
board . . . Since respondent [Phil] has threatened to have his
'staff' of off-duty police officers attack the hotel staff," Ronnie's lawyers advised the court, she wanted the court to en-
join Phil from making any more calls.

Was this a Hollywood-style divorce, or what? The ex-
change of fire continued throughout the summer. At the end
of July, the court ordered Phil to pick up the tab for Ronnie's
stay at the Beverly Crest Hotel, and to pay her $150 a week
for food, as well as any medical bills. Phil got temporary
custody of all the children, although Ronnie was permitted
to see them for six hours on Saturday or Sunday of each week,
at which time Phil was required to make himself scarce. The
judge also ordered the appointment of a court-paid psychiatrist to examine everyone involved.

Ronnie was unhappy with this proposed disposition—she
wanted Phil to kick in a lot more than $150 a week and her
hotel bill. She asked the court to modify its order, and noted
that a certified public accountant hired by her attorneys,
Arthur Linsk, had examined some of Phil's records, and
concluded that in 1971, Phil's various businesses had taken
in an average of $16,250 a month in gross income. Linsk
also concluded that Phil's living expenses for 1971 averaged
about $10,000 a month, including $2,000 a month for rent
on the mansion. So Ronnie wanted Phil to pay her substantially more in spousal support, and also, to pay Linsk's fee,
as well as the legal fees of her lawyers, Jaffe and Stein,
which were mounting fast.

35

MY MONEY

Linsk's analysis of Phil's money—"my money," as he had described it to Ronnie—is one of the more interesting documents found in the court file of Phil's long-ago divorce. On the strength of a court order issued in mid-July, Linsk and his partner gained access to Phil's books. They found that as of mid-1972, Phil had a fictitious business name, Phil Spector Productions. This had once been the front for a corporation, Phil Spector Productions, Inc., which had dissolved, and was replaced by a new corporation, Phil Spector Enterprises, Inc., in 1969—the year before Phil had gone to work with the Beatles. The next year, according to Linsk, Phil had created three trusts: "Phil Spector Family Trust," "Phil Spector 1970 Short-term Trust," and "Phil Spector 1970 Insurance Trust." The "Family Trust" was composed of stocks and bonds, while the "Short-term trust" had revenues from copyrights and other interests in "musical compositions," as Linsk put it. To unravel the financial skein, Linsk said, he would have to examine the account books of a variety of outside enterprises, including Apple Records, Inc., the Beatles' label, and the records of Allen Klein, the Beatles' manager, who was doing business as ABKCO Industries. Linsk also wanted to examine the records "of John Lennon and other persons comprising the so-called 'Beatles.'" Phil had so far refused to provide any of those records, Linsk said.

Phil had paid himself a salary from Phil Spector Productions of $56,000 in 1971, Linsk said, and received additional earnings of $15,818 from the securities held in the "Family Trust," and an additional $40,897 in income from the "Short-term Trust," the copyright owner. Counting interest on various accounts, Linsk said, Phil's "direct income" for 1971 was just over $120,000.

But, said Linsk, that did not include another $75,000 or so of "personal expenses," as Linsk characterized them, "which appear to be improperly charged as expenses of [the] corporation." In other words, according to Linsk, Phil had written off some of his personal expenses as business expenses. This may have included the expense of providing for his sister Shirley's care, as well as his mother, Bertha. Bertha, at least, was listed as a bookkeeper at Phil Spector Productions.

Altogether, said Linsk, Phil had earned about $195,000 before taxes in 1971. Counting the $44,000 or so that Phil had listed as personal expenses with the $75,000 in personal expenses that Linsk claimed were "improperly charged" to the corporation, Phil had spent about $120,000 for his family's upkeep in 1971, leaving an undisposed gross income of about $75,000 for the year. This was, Linsk noted, exclusive of personal income taxes, which would have reduced the gross remainder considerably.

Still, the net effect of Linsk's analysis was to demonstrate that Phil had substantial assets, sufficient to warrant a much larger amount of support for Ronnie than $150 a week and her hotel bill. Linsk noted that in terms of liquid assets—again, not counting any receivables still owing from Klein or the Beatles—Phil had at least $15,000 in cash in a bank savings account, along with securities in the "Family Trust" valued at approximately $372,000.

To the extent that these assets had been accumulated after April 14, 1968—the date of the marriage—they might well be considered community property. Given that the records of the Beatles collectively, and of Lennon and Harrison individually, sold extremely well in 1970 and 1971, one has to conclude that a substantial portion of the assets belonged to Ronnie as much as Phil. That was what Jaffe and Stein were after—"the deep pocket," in lawyers' vernacular. Getting a fat settlement for Ronnie would net the firm a fat fee.

Interestingly, Linsk's analysis did not include any figures for Mother Bertha Records, which was a holder of many of the copyrights, including the words and music of "To Know Him Is to Love Him," and apparently, many of the hits of the Crystals, Ronettes and Righteous Brothers. Every time those songs played on the radio, of course, more money flowed to the copyright holders. The omission of Mother Bertha, however, might be explained by assuming that the rights held by Mother Bertha Music might have been assigned to the "Short-term Trust."

Linsk's analysis of Phil's net worth in 1972 has only limited utility in answering a more current question—just what was Phil worth on the evening of February 3, 2003? That question, propounded to a number of people familiar either with Phil's situation (after the shooting) or the music business, invariably brought a nearly identical if anecdotal response: "A lot." Or, "Millions and millions," or sometimes even, "Tens of millions."

Obviously, one can't take a thirty-year-old financial analysis and convert it to present-day values—too much has changed over the past three decades to make any valid projections. However—it appears that about 40 percent of Phil's personal income (not counting the expenses charged to the business) came from royalties earned by the "Short-term Trust." While some of those royalties were doubtless "mechanical royalties" from the sale of the Beatles' records, some were certainly from broadcast royalties earned by Phil as a "songwriter" and publisher for the Crystals, Ronettes and Righteous Brothers, as well as possible broadcast royalties as a producer from the Beatles' *Let It Be* tapes, along with the individual recordings of Lennon and Harrison.

Those royalties would have continued, to some greater or lesser extent depending on public taste, over the ensuing thirty years, and would have been augmented by more mechanical royalties from the compilation of "oldies" albums, as the nostalgia era gained strength during the 1980s and 1990s. There would also be royalties from other sources—so-called "synchronization rights" for use of the music in movies, videos, television and DVDs. It's worth noting that as of 2004, Phil had songwriting credit for a total of 163 songs (most of them in conjunction with other writers), eleven of them listed as "BMI award winning," and most of them earned publisher royalties for Mother Bertha. The total included a songwriting as well as publishing credit for "Spanish Harlem."[53]

Royalty income is subject to the same inflationary pressures as any other source of money, and the trend was significantly upward throughout the rest of the 1970s and 1980s. In today's dollars, that pre–oil embargo $40,000 would be worth about $400,000 a year. That would mean the total royalty earnings for Phil, counting earned interest, over the past thirty years might approximate $15 or $20 million. If the money had been prudently invested in stocks and other securities, it might be far higher—as much as $40 or $50 million.

In this regard, it's worth noting the $372,000 in securities reported in 1972, which generated a return of $15,818 in 1971, or about 4 percent, annualized. If the returns were reinvested, the stake in the "Family Trust" would have grown considerably by 2003. Assuming that these rough calculations have any bearing on reality, Phil's net worth, including real estate, by February of 2003 might have been somewhere between $45 and $50 million—"a lot," by almost any standard, and not at all shabby for someone who had started out with virtually nothing except his own deep pain.

The bitter divorce continued throughout the summer. In August, Jaffe and Stein wanted the court to hold Phil in

---

[53] Ribowsky, in his list of Spector-written or -produced songs appended to *He's a Rebel*, does not include "Spanish Harlem," although BMI does credit Spector with writing the song, along with Jerry Leiber.

contempt, contending that despite a judge's order, Phil had continued to make late-night telephone calls to the Beverly Crest Hotel; refused to leave the mansion when Ronnie arrived for a visit with the children, and "was verbally abusive"; refused to pay the total of room charges for Ronnie at the hotel; refused to provide her with her clothes, and the clothes and personal effects of Beatrice, who was also at the hotel; and that Phil and his lawyer refused to make additional financial records, including income derived from Apple or Klein, available for financial analysis. A hearing was set to determine why Phil shouldn't be held in contempt of the court's orders, then postponed until October.

This seemed to loosen things up somewhat, at least on the Apple question; by late August, Jaffe and Stein had determined that Phil had been paid $325,000 by Apple over 1970 and 1971 alone.[54] This appears to have been the source of most of the money that came into Phil Spector Productions in those years—the pot that generated Phil's official $56,000 salary, and the $75,000 in expenses. Presumably, much of the rest had gone to taxes, or was invested in the securities found in the "Family Trust."

Jaffe and Stein took note of an interesting event that seems to have transpired that summer: "According to [Phil's] counsel, respondent was robbed Saturday [apparently August 19, 1972], and the thieves purportedly removed $2,800 cash from the respondent's possession."

This was included almost as an aside in Jaffe and Stein's attempt to broker a compromise before the scheduled contempt hearing, one that would net them some of their fees, and provide more money to Ronnie. Exactly what happened when Phil was "robbed" isn't at all clear. Ribowsky doesn't

---

[54] Eventually Stein and Jaffe would learn that Phil had earned a total of $375,366.68 in royalties from Apple, of which $354,015 had been paid through March of 1972. The lawyers contended that all of this money was community property, and that it was the origin of most of the securities found in the "Family Trust."

mention the episode in *He's a Rebel*, and neither does Ronnie in *Be My Baby*. But if this happened, one has to wonder where "The Eye" was when his protectee was strong-armed.

Ronnie's take on the summer of the Spectors' discontent was substantially different from what's portrayed in the court file. Of course, Ronnie was mostly interested in relating a compelling story in *Be My Baby*, which she certainly accomplished. Thus, there are scenes in the book that aren't reflected in the official records, and some are such that one would think a lawyer would definitely include them if he were trying to force Phil to pay up.

In one, just after the divorce was filed, Ronnie said that Phil did send her some clothes—including panties and "an enormous women's bra that obviously wasn't mine." That was when Ronnie's lawyer, Jay Stein, told her that he didn't think Phil was going to be "a good sport about this divorce." In another incident, Ronnie claimed that Phil threatened to have someone "take care of her." Still later, Phil sent George Brand over to the hotel. According to Ronnie, "The Eye" was accompanied by another man. The second man gave her a paper to sign, Ronnie said, and when she read it, she realized that she'd be giving up custody of the twins. She said she told the man that she couldn't sign anything without consulting her own attorney. At that point, according to Ronnie, the man went to the telephone and dialed a number. "It's your husband," he told her, holding the telephone out to her. Phil was indeed on the line, Ronnie wrote. "Phil started raving on about how this guy with George wasn't a lawyer at all, but a trained hit man," Ronnie wrote, adding that Phil said, " 'And he's been paid to blow your brains out if you don't sign that paper right now.' " Ronnie didn't sign, but told them she didn't want custody of Gary and Louis, "because I never wanted responsibility for them in the first place." This seemed to satisfy Brand and the supposed "hit man"; they left.

None of these incidents made it into the court record, which casts some doubt on whether they actually took place, or at least, took place in the way that Ronnie described them in *Be My Baby*. Nor does Ribowsky mention them.

The three adopted children of the feuding Spectors remained in residence at the Beverly Hills mansion. Gary and Louis, slightly older than Donté, were enrolled in a private school, and as the split between their parents unfolded, squabbles developed over visitation rights by Ronnie. She complained that Phil refused to leave the mansion when it was her turn to visit. Phil, for his part, insisted that Ronnie was an unfit parent. Exactly what the kids thought of being made the subject of a tug of war between two adoptive parents wasn't recorded, at least in the court file, but it seems clear that it couldn't have been a happy situation. Eventually, after the divorce was over, it appeared that Phil left the raising of the three adopted sons to the "manservants," most particularly George Brand. Phil spent most of his time in his sacrosanct study, the boys said later, and rarely had any meaningful contact with them—except to use them as a means of striking back at Ronnie.

By late August and early September, both sides were taking depositions from each other at the courthouse in Santa Monica. Phil's lawyers pounded away at Ronnie for her drinking. Ronnie said she'd begun drinking since her marriage only "to shut out his continuous stream of shrieking," in Stein and Jaffe's words. At his own deposition, Phil arrived with his old stenographer's machine; as the deposition progressed, Phil typed not a word. When Stein asked him why he wasn't putting anything down, Phil supposedly replied, "I'm waiting for you to say something important."

Afterward, according to Ronnie's lawyers, Phil pursued them into the courthouse parking lot, cursing them. "Declarants [Stein and Jaffe] learned what petitioner [Ronnie] was referring to [about the 'stream of shrieking'] when they were made the objects of a ten minute stream of shrieking and vehemence by the respondent [Phil], who was literally foaming at the mouth," Ronnie's lawyers told the court.

Once again, Ronnie put this episode in rather more vivid

terms. As Phil followed Ronnie and her lawyers out to their car after the deposition, she said Phil was shouting at her attorneys, "Leech! Why don't you motherfuckers mind your own business and leave us alone?"

Then, according to Ronnie, Phil climbed behind the wheel of his white Rolls-Royce (probably not the same car that delivered Mick Brown to the castle in November of 2002) and tailgated the lawyers' car all the way back to Ronnie's hotel, honking his horn the whole way there. By the time the whole thing was over, months later, Phil—ordered to pay Ronnie's lawyers' fees—arranged to have a $1,250 down payment delivered to Stein and Jaffe's law office by an armored truck—in nickels.

Stein and Jaffe were right: Phil was not a good sport.

36

FIRESTORM

Things got even weirder during that summer. Stressed out by all the animus, Ronnie got tanked again and returned to the detox hospital. She checked out of the hospital and returned to the hotel in mid-September. Her mother left to return to New York, telling Ronnie that she had to help Ronnie's sister Estelle with her newborn. According to Ronnie, Phil called her about two hours later, saying that Donté needed her, that he'd just finished "crying himself to sleep for the third night in a row . . . I'm getting worried." Ronnie said she told Phil to put him on the telephone, that she was never going back to the mansion for the rest of her life. Phil snarled at her, according to Ronnie, telling her that he'd be sure to tell Donté how his mother felt, and then hung up.

Depressed, Ronnie ordered a bottle of vodka from room service. "I drifted off faster than I expected," Ronnie wrote in *Be My Baby*. "I didn't even bother to put my cigarette out." The cigarette started a fire in Ronnie's hotel room bed. The fire department came to find Ronnie comatose from smoke inhalation—she was lucky not to have been burned alive. She woke up the following morning in the hospital.

At that point, according to Ronnie, Stein decided to send her back to New York to stay with Beatrice.

Ribowsky's version of this event is different, and for the most part accurately reflects the court file. After noting that Ronnie passed out in bed at the hotel, almost setting herself afire, he says she returned to New York on September 21. A little more than a week later, Ronnie sent a letter to Stein and

Jaffe, firing them. The letter, in discernibly wobbly hand-writing, also cancelled any fee agreements she may have had with the two lawyers. Stein and Jaffe concluded that some-how, Phil had gotten to her in New York.

Stunned by this turn of events, Stein and Jaffe tried to fig-ure out how to get Ronnie back on their side of the court-room. They decided to ask the court to award them $20,000 in attorneys' fees from Phil's money, which they again claimed was community property. And in a letter to Ronnie dated October 3, 1972, Stein let her know that she couldn't just fire them, not after months of work, and expect that "all agreements have been cancelled," as Ronnie had put it in her letter.

Stein and Jaffe were convinced that Phil had pressured Ronnie to get rid of them so he wouldn't have to pay their fees. But, Stein told Ronnie, they would have to meet with her "personally" before they could agree that they were ac-tually fired.

Stein said Ronnie had no legal right to terminate the agreement hiring them without cause, and that, if she per-sisted, she might find herself liable for the substantial costs already rung up by the law firm on her behalf. Moreover, said Stein, if she didn't pursue the divorce, she stood to lose all her interest in community property, and even the tempo-rary spousal support. That could be very expensive for Ron-nie, Stein said.

Ronnie responded with a letter—actually an affidavit—of her own, sent directly to the court. Executed in New York on October 20, just before the hearing on whether Phil was to be held in contempt, the neatly typed document had all the earmarks of something that had been prepared for Ron-nie to sign. In it, she said she no longer wanted to continue with the divorce. "My reasons," she said, "concerned the fact that I feel Mr. Stein and Mr. Jaffe's actions to have been unethical." She said that under no circumstances did she want to meet personally with Stein and Jaffe.

Reading this, Stein and Jaffe were more convinced than ever that Phil had somehow gotten to Ronnie.

The affidavit continued, with Ronnie accusing Stein and Jaffe of taking "unfair advantage of my emotional and mental problems." Ronnie said the two lawyers had hospitalized her "against my wishes . . . and I was *kept* highly medicated and drugged . . ." This made it sound like the two lawyers had made her into some sort of prisoner.

"I now have a clear view of what went on," the affidavit continued, "and I swear that there was no way, to my knowledge, that Mr. Stein and Mr. Jaffe could have obtained, honestly and ethically, my signature on anything. I know now that all Mr. Stein and Mr. Jaffe were doing was just trying to obtain a large sum of money for themselves . . . from Mr. Phillip Spector and myself, which certainly was not my intention at all."

Ronnie said she was sure she could settle the divorce case herself, and amicably with Phil. "In fact," she continued, "I really do not want nor did I ever want anything at all from Mr. Spector." She had never authorized Stein and Jaffe to hire accountants like Linsk, nor to take depositions from various people, including Phil, all of which, she said, only represented Stein and Jaffe's attempts to pry loose some of Phil's money. "I left California specifically to get away from Mr. Stein and Mr. Jaffe," Ronnie said.

Stein and Jaffe struck back with a long declaration to the court on November 8, in which they essentially contended that Ronnie had been brainwashed by Phil. That was why they'd had Ronnie hospitalized, they said, and evaluated by psychiatrists, one of whom had concluded that Ronnie reminded him of a "recently orphaned child, whose mental state fluctuated from suicide and withdrawal to desperate clutching and clinging to anyone who offered her some assistance." The hospitalization, they said, was completely voluntary on Ronnie's part, and besides, even Beatrice had agreed to it.

Right up until the end of August, Stein and Jaffe said, Ronnie had been advised that she was free to try to reconcile with Phil if that was what she wanted to do, but she declined. In a meeting on the subject of reconciliation when Ronnie was present, a psychiatrist telephoned Phil and suggested that Phil come in to discuss the matter. But he was busy, Stein and Jaffe contended, saying that the kids were sick and he was too preoccupied taking care of them to spend more than a few minutes on the telephone, "whereupon he proceeded to harangue [the psychiatrist] for a considerable period of time."

By November, Ronnie had changed her mind again. She decided to continue with the divorce case, and Jaffe and Stein went back on the job. The case dragged on throughout 1973 and all the way through the next year, before finally being settled in December of 1974. Ronnie got $50,000 of the community property and $2,500 a month for spousal support for three years. In return, Ronnie had to disclaim all interest in any of the businesses, including Mother Bertha, as well as any interest in the three trusts. Phil obtained primary custody of Donté, as well as Gary and Louis. He also agreed to pay Stein and Jaffe a fee of $35,000, agreed to assume any tax liability for the couple for the years of their marriage—an oblique reference to Linsk's belief that Phil had "improperly" charged the Spectors' personal expenses to his business. It was a good result for Phil, because it could have been much, much worse. But if it was so good, why did he feel so bad?

37

LOST WEEKEND

With Ronnie gone, Phil entered into a new period of depression. This began around November of 1972, and would continue for some years afterward. He began to drink, Ribowsky said, and quoted a close friend of Phil's who said that although Phil couldn't drink without getting sick, he did it anyway to "show people he could."

Ribowsky made another prescient observation: Phil had also started wearing a shoulder holster, flashing a gun. Given his bitter mood and his drinking, Ribowsky noted, "the combination was ominous."

The back story on Phil's love affair with firearms remains obscure, although, as we have seen, if one believes Ronnie, it was going on at least by the late 1960s, when Phil escorted Ronnie and Beatrice to the church gospel concert with his "peacemaker" in his pocket. Exactly when Phil obtained his first gun, and why, isn't clear. It may have been as early as 1962 or 1963, about the time that Phil first began feuding with Lester Sill over Philles, or perhaps the following year. Hadn't he told *Time* that anyone who messed with him would be in big trouble? But one thing is apparent: Phil's love affair with guns was as psychologically significant as it was, in Ribowsky's word, ominous.

A firearm has often been called the small man's "equalizer." That Phil believed he needed an "equalizer" seems clear, from all of his behavior, going back to the days of the kids' Monopoly games. What was a stashed-away, orange-colored

$500 Monopoly bill but another form of "equalizer"? Phil's level of paranoia, when combined with his often acerbic tongue, meant that he was continually getting into fracases, then calling on someone to bail him out, as he had done in high school with Marshall Lieb. Later, Lieb's "equalizer" role was filled by Terry Phillips, and then by Phil's bodyguards, including "The Eye," George Brand. But here is an interesting facet: those who were employed as Phil's bodyguards, including Brand, were later to say that the largest part of their job was to get Phil out of messes that he himself had created. A case in point was the melee at the Bangladesh concert; there, the significance seemed to be that Phil had acted obnoxiously, and that not even Brand felt it worth rescuing him under the circumstances.

So Phil had guns—how many and from whom wasn't clear. Somehow having the weapons gave him a sense of power that he needed to have. Left to himself to describe, Phil would have said the guns were his means of protection in a nasty, uncertain world, one in which he'd made a lot of enemies. But it seems that having the guns was reassuring to Phil on a far deeper level—that with a gun on his person, he was a real man. The fact that he began habitually carrying one in a shoulder holster *after* his split with Ronnie speaks Freudian volumes. But just having the gun wasn't sufficient. For it to have any effect, he had to show it to people. What was the good of carrying a gun if no one knew you were carrying it?

Most of 1973 seems to be something of a blank in Phil's history; it appears that he spent much of his time fending off the thrusts of Stein and Jaffe, as the divorce with Ronnie ground on. He produced no records during this period. Then, in the fall of 1973, Phil was reunited with an old pal—Lennon.

It appears that Lennon and Yoko Ono had been having domestic difficulties of their own. Ribowsky, in fact, says that Ono just got tired of Lennon's "misery-laced" drugging and boozing, and kicked him out. Lennon arrived in Los Angeles in October of 1973. He wanted to make another album, and wanted Phil to produce it. They made arrangements to record at the A & M studios in West Los Angeles.

As before, Lennon's personality began to rub off on Phil, who soon began replicating some of John's wild, self-destructive behavior. Was this what was going on back at Tony Hall's house in 1964, when Phil and Oldham began aping people? Was it Phil's way of trying to make sure that the outsider was accepted, to mirror others, monkey-see, monkey-do style?

According to Ribowsky, Phil soon began to out-John John himself. He became assertive, virtually taking control of Lennon, even seizing the complete ownership of the recorded product. Phil booked all the musicians, giving short shrift to most of Lennon's desires in that regard. Lennon, Ribowsky said, couldn't even get through the studio gates unless he told the guard that he was there for a Spector recording session. It was as if Lennon had become one of Phil's "manservants."

Well, maybe not that bad. But it was certainly a far cry from the time they had spent together in London, when John had held the whip hand. In contrast to the London sessions, the new collaboration took hours and hours as Phil continued to tinker with things, making the musicians play over and over again, just like in the old days with the "Phil-harmonic."

One has to wonder what was going on with Phil when he made his hirees work and work and work. Few people, if any, saw any method to Phil's madness. But seen from another perspective, the marathon sessions could be interpreted as evidence that Phil, having control of so many people, relished it, and simply didn't want it to end—the way a nasty little boy might torture an insect.

At one point, according to Ribowsky, Phil kept delaying the recording of Lennon's vocal. Lennon grew frustrated. "When are you going to get to me?" Lennon asked Phil. "I'll get to you, I'll get to you," Phil muttered. Lennon lost his temper. "You'll get to me!" he shouted at Phil—but Phil already had.

Lennon was drinking a considerable amount in those

days, and for some reason Phil tried to match him. Phil had
never been what one might call an accomplished drinker—
although Ronnie was to say later that Phil kept his own
drinking preference, crème de menthe, secret; she said she
only discovered this when she realized that Phil's teeth were
green from his imbibing one day. But Phil's capacity for alcohol was certainly far less than John Lennon's. Ribowsky
said that Lennon was capable of "downing fifths of Cour-
voisier and Rémy Martin in one swallow." Where John, like
Ronnie, was slugging booze to kill the pain, Phil was doing
it to demonstrate his virility.

Ribowsky said the recording sessions got out of hand.
One night, John got so blasted that Phil and "The Eye"
carted him back to the mansion, where they tied him up so
he couldn't hurt himself. Then they left, with the drunken
Lennon shouting "Jew bastard" after the departing Phil.

The drinking continued throughout the fall of 1973, with
Phil and Lennon antagonizing people right and left, both inside the studio and out. At one point, Lennon was unceremoniously pitched out of a Hollywood nightclub after heckling
the Smothers Brothers.

Somewhere along the line, the A & M studios got trashed;
those who were there at the time say it wasn't Lennon and
Phil or their crew, but they got the blame. A & M head Herb
Alpert kicked them out. Undaunted, Phil took the show to another studio, and the sessions began again. But things were
reaching a crisis point for Phil.

"Only days later," Ribowsky wrote, "he snapped. Not
getting what he wanted during a stormy session, he drew his
gun, pointed it over his head, and fired a shot into the ceiling." At that point, a shocked Lennon—Ribowsky said that
Lennon hadn't realized until that moment that the gun was
actually loaded—supposedly said, "Phil, if you're gonna kill
me, kill me. But don't fuck with me ears, I need 'em."

Not long after, according to Ribowsky, Phil had to go to
court on a custody and support hearing. Based on a reading
of the divorce file, this took place in December of 1973. He
brought Lennon as a character witness, but things fell apart

when Phil began cursing at Ronnie. The judge soon found Phil in contempt, and by the time things were calmed down, Lennon had left, embarrassed. "Never again would they be in the same room," Ribowsky reported. And in fact, Phil terminated further contact with Lennon, refusing to come to the telephone to speak with him. That was when Lennon learned that Phil had complete ownership of the tapes they had recorded. Lennon couldn't find a way to force Phil to hand them over.

It seems fairly clear that if Lennon was finally beginning to come out of his psychic swan dive, Phil still had a ways to go. Often when bipolar people reach one or the other of their extremes, bad things happen. And it is not as if there are not indicative signs along the way: Phil's drinking, his sniping at people, his cursing of Ronnie in court, his firing the gun into the ceiling, were all symptoms of classic bipolar disorder. And at such times, it is not uncommon for the person suffering from the disorder to do drastic things in order to bring the cycle to a halt, even dangerous things. That's what happened to Phil. In early February of 1974—almost twenty-nine years to the day before the fatal events at his Alhambra castle—Phil crashed his Rolls-Royce. He was catapulted through the windshield, and was taken to the hospital with severe cuts, some on his face, as well as burns and other injuries. There he had surgery, which at least had the effect of slowing his cycles down while he recuperated.

There was a weird coda to the ancient story. *Rolling Stone* suggested that Phil might have been having a hair transplant. Lennon, it appears, was told that Phil had died in the wreck.

Finally sobering up, Lennon went back to New York. He later referred to his time with Phil in Los Angeles as his "Lost Weekend."

38

BACK TO HIGH SCHOOL

From late 1974 on, Ribowsky was on his own in his interpretation of the legend of Phil. Ronnie moved on in her own life and career, and little of the remainder of *Be My Baby* had to do with the harrowing time she had spent with Phil. Williams, of course, had finished with Phil in 1972, even before the breakup with Ronnie. So it would be Ribowsky alone who would help to create the rest of the legend, with his excellent reporting. As the 1970s segued into the 1980s, Phil withdrew more and more from life outside the mansion; the few excursions he made to the outside world would be best known for their notoriety, their weirdness, which had the effect of making Phil seem . . . nuts. Or as Phil's friends were quick to call it, "eccentric."

It is a curious thing about eccentricity that its definition often depends more on who is acting than what it is being acted. Behavior that might be roundly condemned or even vigorously and harshly prosecuted when engaged in by an uncelebrated person is all too often excused when performed by someone who is famous or rich, or even more often, both. That's not the way the letter of the law sees things, but it's nevertheless true in real life. Many of Phil's reputed antics over the next few years would have resulted in the jailing or involuntary commitment of an ordinary person; but in Phil's case, they were often excused or explained away as the result of his "eccentricity," or even "genius." But what this really proves is that people tend to tolerate pathology in the rich and famous, while vociferously condemning it from the un-rich and the un-famous, and thereby, in rationalizing it or looking the other way, they only insure that the uncivilized behavior continues or even grows. People might say a celebrity is "creative," and so characterize antisocial behavior as amusing, when it really isn't acceptable, to say nothing of not being funny.

Such was the case with Phil Spector.

Ribowsky assembled his tales of Phil's increasingly odd behavior mostly from his interviews of Phil's dwindling band of still-loyal associates. As such they are mostly anecdotal—that is to say, there is little in the way of objective public records, such as lawsuits or police records, to corroborate the stories. But like many yarns that go on to form a legend, or part of one, there is a marked consistency of character in them, although the stories tend to become more sensational as the years recede.

It appears, from Ribowsky's reporting in *He's a Rebel*, that many of the incidents he collected were consistent with the symptoms of bipolar disorder in Phil. As was Phil's wont, when he was on his one of his manic cycles, he tended to become aggressive—cruisin' for a bruisin', as Phil's hair-oiled, jalopy-driving classmates of fifties Fairfax would have put it.

After emerging from the hospital after his accident, Phil began using the two sons of guitarist Barney Kessel—one of Phil's early mentors—as bodyguards/companions. The brothers were Dave and Dan Kessel, who also worked as session guitarists for Phil. The Kessel boys dressed in black, practiced karate, and packed pistols—Phil's kind of guys. Later, the Kessels would become Ribowsky's sources for some of the wilder scenes that emerged about Phil's years in the late 1970s and 1980s; the truth of the tales is hard therefore to evaluate—one has to consider the possibility of fabrication for the purposes of shock or entertainment, something akin to Ronnie's version of her life in *Be My Baby*.

Yet there is a ring of consistency to the stories, and as well a suggestion of a dangerous pattern of increasing, indeed self-destructive provocation on Phil's part. In one tale,

Phil got into a heated argument with a strange man outside of Cantor's delicatessen in the Fairfax district one night. The Kessel brothers were with him. Dan Kessel told Ribowsky that Phil was ready to pull his gun on the man when the man whipped out a badge. It turned out he was an undercover cop. Kessel said the cop had seen Phil's shoulder-holster, and concluded that Phil was some sort of drug-dealing, doped-up weirdo. With his own gun out, the cop put all three up against a car and patted them down for weapons, which all were carrying. Kessel told Ribowsky that all three of them were taken to jail, where they spent the night, although each had concealed weapons permits.

Was this a true story? So many years later, there's no way to say for sure; all the records—if there were any records—are gone, or at least no longer publicly available (arrest records on misdemeanors do not have to be kept for public inquiry beyond ten years in California). Did Phil really have a concealed weapons permit in 1975? There's no way to say for sure: such records are private in the state.

There were other incidents, a number of them involving guns. "Guns, in fact, were becoming a major part of Phil's identity," Ribowsky wrote—an observation that, almost thirty years later, would form much of the publicity surrounding Phil's arrest for the shooting of Lana Clarkson. The Kessel brothers told Ribowsky that when they went with Phil to see Elvis Presley in Las Vegas, there was a "high noon" moment backstage in which bodyguards for both Elvis and Phil eyed each other, as if at any moment everyone was going pull out guns and commence firing, like they were all at the O.K. Corral.

Phil grew more and more aggressive—mean, even. At one point, after signing a lucrative deal to make records for Warner Brothers, Phil was producing a record with Cher, who by this time had broken up with Sonny Bono. According to Ribowsky, the sessions were soon in turmoil, with Phil even throwing a punch at Cher's manager, David Geffen. Geffen, who had been dating Cher at the time, decided that Phil surrounded by his bodyguards wasn't worth taking on,

so he left the studio with a split lip.[55] A few days later, an engineer producing Cher's record decided that Phil and his
guns and his bodyguards were too nerve-wracking to work
around, so he pulled out too. In short, Phil had begun acting
like the gangster he had always pretended he was.

There were other incidents, too. One, at least, resulted in
a public record. In late 1977 Phil was sued by a man named
Gary Woods, who accused him of assault. "On or about the
evening of August 26, 1977," Woods' suit asserted,[56] "at the
Sherwood Oaks Experimental College, located at 6353 Hollywood Boulevard . . . defendant Phil Spector assaulted and
battered plaintiff by threatening to strike plaintiff and violently striking plaintiff in and about the head, face and
neck." Woods claimed the alleged assault by Phil had cost
him $738 in medical treatment. Woods said the alleged at-
tack was "without cause or provocation, in that defendant
Phil Spector first attacked plaintiff from the rear without notice to plaintiff and continued his attack when plaintiff
turned to face him . . ." Woods wanted general damages of
$75,000, reimbursement of his medical costs, and punitive
damages of $250,000.

But afterward, something must have happened, because
the lawsuit was never pursued by the attorney Woods hired;

---

[55] Geffen went on to become a promoter for Crosby, Stills and Nash,
Linda Ronstadt, Jackson Browne, Bob Dylan and Joni Mitchell,
among many others—after he supposedly got punched out by Phil. He
later became a Broadway producer, and was the principal financier behind the musical *Cats*. At the height of his long career in the music
business, he sold his ownership interest in Geffen Records for more
than a billion dollars. He went on to co-found Dreamworks SKG, a
movie studio, with Steven Spielberg and Jeffrey Katzenberg. In the
mid-1990s, Geffen declared himself to be gay—something that Phil
had always considered threatening, which may explain why Phil decided to punch him out. It appears that Geffen had the last laugh, however, split lip or no.

[56] Los Angeles County Superior Court case C 220209.

it seems possible or even likely that an out-of-court settlement was reached.

There is no way to know whether the allegations were
factual, since the suit was never tried. But if the charges
were true, it was an ugly image: Phil charging a man whose
back was turned and attacking him without warning from the
rear, while Phil's bodyguards doubtless stood around, fin-
gering their guns.

As Phil's psychological problems continued through the
mid- and late 1970s, his work suffered. From 1972 to the
end of 1980, he produced fifteen single records, and not
one of them made the charts. Of fourteen albums, eight were
compilations of earlier songs, most from the 1960s. Only
one charted, modestly at that: the Ramones' explosion of
retropunk, *End of the Century*, which made it to number 44
and then died.

Through his depression and withdrawal, Phil kept looking for a glimmer—he wanted someone who had the capacity to turn rock-and-roll away from the cotton candy sound
of disco and back to its roots in the driving beat. He tried
Dion DiMucci, but it didn't take. His work with Cher got
nowhere. He tried Leonard Cohen, the Canadian poet, but
that didn't work either. The two, both beset by their own
demons, couldn't work together. Later Cohen would say that
he was unnerved by all the weaponry around the studio.

As these flops continued, Phil grew ever more bitter and
reclusive. His old friend from New York, the songwriter Doc
Pomus, came to stay with him for a while. The mansion, still
a fortress, began to look even more grim when Phil ordered
many of the windows covered, as if the house were in
mourning. Phil held on to Pomus as if he were a life pre-
server, imploring him not to leave. It was Pomus who noticed that Phil's costuming fetish had taken on bizarre
proportions. "He would change clothes four times a day,"
Pomus later told Ribowsky, "and each time he'd have a different gun." Pomus concluded that Phil had to have a different gun for each costume; this was the origin of the legend,
which would later be disseminated widely following Lana

Clarkson's death, that Phil had a different gun for each set of clothes.

As far as Pomus could tell, Phil and Cohen fed on each other's depression. Both were drinking heavily, Pomus thought. Pomus decided that Phil had to get out of the mansion if he had any hope of returning to normality. He began dragging Phil out to nightclubs. Pomus said he and his driver never carried guns in New York, but when they started taking Phil out, they went armed—mostly because Phil, usually drunk, was likely to pick a fight with someone before the night was over. "'Cause he would walk over to the biggest guy at the bar," Pomus told Ribowsky, "and say, 'You're a faggot.'" On more than one occasion, Pomus told Ribowsky, they'd had to save Phil from getting pounded by some stranger. And Phil seemed to spend money prodigiously—again, another symptom of bipolar disorder. Pomus recalled that Phil would order huge meals, but be unable to eat anything because of his drinking. "[H]e didn't know what he was doin'," Pomus told Ribowsky. "God, it was so sad."

At the sessions with Cohen, Phil was barely under control. At one point a violinist mimicked Phil's occasional lisp, making it sound—well, fruity. Phil pulled his gun from his shoulder holster and told the violinist to make tracks—literally. He did, departing the studio with the impression that if he didn't do so posthaste, Phil was going to plug him. The incident so unnerved the rest of the musicians that the remainder of the session had to be cancelled. Phil was drunk at the time, according to Larry Levine. "[I]t was the scariest thing when he got like that," Levine told Ribowsky. "It was the booze. When Phil started drinking, he was out of his head. That was not Phil. That's not the Phil I knew."

Late in 1978, as the disco wave finally ebbed, the punk movement was beginning its rise. The Kessel brothers took Phil to see the Ramones when they were touring in Los Angeles. The four East Coasters' machine-gun–like style stirred some sort of dormant memory in Phil—a flashback, perhaps, to the gangster-suited Phil Harvey Band of the Rainbow Roller Rink, the idea that had been twenty years too soon. The

Ramones, fronted by a six-foot-nine apparition, Joey Ramone, were a live rage, and had helped ignite the punk scene in the United Kingdom, but their recorded music hadn't yet made it big in the U.S. Watching them perform, Phil was most impressed with their re-interpretation of the early sixties' sound. It was rock-and-roll as Phil had always thought it should be: driving, intense . . . loud! Only it was just speeded up a lot more than Phil was expecting. There was also an undertone of satire to the style. Sometimes it was hard to tell whether the Ramones were laughing with you or at you . . . it depended on what side of the sixties you were born on.

By this point, the Ramones had already finished making *Rock 'n' Roll High School*. The movie was about an out-of-control high school that persisted in giving principals nervous breakdowns because the students preferred rock-and-roll to education. When a new principal takes over and tries to burn rock recordings, the students seize control of the school and make the Ramones honorary students. The cops come and demand that the students surrender. The students come out, but the school is blown up—blowing things up being pretty much the "Me Generation's" uncompromised if mindless symbol for rejection of any kind of authority, the inevitable end of a decade's worth of excessive self-regard. Interestingly, the movie was made by producer Roger Corman, who would six years later give Lana Clarkson her best-known screen role as Amethea in *Barbarian Queen*. Phil eventually received producer credit for mixing the songs for the movie.

Going backstage at the Whisky a Go Go after the Ramones finished their gig, Phil is supposed to have uttered his legendary line: "My bodyguards wanna fight your bodyguards." But then, this is a tale told by the bodyguards, the Kessel brothers, so it comes with the requisite package of salt.

The mano-a-mano safely dispensed with, Phil asked if the Ramones wanted to make a "great album" with him—the choice being, a "great" performance with Phil or a lesser one with someone else.

According to Ribowsky, Phil's main interest in the Ramones was Joey, born Jeffrey Hyman. He apparently had the idea that if he could strip Joey Ramone away from the remaining three, Phil could make him a solo star. The Ramones said no—they were a foursome, all for one and one for all. Phil agreed to take them all, but almost immediately began to cause dissension in the group, according to Ribowsky. "[H]is manic presence at once divided the group and obscured the rock-and-roll bond they shared," Ribowsky wrote.

Phil escorted them to the mansion, still surrounded by its electrified fence and gates, with all the warning signs about flesh-devouring dogs and death. Joey Ramone thought it was all part of Phil's inveterate costuming—an unfilmed scene from *The Godfather*, maybe.

Once inside the mansion, the Ramones found it hard to get out. Phil wouldn't let them leave. Joey Ramone thought it was because Phil was lonely. Every time they indicated that they were ready to go, Joey said, Phil would disappear to another room. At one point, Joey said, he opened a closet door, and a St. Bernard dog sprang out. The dog had apparently been locked in the closet. Then, when Phil finally reappeared, he'd find something else in the house to show them. The visit went on and on and on . . . the Ramones, who had their own weirdnesses to deal with, thought Phil was off-the-wall.

Eventually, however, they assembled in the studio. The plan was to make *End of the Century* for release in 1980. Almost from the start, bad things began to happen. Joey thought it was mostly because of Phil's drinking, which had gotten progressively worse throughout the late 1970s. But a large part of the problem was the Ramones' approach. Used to making live appearances in which the way they appeared was as much a part of the act as the way they sounded, they weren't prepared for Phil's style of making recorded music—the over and over and over again method. "It takes us like a month to record an album," Joey told Ribowsky (although actually they had made their first in under half-an-hour). "But with Phil, this album took forever. It was like a crazy Chinese water torture and Dee Dee [Ramone, born Douglas Glen Colvin, the Ramones' bass player] started crackin' up."

This was the origin of the story about Phil holding the Ramones hostage at the point of a gun until they finished the record. That's not exactly what happened, however, as Ribowsky made clear.

By the middle of the sessions, Phil—apparently a bit unsure of how to fit the Ramones' style with his own ideas of rock-and-roll—began to get frustrated. He would lose his confidence, and from that point, things would degenerate, because he wasn't sure what to do next. At that point, Phil would find excuses for the lack of direction—usually a distraction of some sort. From time to time, in frustration, Phil would start hitting things—the floor, tables, a wall—and let loose a long, incoherent, scatological stream of curses. The Ramones were nonplused.

Dee Dee Ramone—who had begun using heroin while still in his teens—was every bit as edgy a personality as Phil.[57] It soon became clear that Phil and Dee Dee were destined to combust. "Finally, provoked by a drug-blitzed Dee Dee, Phil snapped in his usual manner—brandishing his gun," Ribowsky reported.

"He held his gun to Dee Dee's head," Ribowsky said Joey Ramone told him. Joey added that Dee Dee—"fucked up on Quaaludes or something"—had told Phil he was going to kill him. That was when Phil pulled his gun.

The interesting thing about Ribowsky's account of Phil's gun/Ramones incident is that nowhere does it indicate that Phil actually fired a weapon—in other words, when Dee Dee was later quoted as saying Phil "was a crack shot . . . I'd seen him hit a fly from fifty yards"—there was no corroboration by Phil's most thorough biographer, Ribowsky, that such an incident had ever happened. Given that Ribowsky

---

[57] Dee Dee Ramone died of a heroin overdose on June 5, 2002, about seven months before Lana Clarkson was shot to death at Phil Spector's house.

was able to find people to tell him about myriad other weird incidents involving Phil, the absence of the "fly-killing" episode from his version of the legend seems to indicate that it never took place, and that it was probably Dee Dee's exaggeration. What was true, if Joey can be believed, was that Phil pointed a gun at Dee Dee when Dee Dee said he was going to "kill" him. If nothing else, this indicates Phil's precarious emotional state at the time, and most of all—once more—his willingness to pull guns on people when he'd been drinking. That fact alone would have significance twenty-three years later.

39

AMETHEA AND OTHERS

By the time Phil was thrashing around on the studio floor, spewing scatological curses at the Ramones, Lana Clarkson had already begun her career as an actress.

Born Lana Jean Clarkson in Long Beach, California, on April 5, 1962, Lana was a bright, friendly girl, the oldest of three children of Donna Clarkson, a nurse. The family moved to San Francisco when Lana was 5, then to the Northern California town of Cloverdale when Lana was 9, and it was there, amidst farms and forest, that Lana had most of her childhood. An infant when first the Crystals and the Ronettes were in their heyday, a toddler when the Righteous Brothers were at the top, Lana was barely old enough to appreciate the swan song of the Beatles in 1970, and their breakup in 1971.

Life in the Sonoma Valley was and is bucolic. For her tenth birthday, Lana was given a horse named Breeze, and she soon became an excellent rider. A well-coordinated girl with excellent athleticism, she played basketball at Cloverdale High School. A year later, when her family moved to the Napa Valley, Lana attended Pacific Union College Preparatory School, an institution operated by Seventh Day Adventists in Angwin, a small town located in the mountains about ten miles east of the Calistoga wine country.

While in preparatory school, Lana grew rapidly, adding five inches to her frame in one year. With her height and long blond hair, Lana seemed a natural for a modeling career. Eight months after she turned 16, in 1978, the family moved to the San Fernando Valley area of Los Angeles.

Lana soon found work as an actress, filling small parts on television and in movies. As a model, she also found quick success, and traveled to fashion shoots in Japan, Italy, Argentina, Switzerland, France and Mexico.

Most of her early work as an actress was in television, as she took small roles in a number of broadcast staples: *CHiPs*, *Happy Days*, *Laverne and Shirley*, *The Love Boat*, *Hill Street Blues*, and *Fantasy Island*, where she played one of the island greeters who welcomed each guest star with a lei. In 1981, at the age of 18, Lana obtained her first speaking role in a movie, *Fast Times at Ridgemont High*, starring Sean Penn and written by Cameron Crowe. The movie also featured roles by Jennifer Jason Leigh, Judge Reinhold, Nicolas Cage, Forest Whitaker and Ray Walston. Lana played the young wife of the science teacher, Mr. Vargas. Her line: "Hi."

After *Fast Times at Ridgemont High*, Lana went to Greece, where she had a major role in a film by Nico Mastorakis, once titled *Deadly Seduction* but released as *Blind Date* in the United States. The film featured Keir Dullea, Kirstie Alley and Marina Sirtis (later Deanna Troi on *Star Trek: The Next Generation*) as a prostitute. A horror movie, the plot concerned a blind man with a computerized vision device implanted in his brain, who eventually tangles with a maniacal plastic surgeon.

Over the next year or so, Lana had small parts in three more movies: *Brainstorm*, a science-fiction thriller with Christopher Walken and Natalie Wood (Lana played the uncredited role of the food fantasy girl); *Deathstalker*, a fantasy quest film, in which Lana played the role of Kaira; and *Scarface*, with Al Pacino and Michelle Pfeiffer. Lana played one of twenty-two women at the Babylon Club. She continued her television work, appearing in episodes of *Three's Company*, *The Jeffersons*, *Amazing Stories*, *Mike Hammer*, *Riptide*, *Knight Rider* and *Who's the Boss?*

In *Amazing Stories*, Lana played a bathing beauty dressed in a leopard bikini. The plot had a young science student inventing a chemical solution that brought photographs to life. The student poured too much, and Lana's character grew larger than life.

"The theory was that if I were not kissed within two minutes, I would melt back into a lifeless piece of paper," Lana wrote later. "Though I was beautiful as a photograph, I wanted to stay alive. Needless to say I (the character), had one thing on my mind when he brought me to life! The Art Director had built a mini-set to make me appear to be gigantic. Tom [the director] directed me to seduce the frightened Jon and then become angry when he didn't respond to my 'enormous' advances. He had me up on a crane, throwing things and breaking the furniture into bits." Despite mishaps with the breakaway props that had her reduced to giggles, Lana said she'd enjoyed working for producer Steven Spielberg, and looked forward to another opportunity. This was written in October of 2001.

By the early 1980s, Lana had developed a reputation as a competent actress, albeit one with somewhat limited range. Part of this was the casting for type: tall (six feet), blond, buxom, Lana's roles almost always called for someone capable of displaying sex appeal. But there was more to the profession than just looking good on camera. In the motion picture business, an actor who can get a scene down in a small number of takes is highly prized—he or she is saving the producer money. That means understanding the image the director wants to photograph—how it will appear on the screen, in other words. By hard work and lots of practice, Lana had become very proficient—a professional.

In 1984, the so-called "King of the B's," Roger Corman, cast Lana in what would become a campy cult classic, *Barbarian Queen*. Corman's approach to making movies was radical: he wanted the film to make money, and after an early career as a story analyst at Twentieth Century–Fox in the 1950s, realized that the way to make a profit was to minimize costs. As a Fox director, Corman learned how to shoot films quickly, and how to economize, often by using expensive sets that had already been built for other films. In 1960, for example, he shot the original version of *Little Shop of Horrors* (one of Jack Nicholson's early films) in two days and a night. Between 1955 and 1990 he directed fifty-four movies, sometimes making six or seven a year. Between 1954 and 2004, acting as producer, he racked up a staggering total of 339 movies.

Corman's product was generally pitched to take advantage of the visual imagery generated by sex, violence and horror, comic-book style, but usually in such a way that the viewer knew they were being kidded—something akin to a cinematic stroll down a carnival midway. *Barbarian Queen* was a case in point: good guys (the barbarians), bad guys (Romans), lust, rape and revenge. After working with Lana in *Deathstalker*, Corman realized that she could fill the role as Amethea, who sets out to get even with the raiding Romans after they capture her groom-to-be on her wedding day. After escaping the raid, Amethea and two like-minded women arm themselves with swords and go after the bad guys. At one point, Amethea is captured and tied to a torture rack, a scene that required her to appear semi-nude. Later, the scene would be considered one of the must-see moments among the adolescent sex-and-swords aficionados Corman was aiming for. Even years later, long after Lana had gone on to other roles, fans still remembered her turn on the rack. Just a month before she was killed, in fact, one fan wrote to Lana's Web site, saying, "The torture scene in BQ [*Barbarian Queen*] . . . is intense and stimulating. You demonstrate great Bravery and unwavering courage. How long did the scene take to shoot? How long did it take to build the set? And what was your reaction to script [when] you realized torture was a requirement to get the part?"

"The set was already built when I arrived in Buenos Aires," Lana wrote back, "so I honestly don't know how long it took to build it. I believe it took the better part of a day to shoot the scene. You must know that when working for Roger Corman, one does not have the opportunity to do multiple takes. If an actress is capable of achieving the desired effect of a scene in very few takes, she's sure to work for Roger again. That scene is my least favorite in the film. Not because I had my top ripped off and had to hang there, beat-up, tortured and half-naked. I disliked it because of the way it was shot. It looked as though my torturer raped me . . . I didn't object to the scene, the way it was originally written. Amethea was a very strong and independent woman. If she had to endure a little pain and humiliation to save her future husband and the rest of her village, so be it."

And for good measure, there was Amethea's make-my-day line: "I'll be no man's slave and no man's whore! And if I can't kill them all, by the gods, they'll know I've tried!"

The following year, Lana was cast in *Amazon Women on the Moon*, another cult classic. This film parodied 1950's-style science fiction. The cast also included Michelle Pfeiffer, Ed Begley Jr., Steve Guttenberg, Arsenio Hall, Carrie Fisher, Andrew Dice Clay, Howard Hesseman, Steve Allen and Ralph Bellamy. Some called it a cross between a Corman classic (although he did not produce or direct it) and *Saturday Night Live*, grafting the B movie spoof onto a series of comedy sketches, and sandwiching the whole around television parody, not unlike *Kentucky Fried Movie*. The premise was that the audience was a television viewer compulsively channel-surfing. Lana played the role of "Alpha Beta," one of the Amazon women on the moon.

Over the next two years, Lana had roles in two more so-called "swashbustlers," fantasy swordplay semi-sequels. Both *Wizards of the Lost Kingdom II* and *Barbarian Queen II: The Empress Strikes Back* were intended to display Lana's charms once more, and did so effectively, if campily, once again. The second film put Lana back on the rack again, and she did her part: "Lana can moan and twitch with the best of them and make it look like fun," one fan/critic noted. Both films fell into the "so bad they're good" category, meaning they were hilarious to watch if one did not take them seriously. Another fan panned all the actors except Lana. Anyone watching the film had to be kidding himself if he expected it to be a serious work of drama; the role was intended to let Lana spoof herself.

The following year, Lana was back in *The Haunting of Morella*, based on a short story by Edgar Allan Poe, produced by Corman. In this version of the story, Lana played a tall, menacing evil governess, giving the role lesbian overtones. The film didn't work—another breast exposure exploitation, it left any humor on the cutting-room floor. "When I filmed *The Haunting of Morella*," Lana said later, "I had just gotten my right leg out of a full cast. I had put on some weight after being down for three months. I had an extremely bad break and was not allowed to work out at all. Both Roger and My Director thought that as it was a period piece, it would be good for the role that I was a little more shall we say . . . 'Zaftig.'"

After *The Haunting of Morella*, Lana's movie career went into a decline—it appeared that she had taken the sex symbol gig about as far as it would go. She made appearances on several television shows, including *Wings, Silk Stalkings* and *Land's End*, and found herself drawn to commercials, infomercials and product videos, as well as live theater. She made many appearances at comic-book conventions, reprising some of her campy film roles. Part of the difficulty was finding a way to transition into more dramatic roles—a decade's worth of acting as a sword-wielding "swashbustler" made this difficult. So, too, did her height—finding a dramatic role for a woman who tended to dwarf her co-star (many Hollywood leading men are extremely short) was difficult.

Under such circumstances, many actors would give up and move on, looking for some other line of work. The lucky ones are those who find employment somewhere in the film or television industry, often behind the camera. But Lana persevered, even if some years, particularly in the early 1990s, were lean. With her work as a model and in television commercials for agencies shooting ads for Mercedes-Benz, Nike, Anheuser-Busch, Mattel, Kmart, Honda and Playtex, Lana made a living, one of the few women in Hollywood who could support herself as an actress.

In 1996 Lana had another movie role, as a woman at a Paris fashion show in *Love in Paris*, billed as a sequel to *9½ Weeks*. This followed an action role in *Retroactive*; in both roles Lana was able to escape the breast-baring typecasting that had marked her career in the 1980s. She had television roles in *18 Wheels of Justice* in 2000 and an episode of *Black*

Scorpion in 2001, a science fiction series produced by Roger Corman. In this series, Lana was again cast as a campy sex symbol, performing as Dr. Sarah Bellum (really), a virtual reality specialist who proposes to do something to house the Los Angeles homeless. When the mayor turns her down, Dr. Bellum assumes her VR role as "Mindbender," kidnaps the mayor and assorted other characters and inserts them into a virtual reality game that turns into *real* reality. In this role, Lana had to switch from horn-rimmed-glasses–wearing academic to sex siren—Corman's m.o. transferred to the small screen. The episode became a cult classic among fans of the series. Then, in 2001, Lana obtained a role as psychiatrist Ellen Taylor in *March*, an independent film about a two-timing salesman that received generally very good reviews.

While she often wound up playing "blond bombshell" types on television, she did it to perfection. It was done to market herself, and to take advantage of the opportunities presented to her.

"Anyone who makes a living in this business is a success in my opinion," one of her closest friends said, after she was gone. "Her career was very important to her. She worked at it very hard."

Although she had made a living by playing busty, lusty women, Lana's fondest desire was to be cast as a comic actress. She had a fine sense of timing, picked up from hours of studying movies featuring actresses such as Jean Harlow, Carole Lombard and Marilyn Monroe. Her most abiding wish was that she hadn't become so tall—it limited her opportunities. Still, she kept working, honing her stand-up routine, working hard to use her height as an asset rather than a liability. Done right, comedy as a tall, blond, busty woman could be made very, very funny.

40

GIRL NOW

But all of this was only the public side of Lana Clarkson—the side shown to the outside world. Those who knew her knew that for all her drive and ambition to be successful as an actress, there was more, far more, to her personality. Later, the most frequent observation made about Lana by those who knew her well was that she had enormous energy and enthusiasm, and heart. She was the kind of woman one could not help liking—the sort of person who broke through barriers of shyness and got people involved, even in spite of themselves. She enjoyed living, and made others want to enjoy living too. In a media-centric professional world where being "on" was an occupational disease, Lana's most endearing quality was her genuineness.

If someone needed help, Lana was usually the first person to volunteer; and if more help was needed, Lana got busy and rounded up others to pitch in. If someone was broke, Lana gave them money—even if she wasn't sure where her next paycheck was going to come from. She found a small house on a canal in artsy Venice, California, where she lived with a cat named Midnight, surrounded by the spiritual interests that gave her real life meaning. She had long before—sometime around 1995—had mostly given up alcohol, and certainly recreational drugs. She wasn't rich, but she was successful; her true wealth was in the many friendships that she had made over the years.

Much of this side of Lana would be obscured in the weeks and months after her death, in part because detectives with the Los Angeles County Sheriff's Department asked her family to avoid contact with the news media. The sheriff's department, facing what they believed would be an intense amount of media attention as they investigated the events at the castle, wanted to minimize the public profile of the case as much as possible. Lana's family turned to Los Angeles lawyer Roderick Lindblom for help—Lindblom had represented Lana in her professional endeavors—and he tried diligently to keep Lana's family and her personal life shielded from the media glare as the sheriff's department did its work. Lindblom did not want Lana's friends making a lot of public statements that would make it harder for any criminal case against Phil to be prosecuted.

Still, there were a number of people who had known Lana very well who found themselves taking offense at the way she was portrayed in the media. One of the characterizations that grated most harshly was "B movie actress," or the way some media outlets contended that Lana was "hanging on by her fingernails" to her career. To sum Lana up in such limiting terms was to miss the meaning of her life rather completely, many of her friends thought.

One was Sally Kirkland, a veteran film, stage and television actress who had won many awards, and received an Oscar nomination for *Anna* in 1987, and was also an ordained minister in the Church of the Movement of Spiritual Awareness. Kirkland had first met Lana in the fall of 1999, when she agreed to act in *The Powder Room Suite*, a pair of one-act plays by Frank Strausser, at the Court Theater in West Los Angeles.

As Kirkland recalled, she, Strausser and the play's director were casting the parts of one of the plays, which might best be described as a classroom clash between feminism and patriarchy, when Lana came in for an audition for the second lead in the play, a part that required her to portray a woman in her middle thirties who was just becoming attuned to the issues raised by feminism. Kirkland was enthralled by Lana's performance, so different from her typecast roles as a busty, sword-wielding vixen.

"When Lana walked into a room, she was absolutely charismatic," Kirkland remembered. My response was, 'Who is *that*?' She did what I thought was a brilliant five-minute audition. It was as funny as it was dramatic. And intense. And I stopped her mid-way, and I said, 'Would you try and do this? . . .' —you know, a slight re-direction—and she did it. And I thought she *was* the role."

The play centered on a class on the history of women's rights being taught by a university professor, played by Kirkland. The plot concerned a young male student who had wandered into the class by accident, and who began trying to dominate the character played by Lana, "Girl Now." Armed with the tutelage of the mentor-like professor, Kirkland, Lana's character gave better than she got. "And she's gorgeous," Kirkland recalled. "I mean, you can see, she's the one in the play who *had* to be gorgeous." But the point of the play was that there was more to the woman than simply the way she looked, which was, in a way, the story of Lana's own life.

"And when she does that, she has learned enough from me [the professor] to defend herself with tremendous wit and dignity and strength and taste," Kirkland said.

In another way, too, the play reflected Kirkland's own life—for most of the early part of her career, she had been cast as a sex symbol; it was only when she neared the age of 40, which Lana was approaching, that the film industry began to cast her in other kinds of roles. One was *Anna*, described by one critic as "a fable of fleeting beauty and America's obsession with youthfulness." In *Anna*, Kirkland played an aging stage actress "upstaged by her stunning young protégé." Here was a case, possibly, of life imitating art imitating life.

But Kirkland and Lana almost immediately hit it off, in large part because of Lana's effervescent personality. Both shared similar experiences in their careers, and both were very interested in spiritual things. Kirkland asked that Lana be assigned to a dressing room with her, and as the weeks passed, both got to know one another very well.

At one point in the play, Kirkland recalled, Lana was required to shed tears of sadness, anger and frustration at the way she was being patronized by the male interloper. This indeed was a world away from a sword-wielding Xena prototype. Weeping as part of her role was something new for Lana, so Kirkland gave her some advice: "I said, 'You know, Lana, I would just use it all. Use everything in your life, use your frustration that you don't get more acting jobs, use your frustration that people think that you're— You know, you get looked at or hit on in some way every day of your life, probably,' and she kind of said, 'Yeah.' 'And that probably pushes a lot of buttons in you, because you're bright, you're deep, you're not in any way superficial or a caricature or a cartoon of a woman who has a great body. Use your frustration that we're in Hollywood, which is still patriarchal. You know, which still treats women like objects. This play is about that. This play is about the history of feminism, and when it comes to the tears on cue, if you had your heart broken when your dad died when you were six, use that. Use the fact that you grew up without your father, that that's been a frustration.' So anyway, she did cry, and it was very touching the first day she did it, and here's this tall, beautiful woman like a little child."

As the play's run progressed early in 2000, Kirkland got to know Lana well, often praying together or meditating. The fact was, Lana's real personality was completely different from the roles she had played on-screen for Corman and others. Later, a one-time boyfriend of Lana would meet Kirkland—after Lana was dead—and tell her that, despite the roles Lana had played in the movies, she wasn't like that at all. The former boyfriend, a martial arts expert, told Kirkland that Lana was so non-violent, "she couldn't stand it when I would do martial arts in her presence, because basically, even though she played these roles like 'Amethea' in Roger's film when she was a kid, that's not who she was. Those are the roles she got cast in because she was almost six feet tall."

After the plays ended their run, Lana and Kirkland kept

in touch, often by telephone, and occasionally getting together. "Lana's the kind of person who will call her friends,
if not daily, [then] weekly, because she was constantly wanting to socialize," Kirkland said. "She'd say, 'Sally, let's go
here. Let's go to Two Bunch Palms in what-do-you-call-it,
Desert Hot Springs, and do like four days of the spa.'" So
the two actresses, one older, one younger, grew close, and as
they shared confidences, Kirkland realized they had even
more in common than she had first realized: they were both
lonely.

"Our conversations were generally like this," Kirkland recalled. "'Here we are, we're both beautiful women, I mean
I'm older than you, but we're alone. And isn't that interesting? With all of our girlfriends married, having the white
picket fence and/or at least a boyfriend, and here we are,
we're supposed to be these two gorgeous women—granted
you're a different generation—but we're both tall, we're both
blond, we're both beautiful, we're both talented, and we're
alone.' And we talked a lot about that. That, how sad it is,
somehow, that in America, in Hollywood, that—and we both
loved Marilyn—that actually we could get up and do for you,
together, Marilyn Monroe's songs, her dances . . . and that
was something we shared, and the tragedy of her life [Mari-
lyn Monroe's], that she was so alone."

In early 2000, Kirkland's own life underwent something
of an upheaval. Two of her closest friends died, and then
she broke her foot, and following that, had to have a knee
operation.

"So at this point I said, 'Lana, I've got my foot in a cast,
I've got duh duh duh, and so she says, 'Well, I'll bring you
food. I'll bring— [If] you need me to get you to the doctor,
[if] you need—' So what I got to see now was, here's this
woman, who's like self-promoting every day, in the sense of
trying to keep her career alive, going out on auditions, auditions, auditions, trying to keep her foot in the business, doing commercials and commercials, along with whatever
acting she can get, and she stops everything and said, 'Let
me take care of you. Let me bring you food, let me get you

this, let me drive you here.' And I got to see still this other side of her, that cared deeply about her friends, in this case me, and so I said, 'Okay, I could use some help.'" As Kirkland recuperated, Lana was there for her, not because of what Kirkland might be able to do for her professionally— "she was too dignified for that," Kirkland recalled—but because it was the kind of person Lana Clarkson was. "No, she just knew I was by myself, and I was ordering pizza, and she said, 'Well, I can do better than pizza,'" Kirkland said.

About the only thing that Lana ever asked Kirkland to do for her professionally was asking Corman to look at and agree to be interviewed for a videotape Lana had put together. Kirkland was close to Corman—she was his daughter's godmother—and Corman readily agreed to view the tape. All Kirkland knew about it was that Lana had assembled a series of comic roles, all written by herself. She called Corman, and Corman agreed to meet with Lana to watch the tape.

Then, some time later, Kirkland appeared at some sort of awards ceremony for Corman. "He and Julia, his wife, asked me to go, because they're family. So they were with me, and he said, 'Sally—Lana Clarkson.' And I said, 'Yeah?' And he said, 'Unbelievable.' He said, 'Remember when you called me to set up that meeting?' And I said yes, and he said, 'I looked at her tape. She is *so* talented. I had no idea that she could write like that, so witty, so funny, so comedic, much less this woman I've always associated with Amethea . . . she has turned into a great character actress. She's a female Jack Nicholson.'"

Lana had worked on her tape for the last few years before her death, honing her comedic skills, and writing the kind of parts she would most like to play. As it happened, Kirkland didn't see the tape until after Lana died, and when she did see it, she was stunned—Corman had been right, Lana was a comedic genius.

"She's got a little bit of everybody," Kirkland said of the tape. "She plays Little Richard in it, she plays this bimbo, she plays this dyke. She plays everything. She makes fun of her being her, to the point where you can't recognize her anymore." The tape was so good, it was so far off what everyone had ever thought about the sword-wielding Lana Clarkson, that some thought it would launch Lana into a terrific new career.

But as 2001 came to an end, Lana suffered a severe setback. Dancing with some children at a party on Christmas Day, she fell, breaking both of her wrists. With both arms in casts up until around March of 2002, Lana found it impossible to get work. Her rehabilitation from the injuries would last most of the rest of the year. The tape went back on the shelf while she tried to heal.

In October of 2002, Kirkland was giving a show of her own paintings of famous women—"women as goddesses" was the subject—at a Hollywood art gallery. She'd had little contact with Lana for most of the year; indeed, it appears that Lana had never told her about her accident. Kirkland had a call from Lana, and when Kirkland told her about her art opening, Lana said she wanted to help. Kirkland said she'd be very happy if Lana simply got dressed to the nines and came to the opening.

At the opening, Kirkland took Lana around to look at all of the paintings. "So she came, and she looked sensational," Kirkland said, "and she was with a girlfriend. So I said, 'I had wanted to paint you for this show, but you and I haven't talked that much recently.' And she said, 'Well, I haven't talked to too many people, because I've been laying low, trying to heal. Because I had this accident.'

"And she said, 'Sally, I now truly understand what you went through,' when I broke my foot and had knee surgery. She said, 'It's been so frustrating and debilitating, and it's really caused a financial [drain]. I've been literally bedridden,' or whatever the word is, that says, you know, I haven't been able to [work]. 'I've been doing physical therapy.' And she said, 'Remember you used to tell me how you're going to the clinic, you're going to physical therapy, my past year has been exactly what you described to me, in the latter part of 2000, early 2001.' She said, 'I didn't want to burden you with it.' And I said, 'Too bad. Because I wish you'd called me, because you were so kind to me when I was laid up. I would have turned right around and gone to Venice and said, "Okay, here's your meals, and how do we get you to this doctor, or physical therapy?"' "

But Lana said it hadn't been necessary—her many friends had pitched in to help her, just as she had done for so many others when they needed help. "If I discovered one thing when she passed over," Kirkland said later, "it was the amazing number of friends she had, an amazing number. Anyway, she said to me at this art gallery thing, 'I'm in a bind, I don't know what to do, because I've been out of the loop as an actress, but I've got to pay my bills. And I'm thinking of doing a part-time job.' And I said, 'Well, I do.' " Kirkland did other things besides acting to earn her living, and had in the past taken part-time jobs to pay the rent. She got the feeling that Lana thought it might be seen by others in Hollywood as a step backward.

"I said, 'Don't feel bad. Have you looked at our industry right now? Have you looked at the state of women in this industry? I say, do whatever you have to.' " There was nothing wrong with finding a part-time job, Kirkland told Lana. Others did it—even big stars had done it at various times in their careers. "And I said, 'I strongly suggest that you—you're great with people. You're a great communicator, you're cheerful, you make people happy, you always make everybody feel like, you know, they're special.' " Lana should find some sort of part-time job where she could put her personality to work, Kirkland said.

After the art gallery opening, Kirkland didn't see Lana for some time, although they did talk on the telephone periodically. Then, after the first of the year, Kirkland was asked to appear on behalf of the "I Have a Dream" Foundation at a benefit at the House of Blues, the nightclub/restaurant in Hollywood.

Kirkland arrived with her date, her cousin and her cousin's husband, and while waiting for the program to begin, gave her group an informal look at the Foundation Rooms, the VIP lounge on the top floor of the nightclub. It was while going through the rooms, ornately decorated with a surrealistic motif, that Kirkland heard someone calling her name.

"Sally! Sally! Sally!"

"I turned around and I'm looking and I don't see anybody I recognize," Kirkland recalled. "And then I see this woman, and it literally stopped me in my tracks, because I knew I knew her, but I didn't know *how* I knew her. And it was Lana, playing a role of whatever it was that she thought or was told she had to do, to be the first woman-ever hostess of the VIP Foundation Rooms of the House of Blues."

Lana was dressed in a smart black suit, looking very "corporate," Kirkland thought. Lana was ecstatic to see her, and asked her to come to the House of Blues as often as she could, so they could see each other.

"I saw that she was doing what we had talked about in November," Kirkland recalled. "And I saw that she'd made peace with it, you know, the part-time job. That she, that her personality was that of a cheerleader, so in that moment she was cheering me into coming back and hanging out in the VIP room. So we hugged and we kissed, and . . . she was very, very happy. She was happy. And she was excited, and she said, 'I'm meeting great people.' "

One of whom, it appears, was a famous record producer named Phil Spector.

41

END OF THE CENTURY

The Ramones' version of *End of the Century* fell somewhat short—about twenty years, in fact. The album made it to number 44 in February of 1980, then faded. Over the next twenty years, Phil's only new record products were made from old cuts he had stashed up from his days with Philles, or the material he had left over from John Lennon's "Lost Weekend." He made several attempts to get back into the studio, with Yoko Ono in 1981, and much later, in 1996, with Canadian Celine Dion, but neither effort was successful. With Dion, he feuded with her husband/manager, who thought Phil ought to be able to work a lot faster. Phil sniped back that one didn't tell Shakespeare how to write plays.

From 1980 on, though, it was as if there were two different Phil Spectors—the one described by Ribowsky in his wrap-up of *He's a Rebel*, mostly a collection of outrageous incidents that seeped out from under the increasingly thick blanket of obscurity that Phil tried to pull down around himself as the end of the century approached; and a second Phil, someone who settled into a seemingly somewhat normal life, far from the edgy events of the seventies. Unfortunately, one of the side effects of obscurity is that there is little evidence available to shed light on which Phil was closer to the truth.

Ribowsky's Phil continued to get into various scrapes. There was the time, for instance, when Phil's long-time arranger, Jack Nitzsche,[58] showed up outside the gates of the Beverly Hills mansion, wanting to see Phil. Ribowsky noted that Nitzsche had recently had problems of his own—a nasty arrest for domestic assault. But Phil didn't want to see him, according to Ribowsky—he appeared in an upper window of the mansion, aiming a pistol at Nitzsche, and told him to get lost.

There was the saga of Donté, who ran away from home in early 1980, winding up at a local police station. When the cops called Phil to come get his son, according to Ribowsky, Phil told them he didn't care what happened to Donté. Eventually Donté went to live with Ronnie in New York, and still later with Phil's mother, Bertha. All in all, it had been a rough start in life for the oldest son of one of rock music's wealthiest and most infamous men.

Then there was the story Danny Davis told Ribowsky, the one about LaToya Jackson. According to Davis, late in 1986, he brought LaToya over to the mansion, where Phil greeted her enthusiastically. But the next night, according to Davis, when LaToya returned to the mansion, Phil presented her with a key labeled "Bates Motel," and asked her if she wanted to go there with him. LaToya, raised as a Jehovah's Witness, didn't appear to know what the Bates Motel was, other than what it obviously seemed to be. So Phil proceeded to explain all about the movie *Psycho*. LaToya wasn't sure if Phil was making a joke or trying to unnerve her. Then, according to Davis, Phil went into one of his hours-long rants, periodically disappearing and reappearing from the room, usually evincing a different persona with each entrance. LaToya concluded that Phil had been drinking to excess, and finally made her escape from the mansion. But, again according to Davis, Phil began a series of incessant post-midnight telephone calls to the Jackson house in Encino. The verdict on Phil was—he was around the bend.

Then there was the thirtieth reunion of the Fairfax High

---

[58] Jack Nitzsche died August 25, 2000.

School Class of 1957. Phil arrived with two bodyguards and planted himself at the end of the bar, wearing dark glasses. He had little to say, and most of his old classmates ignored him. Harvey Goldstein, for one, wouldn't give him the satisfaction that he thought Phil craved; Goldstein, like others, thought that Phil wanted everyone to approach him with awed respect, venerating him for his success. So they pretended he simply wasn't there, which was, to Phil, the ultimate insult.

One of those who also attended was Marshall Lieb. Marshall, who had gone on to write the scores for a number of motion pictures, was one of those who was at first glad to see Phil. Phil stood and shook his hand, but wasn't able to look him in the eye. Marshall thought that Phil had things he wanted to say, but couldn't get them out. Marshall realized that beneath his I-don't-need-anyone pose, Phil was incredibly lonely. Then Marshall delivered to Ribowsky an epitaph for his old friend.

"As frightened as Phil was when we were kids, he knew he was going somewhere. Now he has nowhere to go and that probably scares him a hell of a lot more."

But this was the Ribowsky take on the first of Phil's last two decades. He published *He's a Rebel* in 1989, so he wasn't able to include the Phil who was inducted into the Rock and Roll Hall of Fame later that same year. There, Phil, apparently drugged or drunk, went up to the podium flanked by bodyguards who held their hands inside their tuxedos as if they were ready to pull weapons. Phil rambled on with his acceptance speech for almost twenty minutes, making little sense to the audience, until finally the show's producer, Bill Graham, strode out onto the stage and gave Phil a note telling him to shut up and get off. Phil finally ceased, then fell off the stage as he tried to exit.

The available public records cast a slightly different light on Phil's life in the 1980s and 1990s, as do several additional anecdotes. For one, it appears that after his years of depression following Ronnie's departure, Phil found another woman to share his life, Janis Zavala, who had once worked for none other than Lester Sill. Some thought Janis was perfectly suited to Phil: quiet, even-tempered, well-organized. According to reports, Janis became the mother of twins, Nicole and Phillip in 1982.

Following the birth of the twins, Phil finally got rid of the bunkered, razor-wired mansion in Beverly Hills, and moved to a far more bucolic, leafy compound on the edge of the Arroyo Seco in Pasadena. There the new family Spector passed most of the rest of the 1980s and 1990s, and with a few startling exceptions, such as the Rock and Roll Hall of Fame appearance, generally far from the craziness of Hollywood and the venues of rock music that had suffused his former life.

Still, there was more litigation: Ronnie and the other Ronettes sued Phil for back royalties, as well as a cut of the action from synchronization rights, the use of old songs in new movies or commercials. That lawsuit would drag on for years and years, and would still be going on, even in early 2003. Some of the Crystals also sued; so did the psuedo-Crystal, Darlene Love. Warner Brothers sued; Phil countersued. It seemed that Phil was fated to live a life of litigation.

Then there was the clash between Phil and his long-time secretary, Donna Sekulidis: she was fired in 1987, according to Ribowsky, when a dispute erupted over her typewriter, of all things. Phil said he owned it, Donna said it was actually hers. *A typewriter?* But this was yet another example of Phil's need to control everyone and everything around him.

Then in 1991, in the second great tragedy of Phil's life, his son Phillip, 9 years old, died of leukemia. It was on Christmas Day, a day that had always meant something to Phil, even though he was born Jewish, and it was the day before his own birthday. His son's death was devastating, and Phil went into another steep depression. As Phil would put it later: "The most vulgar and obscene four-letter word in this language is 'dead.' It is indecent. It has no redeeming social value." There was the faintest of echoes of Lenny Bruce here, and like Lenny at the end, it wasn't meant to be funny.

By 1992 his relationship with Janis had also soured, and she moved out. Nevertheless, she continued working for Phil

as his principal assistant. Still the bickering continued, and
in the following year he became involved in a series of petty
legal actions against Janis, four separate small claims suits,
in which he accused the mother of his children of stealing a
computer, a television and a VCR, and not performing work
that he had paid her to do. Janis argued in court that Phil had
actually given the items to her, and the judge agreed. This appears to have been yet another spasm over control—property
issues always seemed to become most acute when someone
decided to leave Phil, such as the squabble over the typewriter a few years earlier. It appears that Phil and Janis
patched up their differences, because she returned to work for
him all the way up until late 2002.

In 1994, even his old friends among the Teddy Bears sued
him—Marshall Lieb and Carol Connors claimed that Phil
had licensed "To Know Him Is to Love Him" to a number of
"oldie" record producers, and had failed to cut them in for
their share of the mechanical royalties. Phil claimed that
wasn't his responsibility, that Carol and Marshall should
have made their own deals with the record distributors. It
turned out that the "master lease" that the four [including
Harvey Goldstein] had signed so many years ago wound up
in the hands of some Midwest record producer who had been
using the song without paying anything to anyone for years,
at least until Allen Klein, who was managing Phil's catalog
of songs, discovered this fact. Klein, of course, worked for
Phil, not Carol and Marshall. They were soon joined by Harvey Goldstein. The lawsuit would drag on for the next five
years—it wasn't the money, it was the principle, Carol said
later. The three remaining Bears eventually collected a small
amount of royalties from the record label, not from Phil.

Then, in 1995, Phil's mother tripped over a loose board at
a construction site on Hollywood Boulevard, while walking
near her apartment. In falling, the 84-year-old Bertha broke
her leg. The next day, she sued the state and the construction
company for their failure to properly maintain the construction site. Thirteen days later she was dead.

42

ON THE TOWN

By 1998, Phil was ready to move again—Nicole was 16 and in school, Janis was living apart, Gary, Louis and Donté were all grown. Phil had always wanted to live in his own castle, and now he had the chance to buy one.

This was the Pyrenees Castle, built in 1925 by a wealthy former farmer and sheep rancher, Sylvester Dupuy, who wanted something that looked a bit like a Basque chateau he'd seen in his boyhood in the Pyrenees mountains.

"I wanted a castle," Phil would later tell Mick Brown. "There aren't that many left."

That this castle, with its semi-Moorish appearance, happened to be in Alhambra was simply an accident of geography, although Phil would later say it was something of an advantage, in that there simply weren't any temptations for him in Alhambra, unlike Hollywood. So for the most part Phil stayed in his castle, ignoring the world, and perfectly happy—well, mostly—to have the world ignore him. At one point after the move to the castle, Phil began seeing Nancy Sinatra, and there was some talk about Phil producing some tracks for her, although it appeared that the relationship never really ignited. After moving to the castle, according to Marvin Mitchelson and others, Phil had stopped drinking completely. He told Mick Brown he had begun taking medication to control his bipolar disorder and other psychological afflictions. Mitchelson, for one, thought that Phil was in an excellent frame of mind. "Phil stopped drinking about four years ago," he said. "He's about as together as anyone I know."

But this seemingly quiescent period actually began to end in the fall of 2002, at just about the same time that as Lana Clarkson was visiting her friend Sally Kirkland at the art gallery, and thinking about taking a part-time job.

Reconstructing the events, it appears that sometime during the summer Phil became interested in producing the British band Starsailor. According to various published reports—including Phil's interview with Mick Brown—his interest in Starsailor was whetted by his daughter Nicole, then 20 and apparently living in New York. According to Phil's interview with Brown, he became interested in Starsailor when Nicole took him to a concert by the band in Los Angeles. In October of 2003 he flew to London to produce tracks for them.

According to some, the sessions did not go well—in Phil's view, the band lacked the sort of panache that he wanted, and again the problem of playing things over and over again arose. The sessions lasted almost six weeks—far longer than Starsailor was willing to invest for just two songs, which were all that Phil was able to complete. In November, Phil returned to the United States. It was while he was going through customs with a bodyguard that an incident took place that triggered Phil's decision to go bare, so to speak—doing without any more bodyguards.

Here again the legend collides with facts: according to Geoff Boucher, a *Los Angeles Times* reporter who covers the rock music scene, Phil fired the bodyguard when the customs inspectors discovered a cache of soaps and shampoos from a London hotel in his luggage as they returned from a trip to the United Kingdom. But friends of Phil said that he decided to dispense with the bodyguard's services when he realized he didn't need protection any longer—that his non-drinking, along with the use of his medications, made it unnecessary. One thing everyone did agree on, though, was that Phil's bodyguards were more often employed in keeping him from causing trouble for others than for the purpose of preventing others from causing trouble for him.

The fall also brought several other developments, besides the disappointment with Starsailor. One was Phil's legal triumph when, on October 17, 2002, the New York Court of Appeals ruled that Ronnie and the other Ronettes were not entitled to share in royalty income for "synchronization rights" to the Ronettes' songs. The decision reversed an earlier New York court's ruling that the Ronettes were entitled to the royalties. A second part of the appeals court decision, however, let stand a trial court finding that Phil owed substantial back royalties to the Ronettes for sales of records, the so-called mechanical royalties—a finding that was also upheld in a case involving Darlene Love and others who had performed as the Crystals.

At the same time, just after the first of the year, plans were made to re-issue *Let It Be*, without all the Spector strings and bells. The plan made the pages of the *Los Angeles Times* on the last day of January, just three days before the events at Phil's castle. "It's the de-Spectorized version," Ringo Starr was quoted as saying by *Rolling Stone*, and picked up by the *Times*. "Paul [McCartney] was always totally opposed to Phil. I told him [McCartney] on the phone, 'You're bloody right again. It sounds great without Phil.'"

Without Phil—were there ever more ominous words?

Not long after he gave his "devils inside me" interview to Mick Brown, Phil and Mitchelson began once again to get their movie project together. True, the triumphal return to Abbey Road Studios hadn't worked out with Starsailor, so the ending still needed some thought. But Phil was still not drinking (or apparently wasn't, if the red stuff that Brown saw in his hand on the day of the interview was in fact cranberry juice). Most of Phil's intimates—Mitchelson, Dave Kessel, and others associated with the music scene— thought that Phil was on his best behavior in years. Clean, sober, and in a remarkably stable frame of mind.

In December, Mitchelson and Phil attended a party together in Hollywood, and Phil seemed at the top of his game,
according to Mitchelson: warm, funny, very intelligent. Both
of them were amused, Mitchelson said later, to see astronaut
Buzz Aldrin at the party, and, they thought, apparently a little
tipsy. Phil rolled his eyes at Aldrin's behavior, Mitchelson
said.

Then came the Christmas holidays, always an emotional
time of year for Phil, especially since the death of his son.
Turning 63 probably made the sober Phil realize that he
wasn't a kid anymore—that in fact, he hadn't been one for
decades.

Sometime after the first of the year, Phil seems to have
gotten into an argument with Janis. According to Boucher—
apparently relying on sources close to Phil—Phil fired her,
and she left the castle. It likewise appears that Phil may have
stopped taking his medications; and he began to drink again.

That's what he was doing, certainly, on the night of Sunday, February 2, 2003, when he decided to go out on the town.

At some point that afternoon, Phil made a telephone call to a
woman in Hollywood, an old friend who now ran a business,
Hollywood Basics, a sort of orientation school for people
who wanted to know where the hot restaurants and nightclubs
were, usually for the purpose of seeing and being seen by entertainment industry types. The friend, Kaylee Kiecker, later
said that Phil had invited her to join him at dinner, but that
she was unable to make it because of a prior commitment.

Nevertheless, at some point that evening, Phil got into the
back seat of his new black Mercedes S430 limousine, and
his driver, later identified as Adriano Desouza, drove him to
a number of places in West Hollywood and Beverly Hills.
During the evening, Phil made stops at Trader Vic's, The
Grill, and Dan Tana's, all restaurants/bars in Beverly Hills or
West Hollywood, before winding up at the House of Blues a
bit after 2 A.M.

At The Grill Phil met with Rommie Davis, who had in
the past provided catering services for Phil's annual bowling

party, an event Phil usually held for selected music business friends in Montrose, a Los Angeles suburb. According to Phil's telephone records, subsequently seized by the police, Phil had called Davis earlier in the day to make a date so they could talk about the upcoming party. According to what Davis later told the sheriff's detectives, Phil ate dinner, and also consumed some alcohol, as he had earlier at Trader Vic's. He would continue drinking the rest of the night, at Dan Tana's and eventually, at the House of Blues.

At Dan Tana's, a popular hangout for Hollywood celebrities, Phil actually surprised the bartender by asking for an alcoholic drink—people at the trendy restaurant had known that Phil hadn't been drinking for the last few years. He'd often come there with Nancy Sinatra, before Sinatra had ended her relationship with Phil to work on a new record with . . . Lee Hazlewood, a decision that probably contributed to Phil's unhappy mood. The bartender first thought the waiter had gotten the order wrong, according to Robert Sam Anson, a writer for *Vanity Fair* magazine who subsequently looked into the sequence of the fatal evening's events. The bartender came to Phil's table to make sure, Anson said. Phil said he was sure—he wanted a drink. The bartender made him a daiquiri. The price was $8.50, which probably meant it had a double shot of rum.

After conversing with the caterer for some time—and apparently consuming a salad, if Anson's sources were correct—Phil left Dan Tana's for the House of Blues, accompanied by Davis, according to Anson. He signed a credit card slip for the tab, and, left a tip of either $450 (according to the sheriff's department) or $500 (according to the *Los Angeles Times*). In any event, it was a substantial amount of money for a total tab of $55. On the other hand, such profligacy is often a symptom of mania's grandiosity.

So, too, was the drinking—after several years of sobriety, suddenly plunging into booze was likewise a symptom of Phil's bipolar disorder, particularly in the way the disorder erodes self-control. More significantly, after years of detoxification from alcohol, having at least three stiff drinks before midnight, if not more, was likely to make Phil fairly drunk, especially given his 135-pound body weight.

Arriving at the House of Blues sometime between 2 and 2:30 A.M., it appears that Phil had still more alcohol. According to Anson (who wrote his piece for *Vanity Fair* about two months after the fatal events), Phil ordered a $250 bottle of champagne, and a shot of 151-proof Bacardi rum, the first of at least two more drinks he had at the nightclub.

It was when he and Davis came into the House of Blues, almost everyone agreed later, that Phil first met Lana Clarkson. And once again the conventional wisdom seems to conflict with, if not the actual facts, at least the most likely facts. Because, contrary to the sheriff's department, the *Times* and Anson, it appears that Lana and Phil Spector had actually met for the first time some weeks before the night of February 2.

For the support of this notion, there is first the recollection of Sally Kirkland, who later said she was "one hundred percent sure" that Lana had mentioned Spector's name on January 19, 2003, at the "I Have a Dream" Foundation benefit at the House of Blues. She couldn't later recall whether Lana had said she was going to meet him, or had already met him. At the time, it meant little to Kirkland—it wasn't as if Lana was saying that she'd struck up any sort of special relationship with Phil, only that he had been to the House of Blues, and that she had been introduced to him, or would soon be introduced to him, as she had been introduced to other well-known people as part of her new job.

Second, there is the fact that Phil was reported to have gone to the House of Blues on at least two occasions in the month or so preceding the shooting, almost certainly in an attempt to scout talent for someone to replace the Starsailor hopes, and to demonstrate to the music world (and himself) that he was still a big player in the rock-and-roll scene. Because Lana began work at the club on January 6, 2003, there is every reason to suspect that they had been introduced to one another prior to February 2.

Third, there is the version of this initial meeting recounted by Anson in *Vanity Fair*: that when Phil and Rommie Davis arrived at the club between 2 and 2:30 A.M., Lana supposedly did not know who he was, that in fact, he had entered by the wrong door, and that Lana was getting ready to give him the heave-ho.

At this point, according to Anson, a waitress supposedly told her, "Don't you know who that is? That's Phil Spector."

After downing his two rums, according to Anson, Phil tried to pick up one of the waitresses, but she declined. Rommie Davis had by this point disappeared, according to Anson. The club was getting ready to close. Phil asked how to get to the men's room, but stopped short. According to Anson, he saw Lana leaving the club, her work shift over. He got into the elevator with her.

"Bet you won't forget *me* again," Phil supposedly said to Lana, as they left. Anson then had Lana offering to walk Phil to his car.

The story rings somewhat true, but not completely. For one thing, if Phil really had left Dan Tana's at about 2 A.M., arriving at the House of Blues some minutes later, he wouldn't have had very much time to order and drink two 151 rums, not to mention a $250 bottle of champagne. The evidence collected by the sheriff's department seems to indicate that Phil and his limousine, with Lana in it, left the House of Blues between 2:30, when Lana's shift ended, and 2:45 in the morning. That's a lot of drinking for just fifteen to thirty minutes.

What seems more likely is that Anson inadvertently combined the events of two different nights—one night when Phil arrived at the House of Blues through the wrong door, and Lana was getting ready to throw him out before being told who he was, and a second night, the early morning hours of February 3, and that the two different nights might have been mistakenly conjoined by witnesses when they talked to Anson and others. It also seems possible that Phil acquired the champagne for Lana, given that, on the few occasions that she did drink, champagne was her beverage of choice, and that Phil himself had been imbibing rum all night.

Added to that is another important fact that Anson did not have access to at the time he wrote his article for *Vanity Fair*: the sheriff's department eventually came to suspect that Phil had actually been "stalking" Lana, possibly via her Web site, in the days and weeks before the shooting. That was one reason they later seized his computers and his phone records—to see whether he had tried to make any sort of contact with her, or her Web avatar, in the days prior to the fatal event. That potential fact could indicate that Phil knew who Lana was before he got to the House of Blues on the night in question.

43

THE NIGHT THE MUSIC DIED

Based on the sheriff's department's reconstruction of the events, it appears that the limo bearing Phil and Lana arrived at the castle at approximately 3:30 in the morning—that would include time to get out of West Hollywood, make it to the nearest freeway, and drive to Alhambra, plus another five or ten minutes to get to the castle. Altogether, it would take somewhere between forty and fifty minutes, depending on the traffic. Lana's Cougar was left behind in the parking lot, suggesting that Phil had told her that he would have Desouza drive her back to pick up her own car later. According to Lana's closest friends, she made it an ironclad rule to drive her own car to social events—just in case she wanted to leave early. And here one is forced to wonder whether Anson's informant didn't have the story somewhat garbled: that rather than Lana offering to walk Phil to his car, it was Phil offering to do the same for Lana. Because there is evidence that they stopped at Lana's car first, as we shall see.

According to Desouza's statement to the police, once at the castle, Phil had him stop the limo at the heavy iron gates at the bottom of the hill. Then Phil and Lana climbed the steps to the castle, similar to Mick Brown's initiation into the cult of Spector the previous November. Desouza took the limo up to the top of the hill, parked it in the roundabout near the back door, and settled down to wait.

About fifteen minutes later, according to Desouza—say, around 3:45 A.M. or so—Phil emerged from the back door and went into the rear seat of the limo. He emerged carrying what has been variously described as a briefcase or a valise. Phil then went back inside, Desouza told the police later.

At some point after that—no one later made clear the exact time, at least publicly—Desouza said he heard a loud report, a noise that sounded to him like a gunshot, a "popping noise," as he put it later to police. He got out of the limo, apparently thinking that the shot had come from inside the house, and wondered what to do.

Within a short period of time, Desouza later told the police, Phil came to the door with what Desouza thought was a gun in his hand. At the point, Desouza said, Phil told him that he thought he had killed someone. In fact, Desouza told police, Phil's exact words were: "I think I just shot her." Phil then went back inside the house, closing the back door behind him.

Based on documents later filed in court by the sheriff's department, it appears that Desouza did not immediately dial 911 for official assistance. Instead he called Michelle Blaine. It seems likely that Desouza told Blaine about hearing the possible gunshot and what Phil had said. Subsequently—"ultimately," to use the sheriff's department's word—Desouza did call 911.

The Alhambra Police Department received the call shortly at 5:02 A.M., but were unable to get in, "due to the uncooperativeness of the suspect," as the coroner's report put it later. After getting organized at the bottom of the hill, at 5:20 A.M. they broke through the rear door of the house—it isn't clear whether it was actually locked—and there saw Lana Clarkson, apparently dead in a chair in a foyer leading to the rear door. Phil was standing next to her outstretched legs with his hands in his pockets. When the Alhambra officers told Phil to remove his hands from his pockets, Phil apparently didn't respond, or at least respond quickly enough. That was when the Alhambra officers Tasered him to the floor, "for their own safety," as the police put it later.

It took the Alhambra police nearly an hour to go through the house in search of other possible suspects before they would allow the paramedics to come in. After trying to find signs of life, the paramedics concluded that Lana was dead, and had been for some time. It appeared that she had been shot through the mouth; broken teeth were scattered about the floor, and there were blood spatters in a variety of places on the floor and on the stairs. A gun was found on the stone floor near her left leg. The Los Angeles County Sheriff's Department's homicide investigators began to arrive to begin their search for evidence. By that time, Phil, handcuffed, was in the Alhambra jail, waiting for Robert Shapiro.

Later the sheriff's department's search effort would engender controversy from Phil's lawyers, who accused them of losing control of the crime scene. An attorney for Phil was to claim that "192" officers were logged into the scene during the two days of searching. That figure was untrue—there were 192 separate entries into the crime-scene perimeter log during the two days of searching, as many of the same officers came and went multiple times.

The crime scene had elements of the macabre—in fact, it might have been a scene from one of Lana's old movies, given the dark spookiness of the castle.

"In a living room next to the foyer," Sheriff's Detective Mark Lillienfeld reported, in an affidavit for a search warrant later served in connection with the shooting,[59] "[I] saw that candles had been lit atop a fireplace mantel. The coffee table between two couches had a brandy glass partially filled with alcohol, and atop the table was a Jose Cuervo Tequila bottle and a partially empty Canada Dry soft drink."

---

[59] Two affidavits and their returns—that is, the list of items seized—were obtained by the Los Angeles County Sheriff's Department after the shooting. Both were immediately sealed by the issuing courts. Seven months later the author filed a motion to unseal these records. The sheriff's department and Los Angeles County District Attorney's Office initially opposed the unsealing, then withdrew their opposition when Phil Spector was charged with Lana Clarkson's murder. The quotes from police records are taken from the formerly sealed affidavits.

When he arrived at the scene, Lana was still in the chair near the back door. "[I] saw the victim slumped in a chair in the foyer of the home," Lillienfeld said. "She was wearing a black nylon slip/dress, black nylons, and black shoes. A leopard print purse with a black strap was slung over her right shoulder, with the purse hanging down on her right side by her right arm.

"She had what appeared to be a single entry gunshot wound to the mouth. Broken teeth from the victim were scattered about the foyer and [on] an adjacent stairway.

"Lying on the floor under the victim's left leg was a Colt 2-inch, blue steel, .38 caliber, six-shot revolver. This weapon had five live cartridges in the cylinder, and under the hammer, a spent cartridge.

"A check of the weapon's serial number via the Automated Firearms System [the state's computer data bank, also linked to the federal Bureau of Alcohol, Tobacco and Firearms (ATF)] was negative. There was blood spatter on the weapon.

"On a chair next to the victim was a brown valise that contained a wallet with personal identification and other documents belonging to Phillip Spector." The valise, said Lillienfeld, included two cellular telephones.

"Blood smears," Lillienfeld continued, "were seen . . . on the back door handle, and on a wood railing for the stairway, about seven feet west of the victim's remains.

"A level for a dead bolt lock in the back door was lying on the floor, amidst the broken teeth material previously described. This lever was brass, about two inches long, and a part of the interior portion of the lock.

"In an upstairs dressing room, [I] saw a white men's coat that had blood smear on the sleeve and blood spatter on the lapel area.

"In a bathroom next to the foyer, [I] saw a blood soaked cloth lying on the floor, and a wet hand towel lying on the sink top."

The specificity of Lillienfeld's observations is interesting, particularly his description of the blood spatters, the broken teeth, and the arrangement of the purse over Lana's shoulder.

Since Lillienfeld was only trying to get a warrant to seize Phil's telephone and credit card records, it would ordinarily have been sufficient merely to indicate that there was a suspected homicide in the house of Phillip Spector, and that Phil had been arrested for investigation of the crime.

But his careful description seems to indicate, without overtly saying so, that Lillienfeld—a veteran of over two hundred homicide investigations—had an idea there was something phony about the scene, that it might have been arranged by someone, probably an amateur, to make it look as though the death were a suicide. Moreover, noting that the fatal weapon had five live rounds in its cylinder, and one expended shell casing, effectively ruled out any claims that a game of Russian roulette had been under way.

The careful attention to the location of the blood smears, the mention of bloody towels and a "men's coat" upstairs, and especially the fact that Lana's purse was "hanging" from her right shoulder while she was "slumped" in the chair, the gun under her "left" leg, suggests that Lillienfeld was calling attention to some anomalies in case someone later wanted to claim that Lana had shot herself. While not mentioned by Lillienfeld, the search by detectives had also netted an empty but bloody gun holster in a drawer next to the chair Lana had been sitting in. When combined with the assertion that driver Desouza "ultimately" notified 911 of the shooting, it suggested that someone had had enough time to try to arrange things the way he or she thought a suicide might look, preparatory to making such a claim.

Which would soon happen.

The sheriff's department searchers—"192" of them or not— went through the entire thirty-three-room house looking for evidence. According to the inventory of items seized, later filed with the court, the searchers found, altogether, twelve different handguns in various places in the castle, including the unregistered two-inch Colt .38 that was apparently the fatal weapon. It appeared that the tales about Phil having a different gun for each suit of clothes might actually have some validity.

But there were other things found in the search that pose some peculiar questions: for one, how did blood get on the broken striker plate from the back door dead bolt lock, the remnants of which were found on the floor? It was certainly possible that the police, in breaking through the door, had shattered the lock, but if that were the case, how did it get blood on it, if Lana were sitting in the chair? The blood on the striker plate suggested that there was a sufficient amount of blood on the floor near the back door to support the notion that Lana's body might have been moved into the chair by someone. Alternatively, the blood could have been put on the plate by Phil as he opened the door to call out to Desouza, the chauffeur. One thing was certain: *Lana* hadn't opened the door herself after she was shot.

The Jose Cuervo bottle and brandy glass "partially full" of "alcohol" suggests that when they arrived, Phil poured himself yet another drink—this one of tequila in the brandy glass, and that he had consumed some of it. The presence of a Canada Dry soft drink container suggests that the light drinking Lana had a ginger ale—a significant observation in light of claims that Phil would later make about Lana's behavior that night. And there was another interesting fact—that in the kitchen sink, there was an empty brandy glass. It appeared that a person who had drunk from that glass had then washed it out, possibly preparatory to leaving.

Leaving? Where have we heard about this before? The fact is, if there was one thing predictable about Phil when he was on one of his manic cycles, when he began drinking and waving his guns around—when he was at his wildest, as Ronnie and countless others could attest—it was his anger at those who wanted to leave before *he* was ready to let them go.

As dawn arrived on February 3, 2003, it was forty-four years to the day since Buddy Holly, Ritchie Valens and the Big Bopper had died in their Iowa plane crash—in songwriter Don McLean's words, "the day the music died." Now Lana Clarkson was dead, and the one-time "Tycoon of Teen" was in jail, suspected of her murder.

SPIN CYCLE

44

THAT LOVIN' FEELIN'

As we have seen, the arrest of Phil Spector gave a wide assortment of interested parties a chance to resurrect their various takes on the Spector myth, as well as the opportunity to embellish it, or spin it in whatever particular direction the spinner might believe was advantageous. A series of crypto-facts was soon grafted onto the legend, usually embellishing it in ways even more baroque than usual.

All the old canards were trotted out: Phil getting cheated of his money from "To Know Him Is to Love Him"; Phil's supposed career as a court reporter at the Cheryl Crane inquest; producing for Elvis Presley; creating "Spanish Harlem"; Phil as a "genius," "a mad genius," "a recluse," "the Howard Hughes of rock-and-roll," along with Lennon's "save me ears," and the Ramones. It was widely reported that Phil was a multi-millionaire, but no one ventured to say what he was really worth—in dollars, that is.

Phil's defenders—there were a number of them—said it was impossible that Phil could have shot anyone, much less committed murder. The day after Phil was released from jail, even Ronnie at first came to his defense. Interviewed by the television show *Good Morning America*, Ronnie said, "I don't think he would murder anybody. I'm still, like, in shock, you know? I haven't slept all night."

Ronnie said that while she'd had her problems with Phil, "I never thought he would ever kill anybody. I ran away a lot of times when I was married to him because he would yell, but he would never hit me. In the first three months of our marriage he pulled a gun and I ran away because I was afraid, and I never saw him with a gun again." That of course was different from what Ronnie had said in *Be My Baby*, when Phil had brought his "peacemaker" to the church in South Los Angeles. Then, a week or so later, Ronnie changed her tune slightly: "My heart goes out to the woman [Lana] and her family. I don't know what the circumstances are; I can only say that when I left in the early seventies, I knew that if I didn't leave at that time, I was going to die there." That made it sound like Ronnie was afraid Phil would kill her, but what she probably meant was that Phil was psychologically suffocating her.

Gene Pitney, Phil's old rock-and-roll friend from the early 1960s, songwriter of "He's a Rebel," was in England when the news broke. Reached there by reporters, Pitney said it was his guess that Phil had been under the influence of "anti-psychotic drugs and alcohol . . . He probably doesn't even know what happened, doesn't even know where he was."

Others were more stalwart on Phil's behalf. Typical of this school of spin was Marky Ramone, who soon asserted, "He wouldn't hurt a fly," only to be immediately contradicted by another Ramone, Johnny, who had the band-as-hostage legend a bit different from what Joey Ramone had told Ribowsky years before. The way Johnny now told the tale, Phil had kept them prisoner at the point of a gun at the *mansion*, not, as Joey had told Ribowsky, that he'd pointed his piece at Dee Dee Ramone in the studio, after Dee Dee had said he felt like killing him. Johnny told the *LA Times*: "We were prisoners in his house, he wouldn't let us leave. Dee Dee said something and he pulled out a gun and started waving it around, he kept saying, 'You're not leaving, nobody's leaving.'"

Still, Phil's long-time friends tried to tell people that the idea of him shooting anyone was completely out of Phil's most recent character.

"I'm hoping that this is not something he's guilty of," Larry Levine said. "In the old days, I could have seen it as accidental, waving a gun around. But he hasn't been that way for a long time. He was in a really good place."

"Phil became a pussycat," Los Angeles artist Hudson Marquez told *USA Today*. "Over the past ten years I've seen him go from a madman on the loose to a complete gentleman, generous beyond belief and overly polite. He no longer had bodyguards, just a driver. The change was enormous. I can't believe what's happened." Marquez said he thought that much of Phil's menace was nothing but bluff. He told of visiting Phil at his Pasadena house and being warned about the danger from guard dogs. What Phil actually had, Marquez said, were two Irish setters "who might have licked you to death . . . he has been in great spirits and great shape, and feeling so good about everything. This doesn't fit into what I know about him and where he is."

Bob Merlis, a music publicist, said that despite all the stories about guns and bodyguards, he'd never, ever seen Phil with a gun. Merlis said he was dumbfounded by Phil's arrest: "I'm devastated. It's pretty overwhelming."

"I haven't seen him drink in years," Merlis told the *Times*. "The Phil I have known in that time is charming and witty. He's a unique character. I've never known anyone like him. You know how they say you shouldn't meet your heroes because they will disappoint you? Phil didn't disappoint."

One of the Kessel brothers, who had once posed as bodyguards for Phil, now reversed himself and said most of the legend was simply hyperbole. "A lot of the stuff in the old days was just show biz, theater," Dave Kessel said. He added that when Phil had finally realized that drinking was destroying him, physically and emotionally, he'd quit.

Marvin Mitchelson was among the most adamant that Phil wouldn't harm anyone, ever. "It's inconceivable to me that Phil would meet someone, take her home and shoot her dead," he said. "There's no motive. I think the police are having trouble with that. I know a different Phil Spector. If you knew Phil, you loved him. No matter what his reputation was in the past—all these stories about him waving a gun around—he never shot at anyone."

But even Mitchelson realized that the shooting death had already had an effect on the prospects for the movie about Phil's life. Mitchelson seemed to have two minds about it. At first he told the *Times*, referring to the ending that would have Phil getting back to the studio with Starsailor, "So we started working on a treatment, and we thought this was it, this was the ending. We'd found it. After all those years and all those troubles, he was happy. Honestly, I don't know what happened in that house on Monday morning. I just can't believe he would kill someone. We thought we had a happy ending to the story. Now I don't know what's going to happen, but it doesn't look like it's going to be a happy ending." The movie was to have been titled *Wall of Sound*, Mitchelson said.

Then, a few days later: "I wanted to produce a story on his life. I spent hours digging into his psyche, and the net result is, no real violence at all. This is such a tragic thing, so shocking. I won't believe it was intended, if he even did it. It's untoward and unlikely he'd do this without some reason we can't understand yet. He'd never take out a gun and shoot anyone."

And by the following week, the Hollywood gossips were saying that this actually *was* an ending: Phil being arrested for the shooting death of an actress at his castle, and having to go on trial for his life. Was that a boffo ending, or what? One gossip sheet reported that producers and television companies were "racing" to "tell the bizarre tale of Spector's life, with some of Hollywood's hottest stars, including Leonardo DiCaprio, tipped to take the lead."

The Tom Cruise angle was played big, with the note that while Cruise had been interested in the role, he was now considered "too old." Hence DiCaprio. Some said Cruise had tried for years to convince Phil to authorize the movie, only to have been turned down. That was just the opposite of the facts, though. Cruise's publicist told the news media that the problem was, the script had never been finished. "There was no further interest in Spector, who became a virtual recluse given to bouts of increasing violence," a movie gossip Web site reported. Take that!

At that point, Mitchelson weighed in once more: "This alleged murder is a major development in Phil's life, and like any life-changing event, it makes his story even more gripping," he said, sounding like a Hollywood pitchman of old. "The Crowe and Cruise film didn't have an ending Phil approved of, but we're now getting a treatment together that Phil feels is much more appropriate." But then Mitchelson added that he hadn't seen or talked with Phil since his arrest, which seemed to contradict the notion that Phil felt the new ending—an "alleged murder"—was "much more appropriate."

Meanwhile, UK *Daily Telegraph* columnist Mark Steyn had an altogether different take on the events. He thought people made much too much of rock musicians—the more people made of them, the worse they behaved, Steyn said, pointing to Phil, Michael Jackson and Courtney Love. And, said Steyn, it wasn't as if they had anything profound to say. Borrowing a page from David Susskind in the ancient past, he reprinted the words from "Da Doo Ron Ron", mocking its cliched rhymes ("my heart stood still"/"his name was Bill") and sing-song refrain:

Da-Doo-Ron-Ron-Ron Da-Doo-Ron-Ron

Steyn was missing the beat, of course.

Cramming a bunch of overworked musicians into a small room took no genius, Steyn observed. And "the less Spector did the more the aura of his 'genius' grew. For the last 30 years, the 'troubled genius' has been more trouble than he's worth . . . That's another rock exception to the general rule: celebrities are supposed to age well, but the Phil Spector staring out from *The Telegraph* masthead last weekend is a shriveled little prune under a Status Quo fright-wig, like

someone auditioning for a [regional theater] production of
This is Spinal Tap. . . .

"My advice to Nancy Sinatra [now that] Phil's out on
bail . . . Da-Doo-Run-Run-Run"—meaning that she should
make fast tracks away from Phil, and not the kind used on
records.

45

A DOUBLE NEGATIVE

Worse was soon to come, and from much closer quarters: Two of Phil's three adopted sons soon lambasted him as a greedy, neurotic, abusive father. Donté went on television and said, "While we don't know if Dad killed this lady, he should be locked up. He's a sick man." Gray had even worse to offer, contending that Phil had kept the boys locked in their room, and that he had even forced them to "perform sex acts" with Phil's girlfriends. Donté added that when Phil went out for dinner, he brought the leftovers home for the boys to eat. When he'd heard about the shooting death, Donté said, his first thought was that Phil had finally, actually made good "on one of his threats."

Was this a slap, or what? Who knew what was really true, especially with the movie sharks hanging around, salivating at the chance to tell Phil's life story? Gary was quoted as saying that their lives were essentially managed by the "manservants," including the governess and George Brand. Brand, in fact, probably became the closest thing to a father that Donté ever had. Gary said that Phil would often send the word to them to get ready to go somewhere for an outing, then never show up. The boys would wait for hours, all dressed up with nowhere to go.

With these statements, things were getting even more ugly. Mitchelson soon tried to right the ship. "I understand," he said, "his defense will be that this was a tragic accident. I've spoken with various individuals connected with the case, and I'm one hundred percent certain it's not a homicide." But because Mitchelson said again that he hadn't talked with Spector since his arrest, and since Phil and Lana were the only two people who knew for sure what had happened, and Lana wasn't around any longer to say what that was, it was hard to see how Mitchelson could be "one hundred percent certain."

What was somewhat significant about this statement—if one assumed that one of the "individuals connected with the case" was Phil's lawyer, Robert Shapiro—was that it seemed likely that Shapiro was preparing his defense on the premise that the shooting was accidental, not deliberate. That seemed to eliminate the possibility that some unknown person had done it, and had then fled. Given Phil's long, well-documented history of brandishing firearms, especially when he'd been drinking, people would probably be willing to accept this—it seemed a more likely explanation for Lana's death than cold-blooded murder. In this scenario, Phil might have been fooling around with his gun, perhaps twirling it around his finger to show off, cowboy-style, when it went *bang*, much to his shock and surprise. So, an accident might work—Phil might get placed on probation for negligent, involuntary homicide, but it would be almost the same thing as getting drunk and driving into a fatal collision. It wasn't a happy outcome for Phil (to say nothing of Lana), but it was a lot better than spending the rest of his life in the slammer. Of course, Phil would have to admit his idiotic negligence—that would be inherent in claiming that the death was an accident.

The sheriff's department's homicide investigators kept their own counsel, saying that they intended to work on the case carefully and thoroughly, and that it was too soon to reach any conclusions.

Then, in March, Mitchelson struck again.

Spector's Attorney Says He'll Be Cleared, read the headline. Associated Press reporter Linda Deutsch, who covered the Los Angeles County courts, said she'd had a conversation with Robert Shapiro. "Ending weeks of silence," she wrote, "an attorney for Phil Spector said Tuesday [March 11, 2003] the music producer will be cleared in the death of an actress found shot to death at his mansion."

Deutsch said that Shapiro had told her that he was convinced "a thorough and accurate investigation of the evidence will prove that Phil Spector is innocent of any crime."

Shapiro's first substantive statement about the shooting hadn't actually been his idea—it appeared that Phil and Mitchelson had forced his hand. When the root of the report was excavated, it turned out that Phil had sent an e-mail message to Mitchelson after the sheriff's department had returned his computer. Phil somehow got the impression that this meant the sheriff's department did not intend to file charges against him. Mitchelson, in turn, had provided a copy of the e-mail to a local radio station, which then precipitately broadcast that Phil had been cleared of any possible charges.

"I hate to use the words I told you so," Phil's e-mail read. "But I did tell you so. After seven weeks of silence, we can say with certainty, this will speak for itself, and boy, does it speak volumes." The death, Phil said, was "an accidental suicide."

An "accidental suicide"? What the heck was that? That Lana had accidentally intended to kill herself? It made no sense.

Hearing the report on the radio, Deutsch called Mitchelson, who confirmed that he'd received the e-mail from Phil, and then called Shapiro to get his comment.

Shapiro was in a bad position, especially hearing that his client had put the sheriff's department under the gun like that, so to speak. He couldn't very well say that Phil was wrong—that might be tantamount to calling his own client a liar. But on the other hand, he certainly couldn't confirm that the sheriff's department had "cleared" Phil, either, since they hadn't. But Shapiro wasn't one of the best criminal defense lawyers in Los Angeles for nothing. He crafted his statement carefully, saying that he believed "a thorough and accurate investigation will [clear Phil]," using the future tense rather than the conditional. That backhandedly confirmed that the investigation had not yet done so, but it also had the unfortunate effect of suggesting that the sheriff's department might not be performing a "thorough and accurate investigation" if they didn't "clear" Phil.

The sheriff's department retaliated the next day. **Authorities: Death of Actress at Spector Home Not Suicide,** the *Los Angeles Times* headlined. "If we had come to a conclusion as monumental as suicide," said Captain Frank Merriman, the head of the sheriff's homicide division, "we would have a duty to say so publicly." Merriman said he suspected that some people were trying to spin the media. "My opinion is that someone is orchestrating this to plant seeds of doubt with potential jurors." The *Times* reported that Shapiro was unavailable for comment.

In truth, Shapiro must have been extremely irritated with both his client and Mitchelson. In addition to alienating the sheriff's department, the statements—particularly about the "accidental suicide"—had foreshortened Shapiro's playing field considerably, taking away his ability to argue negligence, that the shooting had been some sort of "tragic accident," as Mitchelson had described it only the month before. With Phil contending that Lana had shot herself, accidentally or otherwise, it would be much more difficult for Shapiro to negotiate a plea with the Los Angeles County District Attorney's Office that the shooting *was* an unfortunate accident—one that Phil might have taken responsibility for. The only living witness was in effect saying that Lana had done it to herself, that he'd had no share of the blame, and the only way for the DA's office to make a deal now would require Phil to admit that he'd lied. That in turn wouldn't inspire much confidence in the DA that Phil was telling the whole truth about the "accident."

By this point, Phil had paid Shapiro a rather substantial sum on retainer, and Shapiro had already moved to get some heavy-duty witnesses in for the defense. The defense experts included New York pathologist Dr. Michael Baden, and forensic scientist Dr. Henry Lee, both of O. J. Simpson trial fame. That was one of the great advantages of being a rich defendant—an accused person with money could sometimes out-expert the government. According to some reports, Baden and one other pathologist had flown into Los Angeles to attend the Lana Clarkson autopsy, which was conducted shortly after the shooting. Shapiro soon let it be known that tests on Lana's hands showed gunpowder residue, and that Baden had informed him that the results were "not inconsistent with suicide."

This careful phrasing sounded good, that is, if one were in Phil's corner, but what did it really mean? The double negative was the key, "not inconsistent," which wasn't quite the same thing as saying, "It was consistent with suicide," or, "It was definitely, indisputably suicide." It only meant that as an expert, if asked, Baden could truthfully testify that the residue "was not inconsistent with suicide." Naturally, if a prosecutor then asked on cross-examination whether the gunshot residue was "not inconsistent with *homicide*," Baden would have to say yes, it was also "not inconsistent" with homicide. It was just another way of saying the gunshot residue was not conclusive to establishing what had happened, only with a pro-Phil spin.

But at this point Shapiro probably felt that if there were any chance to get Phil off, especially now that the only witness—Phil—had said that Lana had shot herself, he had to do it by muddying up the scientific testimony. Now, if he could only get Phil and his pal Mitchelson to stay away from the news media, there was a chance that Shapiro could still negotiate a deal with the district attorney's office, one that wouldn't have Phil going to jail for murder. He had to make it hard for the DA to prove his case, and to do that, he needed reasonable doubt. He apparently believed that he had some with Doctors Baden and Lee.

Was the gunshot residue found on Lana's hands significant? This was a complex area, but the short answer was, not really. There might be all sorts of reasons why Lana's hands might test positive for gunshot residue. One might be that, just before she was shot, she could have thrown up her hands in a defensive gesture. Or, it was possible that someone wiped her hands on the gun after the shot was fired—the chemicals found in gunpowder residue are easily transferable. There were, in fact, any number of possible explanations for this finding. For Shapiro to base his defense of Phil on this was to rely, in the end, on a very weak reed. Again the sheriff's department suggested that someone—unnamed—was attempting to influence the jury pool. But Shapiro had to play the cards he had been dealt, and make it look like he had the top hand in the game.

Left unreported was whether *Phil's* hands had been tested for gunshot residue, too. That would have been standard procedure for the police. If Phil's hands had tested positive, it would be a fact "not inconsistent" with homicide. But if Phil's hands had no such residue, it might not have meant anything anyway: he'd had plenty of time to wash up afterward, and in fact, there had been a bloody towel (actually, a baby's diaper) in the bathroom near the back door, and it wasn't likely that Lana had left it there. So the gunshot residue question wasn't really very meaningful.

The suggestion that Lana had shot herself was met with fury by her family and friends. "That's ridiculous," Ray Cavaleri, her agent, told the *Times*, and others soon chimed in: the idea that Lana Clarkson had killed herself—had in fact chosen Phil Spector's house to kill herself—was so far off the wall as to be unbelievable; in fact, it was downright insulting. It was totally inconsistent with everything that anyone who knew Lana knew about her—she simply was incapable of doing herself in, she was far too bright, energetic and happy, and far too much of an optimist. She was the sort of person who made everyone happy, not least herself, and she had much too much to look forward to in life.

But the suicide theory would soon gain even wider circulation, no matter how implausible it was.

46

KISSING THE GUN

The June, 2003 issue of *Vanity Fair* magazine gave its readers a rather long look at the Spector situation. It wasn't the first time the magazine had addressed the shooting, but it was its first attempt to be comprehensive.

This was Robert Sam Anson's article, titled "Legend With a Bullet." In his first paragraph, Anson suggested that he had interviewed "some 88 people in all" to prepare his account, which certainly made it sound like a vast and thorough undertaking. But after reading it, a reporter for the *LA Times* noted snidely that whenever a piece of journalism starts by listing the total number of people interviewed, it's probably because those interviewed didn't have much to say.

Relying almost exclusively on unnamed sources, Anson set the scene at the House of Blues. As noted, he had Phil meeting Lana for the first time that night, and ending with Phil's supposed line, "I bet you won't forget me again."

Because Anson didn't have access to the search warrant affidavits, he got a few things wrong with the scene at the castle. Like everyone else, he reported that Lana's body had been found on the floor, not sitting in the chair. But that may have been because the police may have believed that Lana's body had previously been on the floor, and that it had been moved to the chair after the shooting as part of the staging to make it look like a suicide.

Anson went on to sketch in some of the things people were saying about Phil, in print and on the airwaves, including some of the statements made by Gary and Donté. He

noted that several women had previously complained that
Phil had threatened them with guns, including one who contended that Phil had used his gun to prevent her from leaving after sex. He located yet another woman—a "rock icon,"
he said, without naming her, who said that she'd been res-
cued from the Beverly Hills mansion by a private patrol,
which had then admonished Phil about his propensity to
hold women at gunpoint. The "icon," whoever she was, told
Anson that it was her impression that Phil had been warned
before.

Anson also referred to Mick Brown's "devils inside that
fight me" interview, and observed, "The case appeared open-
and-shut . . . All that seemed left was an insanity plea."

So far, so good, relatively speaking. But then Anson
veered sharply away from the conventional wisdom. "Second thoughts tiptoed in," he said. He had Ronnie and
Mitchelson saying they didn't believe that Phil would kill
anybody.

"Lana," he continued, "also turns out to be more complicated than first thought." And with this, Anson took a sharp
turn away from reality, and began to rely on some rather du-
bious sources, some of whom were clearly attempting to
coattail on the tragedy in time-honored Hollywood fashion,
working to thrust their own names to the forefront of the
mix, even if they had to smear the victim in order to do it.

He quoted Edward Lozzi, a Hollywood publicist, as claiming that he had dated Lana, and that she was trained and proficient in the use of firearms. Lozzi told Anson that Lana
sometimes carried a pistol. "She could shoot the eye off a fly
at a thousand yards," Anson said Lozzi told him.

Lana's friends and family were first flabbergasted by this
assertion, then outraged. Not only had Lana never carried a
pistol, she had never even owned one—and in no way was
she trained in firing a weapon, let alone having the ability to
"shoot the eye off a fly at a thousand yards." This was so
completely off the wall as to be absurd. "She hated guns,"
one of her friends said, which sounds about right for someone who was spiritual and didn't like it when a boyfriend

practiced his martial arts. Not only that, no one who knew Lana—and who had known her for decades—had ever heard of Edward Lozzi. But there was worse to come.

Anson asserted that Lana had been "chums" with Jack Nicholson, Warren Beatty, and a variety of other Hollywood luminaries, which was a considerable overstatement. She had met many famous people, but to call her their "chum" was to imply a level of intimacy that did not exist. Anson also said that Lana had "done the scene" in Paris, Monte Carlo and Cannes, and generally portrayed her as a party girl. Then he got very nasty: "And for a time in the early 1990s, according to a source who spoke to *Vanity Fair*, she was a $1,000-an-hour call girl, working under the name 'Alana' for Beverly Hills madam Jody 'Babydol' Gibson."

Not only was this last untrue, it was scurrilous. If the source was Lozzi, Anson failed to note that Lozzi had been a publicist for a Los Angeles lawyer who had defended "Babydol" Gibson on the pandering charges that made her infamous, that Lozzi had put up a photo and a brief biography of the madam of his Web site, and that Gibson was trying to flog her memoirs to publishers. Getting publicity for his clients, after all, was Lozzi's business.

Later, Lozzi denied that he was the source for Anson's "Babydol" information, and said he doubted whether it was true. Nonetheless, Lana's friends and family were furious, and later could not mention the name Lozzi without growing apoplectic. Nowhere in Anson's article was there any indication that he had talked to anyone who really knew anything about Lana, such as her attorney Roderick Lindblom, or her friends, to see whether any of this nasty material had any substance.

Much of the rest of Anson's piece was a run-of-the-mill recitation of Phil's legend, with a few embroideries thrown in, such as Phil getting "beat . . . to a pulp" while a Teddy Bear, and the I-was-cheated-out-of-my-Teddy-Bears-money story that had emanated from Wolfe so many years earlier. There was no mention of payola.

But Mitchelson's movie project was still on: "It makes

the story even more gripping," Anson said Mitchelson told him, meaning Lana's death and Phil's arrest.

Near the end of the piece, Anson returned to Lana once more, referring to her recovery from the broken wrists, and her hesitancy in taking a part-time job. A passing mention was made of the comedy tape, the one Corman had praised so highly; Anson apparently was unable to talk to Corman himself, because he provided no details of the project Lana had invested so much of herself in. Then he had Lana deciding, by late January, "that the House of Blues was turning out to be a great place to meet the people who would make her career." That made it sound like she had no career, and worse, that she had taken the job at the House of Blues for the wholly mercenary purpose of finding some rich angel she could cajole into backing her return to the screen.

All in all, it was a rather shoddy performance by Anson, who, despite having talked to "88 people in all," seemed to have missed some of the most pertinent facts, and was even used to smear the victim for someone else's benefit.

But there was even worse in store. The month after Anson's *Vanity Fair* piece was published, *Esquire* magazine weighed in with its own assessment of Phil's difficulties. "Writer at large" (writer on the loose?) Scott Raab didn't have to interview "88 people in all." He had the mouth of the man himself, Phil Spector.

In "Be My, Be My Baby," Raab compiled—well, it wasn't an article, really, and it wasn't even actually an essay; it was more a slug of gonzo journalism, heavy on the first person, so that by the end, the reader knew as much about Raab as he or she did about the subject, which was supposed to be Phil. Written in the present tense, sprinkled with colloquial obscenities—a page from that *Esquirian* of old, Tom Wolfe, doubtless pitched to make the language seem hip—Raab told of his post-shooting encounter with Phil, in which Phil had invited him on a trip by private jet from Los Angeles to New York. Told *cinema verite* style, the words soon got in the way of the facts:

I want to take him in my arms and hug him, and so I do. I kiss him on the cheek and, still holding his narrow shoulders, I say, "Phillip, how are you?"

He brightens, grins his wicked grin, his eyebrows raise and waggle, and he cocks his head and looks up at me as if I must be slightly slow.

"Yes, Mrs. Lincoln," he snickers. "Other than that, how was the play?"

For Raab, Phil was A-OK, never mind what everyone else said about him.

"Myth? Vanished? Puh-*leeze*. I've read everything ever written about the bodyguards and the guns and the insanity, all the campfire tales of the recluse-zombie-maniac-dwarf self-imprisoned behind locked-around-the-clock gates, dragging his chains and howling at the moon—but I've also been to the castle. And I'm here to tell you: He's a very nice man."

Of course Raab failed to point out that just because Phil was a very nice man to a writer for *Esquire* magazine didn't mean he was a very nice man to someone without a large reader circulation behind her.

Lana, wrote Raab, was "a chronically aspiring buxom blond B-movie actress/model/comedienne/hostess—a type always common in Hollywood and not unknown at the castle."

So Raab's subtext is quickly made clear: the real victim here is Phil.

Eventually Raab gets down to the nut of the matter—Phil's version of what happened early in the morning of February 3.

Phil told Raab:

It's "Anatomy of a Frame-up." There is no case. They have no case. I didn't do *anything* wrong—I didn't do anything. I called the po-lice myself. *I called the police*. This is *not* Bobby Blake. This is *not* the Menendez brothers. They have no case. If they had a case, I'd be sitting in jail right now.

She kissed the gun. I have no idea why—I never knew her, never even saw her before that night. I have no idea who she was or what her agenda was. They have the gun—I don't know where or how she got the gun. She asked me for a ride home. Then she wanted to see the castle. She was loud—she was loud and drunk even before we left the House of Blues. She grabbed a bottle of tequila from the bar to take with her. I was *not* drunk. I wasn't drunk *at all*. *There is no case*. She killed herself.

This was Phil's story, finally, and he would be sticking to it.

47

LIAR LIAR

Phil's "She kissed the gun" remark set the case on its ear. Now it was clear that Phil would never be able to claim the shooting was a tragic accident, let alone that someone else did it, he knew not who. In essence, Phil was saying he was right there when Lana supposedly pulled the trigger on herself, that he was a witness, for Pete's sake.

But Phil had to be in some sort of fantasy land if he thought this was going to fly. His statement to Raab was larded with facts that could be checked, and quickly were. He called the police? It wasn't so, the limo driver, Adriano Desouza called, and the records proved it. He had no idea who Lana was? What about the several times he had been to the House of Blues while Lana was hosting at the Foundation Rooms? The only reason he wasn't sitting in jail "right now" was that he was rich, not because there was no case—someone named Jose Garcia from East Los Angeles would have still been in jail, and maybe even on his way to state prison. She asked for a ride home? Really? Why—when Lana had her own car in the parking lot at the House of Blues? She wanted to see the castle? Not very likely—the only way Lana would have known there was a castle was if Phil or someone else had told her about it; it wasn't as if Lana Clarkson was some sort of Phil Spector groupie, up-to-date on all of Phil's doings. She had the gun? Where did she get it? All the evidence indicated that the gun came from inside Phil's house. Why would she have a gun at all, when everyone who knew her said she had never owned one? Besides, who was well-known for carrying guns when he went out on the town, and even brandishing them at his guests? It wasn't Lana Clarkson.

She was "loud and drunk" at the House of Blues? Phil didn't know that Lana was an infrequent drinker, and in any case, witnesses who saw them leave together said Lana hadn't touched a drop of liquor all night, and never had while working at the House of Blues. She grabbed a bottle of tequila? *If* she did, it could only have been at Phil's request, since she ordinarily didn't drink the stuff herself— her beverage of choice, when she did drink, was champagne. He wasn't drunk? After all the booze he had consumed that night, was that even possible? She killed herself? For those who knew Lana, there was simply no way.

The day after the shooting, in fact, sheriff's detectives went to the House of Blues, and there recovered and searched Lana's car. Later they went to Lana's small house in Venice, accompanied by Roderick Lindblom, to search it—they wanted to see if there was any evidence of Lana having had any prior significant contact with Phil. Not only was there no such evidence, they discovered Lana's work records neatly laid out, all ready for her to prepare the tax return she would never have an opportunity to file. Was this the act of someone who was suicidal? It told eloquently of a well-organized woman who planned to be around for some time to come.

And when detectives checked with Ray Cavaleri, her agent, and Roderick Lindblom, her lawyer, they found that Lana had several commercial deals in the works—Lindblom was vetting the contracts—and a possible comedy series under consideration. Altogether, it looked as if Lana was on the verge of doing quite well, if not becoming a big success, just as she had always wanted. Why on earth would she have even wanted to kill herself, much less actually done it? Where was there a shred of evidence, other than Phil's own words, that showed that Lana's shooting was a suicide?

Here were two people—one with a reputation for telling

the truth, someone who rarely drank, a bright, effervescent
personality, a person who prayed and meditated and who
cared deeply for other people, and the other a man with a long
history of drinking to excess, of waving guns around and even
pointing them at people, of making self-aggrandizing statements that could later be proven false, who was desperately
trying to cast someone, a victim, as a drunken, simple-minded
bimbo, a cardboard cut-out in the wonderful world of Phil
Spector, when nothing could have been further from the truth.
Who had the better credibility, Lana Clarkson or Phil Spector? Who was more likely to be a liar?

Having read Phil's latest pronouncements about his
predicament, Shapiro had to have been tearing out what little hair he had left. How was he supposed to get Phil out of
this mess when Phil kept handing ammunition to the authorities in the form of out-of-court statements that could be
proven to be wrong, or even lies? And there was this zinger
in Raab's piece: not only was Phil mad at Mitchelson for his
talking to the media, he was mad at Shapiro "for charging
him a huge fee," and at Nancy Sinatra, for "failing to stand
by him."

The worst of it was, for Shapiro, if the case ever went to
trial, there was only one person available who could say un-
equivocally that Lana had shot herself in the mouth: Phil,
who seemed to be claiming that he'd been right there when it
happened. That meant, unless Shapiro could stop the case in
its tracks by coming up with some irrefutable piece of evidence that showed there was a suicide (like a suicide note,
maybe?), or unless he could head it off with some sort of
plea deal, Phil would have to take the witness stand to tell
the story to a jury. If that happened, Phil was sunk: a prosecutor would be able to tear his credibility to shreds after all
the years of tales, yarns, anecdotes and stories that could be
demonstrably shown as false. On the Crystals and Ronettes'
royalties alone, courts had already decided that Phil had
been less than candid. And even worse, there were all the
stories about Phil keeping people prisoner at his house at the

point of a gun. It would be child's play for a prosecutor to suggest that when Lana wanted to leave, Phil shot her.

There was another problem with the suicide idea, as well: statistically, it is a fact that very few women commit suicide by firearm, and of those who do, the vast majority shoot themselves in the heart, not the face. An actress would be even less likely to shoot herself in the part of her anatomy that would be most closely linked to her public identity, in other words, her face.

There was simply no way to get Phil out of the box that he'd put himself in with his own mouth. It was self-destructive behavior at its near-worst, the same sort of persecution mania that Phil had always felt, that had also been present in Lenny Bruce, the idea that someone was coming after him because he was misunderstood, because he was a "genius," because he was special, because he "didn't fit in." Because the truly talented people are always persecuted. And here was the most subtle point of all: it was as if Phil *needed* to feel persecuted in order to feel alive, to validate the proposition that he *was* talented, despite all his deepest self-doubts.

48

AN ABANDONED AND MALIGNANT HEART

The spring of 2003 turned into summer, and still nothing had been decided—at least officially—by the sheriff's department. When pressed for when a decision on Phil's fate was likely to be made, Captain Frank Merriman, the unit's administrator, said more time was needed to complete tests.

Some thought this might mean there was merit to Phil's "She kissed the gun" defense. After all, if it was taking so long, there must be something to it, right? But it wasn't necessarily so. What most people did not realize was that the case was only one of an average of four hundred suspected murders committed every year in the sheriff's jurisdiction. All of them had greater or lesser degrees of complexity, and most of them required at one point or another some sort of laboratory analysis before a final determination could be made. And the cases generally went through the chronically understaffed crime lab in the order in which they came in. There was no way to jump the queue just because the suspect was Phil Spector.

There were a number of lab tests that had to be performed. The gunshot residue issue needed to be resolved, and there were ballistic tests to perform, not just on the supposed fatal weapon, but also on the other eleven pistols that had been seized from Phil's castle (What if the supposed fatal weapon turned out to be a plant, and the real gun had been someplace else in the house? There had been plenty of time between the shot heard by Desouza and the arrival of the police for the guns to have been switched). Chemical analysis of the powder in the unexpended shells had to be compared to the gunshot residue to make sure they had the right gun. DNA tests had to be performed on the bloodstained articles taken from the house. The beverages consumed by the two parties might be tested for other substances, such as illicit drugs like hypnotics. Rape kits that had been taken from both Phil and Lana had to be tested. All of these would take time.

And there were other things that had to be done—examining Phil's computer, for example, to see if he'd logged on to Lana's Web site, or if he'd exchanged any e-mails that shed light on the matter. Fingerprints—that was a potentially fruitful area. If Lana had killed herself, why weren't her prints on the gun? What about Phil's? Phil's voluminous credit card accounts had to be analyzed, along with his purchases of alcohol on the night Lana died. Another analysis had to be done of all of Phil and Lana's telephone records, and people whom either had talked to on the night of the event had to be tracked down and interviewed.

It took time, Merriman kept telling people. They wanted to do a thorough, professional job. They didn't want to rush to judgment.

On September 18, 2003, the case was finally forwarded by the sheriff's department to the Los Angeles County District Attorney's Office, where it was routed to the major crime section. A few days later, the Los Angeles County Coroner's Office finally released its own findings in the Spector/Clarkson case: the death was a homicide, the coroner ruled—not a suicide. Since there were only two people in the castle at the time, and one of them was dead, that meant the coroner had decided that Phil had done it. But the coroner's office refused to make its complete report public, at the request of the district attorney's office.

The suppressed report was actually quite voluminous—nearly 100 pages. Its most fundamental finding was shocking: that the two-inch barrel of the pistol had actually been inside Lana's mouth when the gun had been fired. The bullet's track scored the top of the tongue, struck the rear of the throat, severed the spinal column at the top and caused a massive fracture to the rear of the skull. The blowback from the explosion caused the caps on Lana's front teeth to spew out of the front of her mouth. There was a substantial amount of gunshot residue on both of her hands.

On paper like this, the coroner's findings seemed strongly supportive of the suicide theory—especially if, as Phil would eventually claim, there was no gunshot residue at all on the clothing he'd been wearing at the time. If Phil had placed the gun in Lana's mouth and pulled the trigger, and if he'd been standing directly in front of her, the explosive blowback that had dislodged the caps almost certainly would have coated his own clothing with gunshot residue.

But there were a number of anomalies that had to be accounted for. One was the "teeth material"—part of Lana's front incisor caps—that had been found on the stairway opposite the death chair. This material was found ten to twelve feet away—a very long distance, especially considering that other "teeth material" had been found at her feet. How did the evidence on the stairs get there? One possibility was that Phil—or someone—had inadvertently tracked it there after the shooting. In that regard, it was interesting to note that evidence technicians had found Lana's blood on the stairway railing. It seemed possible that Phil had left this there as he went upstairs to remove his bloody coat. But this would cast doubt on Phil's claim that there was no gunshot residue on his own clothing.

A second significant anomaly was found in the toxicology report. Lana, it appeared, had consumed—enough alcohol to have a blood alcohol level of between 0.12 and 0.14—well over the limit for being declared legally drunk. In addition, she had a significant level of hydrocodone, the painkiller Vicodin, in her bloodstream. Alcohol and hydrocodone don't mix well. Thus, there was a chance that Lana may have been too woozy to resist if someone had chosen to put a gun in her mouth.

There were other unexplained injuries as well, including recent bruises on her legs and arms, and a swelling of the brain, along with a second, seemingly unrelated skull fracture, that seemed to indicate another possible blow to the head, not connected with the firing of the gun.

A deputy prosecutor now examined the complete file, and realized that there was something missing—a tiny piece of evidence, what appeared to be a portion of an acrylic fingernail, possibly a thumbnail, which appeared to have been charred by burned gunpowder. The portion of the nail had supposedly been discovered by a man named Stan White, a former sheriff's department homicide investigator who had been hired by Shapiro to inspect the castle after the police were finished with it. White subsequently told Detective Lillienfeld about the recovery of the fragment at a sheriff's department barbeque in July.

Lillienfeld, in turn, noted in the case file that the defense side had possession of the fragment. The deputy DA, Michael Latin, read that, and then called Shapiro to ask that the supposed evidence be turned over to the sheriff's department for custody, pending the decision on whether to charge Phil. Shapiro was noncommittal. There the matter rested for some weeks; then Latin was named a superior court judge by just-recalled Governor Gray Davis in the waning hours of Davis' administration. That meant a new deputy DA would have to take over, which meant more time would go by. Sometime later, after he read the file, Latin's successor, Deputy District Attorney Kevin McCormick, renewed the demand for the supposed fingernail, and again Shapiro was noncommittal.

The significance of the fingernail fragment would be hotly debated by prosecutors and Phil's lawyers over the next six months. The main issue was whether it shed any light on Phil's claim that Lana had shot herself. Exactly how shooting herself would cause a broken acrylic fingernail or thumbnail wasn't made clear; it wasn't very likely that she'd had her nail in front of the barrel when the gun went off, at least if she shot herself. In that case, the nail fragment would most likely have been embedded somewhere in her lips or inside her mouth, not someplace in the foyer. On the other hand, it *was* possible that it might have been broken off if she'd thrown up her hands to shove the gun away, which would have also been "not inconsistent with" having gunshot residue on her hands. In any case, Phil's lawyers began playing a game of hide-and-seek over this supposed nail fragment that would go on for the next year. Eventually they would contend that the nail fragment was illusory—that it did not in fact exist.

After reviewing the case file for two months, and after apparently deciding they had enough even without the nail, the district attorney's office filed a murder charge against Phil Spector on November 20, 2003.

The actual formal charge must have been sobering for Phil—he was actually accused of two separate crimes: murder, defined as the unlawful taking of a human life "with malice aforethought," and use of a gun in the commission of a violent felony, a so-called "sentencing enhancement" that could add as much as 10 years to the term for murder, which itself was 15 years to life. If Phil were to be convicted, and the sentences were served concurrently, that meant he was looking at being in state prison until at least the age of 75, even with time off for good behavior. If the sentences were made consecutive, that was it—Phil was likely to die in prison.

The most interesting aspect of the murder charge was in the definition of "malice aforethought." Under California law, "malice aforethought" could be either expressed or implied. The definition of expressed malice was obvious: when a person says something like, "I hate you and I am now going to kill you," a deliberate intention to take the life of another is manifestly "expressed." Implied malice was more subtle. According to Section 188 of the Penal Code, malice can be implied "when no considerable provocation appears, or when the circumstances attending the killing show an abandoned and malignant heart."

Both of those definitions of implied malice appeared to be present in the death of Lana Clarkson. After all, Phil had never claimed that Lana had given him any kind of provocation—according to him, in fact, she had shot herself. At the same time, a prosecutor could also argue that Phil's presumed shooting of Lana showed "an abandoned and malignant heart."

What was an "abandoned and malignant heart"? California courts had grappled with that somewhat archaic definition for some years before eventually concluding that an "abandoned and malignant heart" was obvious when "a defendant does an act with a high probability that it will result in death and does it with a base antisocial motive and with a wanton disregard for human life." That meant, the State's Supreme Court held in 1992,[60] that even the act of "brandishing a weapon" could, under some circumstances, be evidence of implied malice.

Under this theory, then, the district attorney's office would almost certainly be able to point to all the other times that Phil had "brandished" a gun at someone—the Ramones, for instance, or in the various studio sessions—and that would be supportive evidence for Phil's "abandoned and malignant heart."

And if they could prove that Phil had an "abandoned and malignant heart," because he'd brandished a gun in Lana's face and then killed her, he was going to be convicted of murder.

---

[60] *People* v. *Nieto Benitez*, 840 P.2d 969.

49

THE WHOLE CIGAR

In late January of 2004, Robert Shapiro withdrew as Phil's lawyer. Phil hired Leslie Abramson to replace him. Abramson was best known for her cacophonous defense of the Menendez brothers. What was it Phil had told Raab? "This is not the Menendez brothers"? It might not have been the brothers, but now Phil had their lawyer.

Neither Shapiro nor Abramson explained why the switch had been made. As for himself, Phil was finally not talking. But it wasn't long before speculation arose. Shapiro, who had obviously had problems keeping his client under control, was a consummate insider—if one wanted a deal, a plea bargain, Shapiro was your man. He was, some said, the best in the business at negotiating charges down to the barest possible minimum.

Abramson, on the other hand, was a trial lawyer. She liked nothing better than to get into the courtroom and mix it up with the opposition. She was loud, strident, irritating—an act that was calculated to get under her opponents' skin, and often did. What this meant, ran the speculation, was that Shapiro had tried to convince Phil to take some sort of deal—perhaps for manslaughter—but that Phil had turned this down, possibly because such a deal would probably require Phil to serve at least some time in prison, perhaps the minimum of 3 years for manslaughter. Naturally, Shapiro would have said no deal could be made unless the DA's office also agreed to drop the "gun enhancement," which carried a minimum of another 3 years. But Phil had no intention of serving any time. He wanted a trial, and for that, Abramson was his instrument of choice.

Eventually, Phil and Shapiro's parting would turn nasty—Phil would file suit against Shapiro, demanding the return of part of his retainer fee, reportedly a million dollars. In fact, according to the lawsuit, Shapiro was taking the position that Phil still owed him $500,000, and contending that he'd earned the money for his services. The blow-up between Phil and Shapiro seemed to be just one more example of Phil's capacity to turn on even his oldest friends.

Abramson quickly began by attacking the prosecution at a hearing on February 17, 2004, more than a year after Lana was killed. She used the fingernail issue as an opening wedge. She told Judge Carlos Uranga—scheduled to hold Phil's preliminary hearing, if and when it even finally took place—that the defense considered Stan White, the man who had found the supposed fingernail, a "plant," in other words, a police spy in the camp of the defense sent to clandestinely gather evidence while appearing to work with the defense team.

Parsing this was difficult, because Abramson refused to discuss it in open court. She wanted to tell Uranga the defense side of the story in chambers, contending that attorney–client privilege was involved. It appeared she was contending that Shapiro had discovered things about White's true loyalties, and wanted Shapiro to explain all this to Uranga behind closed doors.

The district attorney's office objected to this procedure, but in the end, Abramson got her way. As a result of the conference in Uranga's chambers, the DA's office and the defense side met in the jury room in the nearby courtroom to hash out their differences over the supposed thumbnail.

Afterward, Abramson—who appeared to like television cameras—told a media mob assembled outside the courthouse that the police were playing fast and loose with the facts, especially about the fingernail, which she suggested never really existed. This was all the work of the police "plant," Stan White, she suggested. And even if the fingernail existed, she said, there was no requirement that the defense turn it over to the prosecution. There had to be some indication that it was in fact evidence in the case.

Abramson then moved on to her peroration: Phil did not kill Lana Clarkson— "There's no motive," she said. And besides, the gun wasn't registered to anyone, which meant it *could* have belonged to Lana. And, she said, the police had botched the case, almost from the beginning, by sending "192" police officers through the house during the search.

That was clearly an erroneous statement—there were never "192" separate police officers going through the castle, that would have been impossible. The sheriff didn't have that many people available, for one thing. After all, it wasn't as if the only crime occurring in Los Angeles County that morning was at Phil Spector's house. Abramson must have known that there were really only 192 separate logged entries into the crime scene by the search teams over two days, as the same teams of investigators came and went from the castle on numerous occasions. But the fact that she had fuzzed this up in front of the television cameras meant one thing: Abramson was prepared to pull out all the stops in the interests of her client.

"He's my idol," she said, when she was asked why she had decided to defend Phil.

Two months later, as both sides continued to wrangle over the supposed thumbnail in a hearing before Judge Uranga, Abramson and Phil went on the offensive, after a deputy prosecutor suggested in court that Phil had a history of threatening women with firearms.

Abramson took heated exception to this assertion. In an impromptu news conference in the hallway outside the courtroom minutes later, she complained that the district attorney's office was trying to poison the well against Phil, especially with the reference to other women, other gun incidents.

"This has been going on from the beginning of the case," she said, referring to women coming forward to authorities with information about Phil's prior behavior. "Like I said, every rock that gets turned over, another one crawls out. So I mean that's the kind of thing that—you know, for years, ladies and gentlemen, I have resisted publicity on my cases, and the main reason was not that I didn't trust *you* [the news media, but] that the volunteers start crawling out of wherever it is they skulk, and claim to have knowledge, claim to know the client, claim to have seen something, and it's happened in every high-publicity case.

"And that is one of the burdens that any accused person who has a case that's getting any attention has to bear. That anybody who ever had a grudge, anybody who wants their money, anybody who's trying to curry favor, anybody who wants their fifteen minutes, can come forward and say anything they want—anybody—can say anything—at any time. And they're not carefully scrutinized. There was one witness, so-called witness in this case, that the Sheriff's Department interviewed, who made one of these outrageous claims, which she claims happened several years ago, and they were taking her seriously enough to re-interview her, to interview her mother, and only after all this did they check her psychiatric record. And she had three prior commitments."

This sounded like an oblique reference to Ronnie, and a flashback to the bitter divorce allegations of parental fitness.

"One other thing I would say," she continued. "When a person is accused of a crime, whether they are a good person or not, is not the issue. Every one of us has people who would say negative things about us, and the larger celebrity you are, the more famous you are, and the more of a genius you are, and the richer you are, the more people want to knock you down. He's not on trial here for whether or not people lied about him thirty years ago or twenty years ago or ten years ago. He is on trial solely for the issue of whether or not he shot Ms. Clarkson or she shot herself."

The autopsy report, Abramson said, indicated that Lana's

hands were coated with gunshot residue, while there was almost none of Phil's own hands. To prove her point, Abramson said, they had just released their own copy of the long-suppressed autopsy report to the news media.

"Our pathologist, Dr. Michael Baden, was present during that autopsy. And it was perfectly clear at the end of the physical examination that all the evidence they could physically see was consistent with a self-inflicted gunshot wound. And when the earliest forensic science testing came back and found that her hands were covered with gunshot residue, that the gun was covered with her DNA and her DNA alone, and that when their investigation indicated that she was familiar with and liked guns [this seems to have been a reference to publicist Ed Lozzi's quotes in the *Vanity Fair* article, but was contradicted by statements of Lana's family and friends], all of that came out within the first few weeks, they did not at that time rule this case a homicide.

"The reason they ultimately gave, in the autopsy report, for saying this was a homicide were things they knew on February 5, 2003," Abramson continued. "And yet they did not come to that conclusion until September 20, 2003. And we can only conclude therefore that their reason for saying [it was] homicide, were not those things about which they knew for seven months, but political pressure from whatever source. We know there were many meetings with the sheriff's department and the district attorney before that conclusion became the signed version of the autopsy. So they can fling as much mud as they want, but A, the mud won't stick, and B, this isn't a contest for who can sling mud the furthest, but who has the best evidence on their side. And we do. Or else, *they* would have released the autopsy report. They have kept it locked up and secret all this time."

Indeed, said Abramson, the coroner only concluded that the death was homicide after being convinced of that by the sheriff's department investigators; there simply wasn't any physical evidence from the autopsy alone to support that conclusion, and what evidence there was pointed in the direction of suicide.

It was politics—pressure to put a rich, famous person away for a crime so the DA wouldn't look like he had different standards for the rich and the poor, the famous and the unknown, Abramson implied.

It was almost a reverse Lenny Bruce, but the net effect was the same: injustice, or so Abramson sought to persuade.

Phil by this point could no longer restrain himself.

"He works for the sheriff," Phil said, referring to the corner. "He stated in the *LA Times* he would not have ruled it a homicide were it not for the sheriff. He said that in the *LA Times*."

Abramson was probably wishing that Phil would keep quiet, especially in front of television cameras, since anything he said there could later be used against him if he ever had to testify.

"Phillip, darling . . . " she said, trying to shush him. Phil made a face, as if accepting his chastisemet.

"He [Phil] is very aware of his case," she went on, trying to explain Phil's interjection. "He takes it very seriously. And that is absolutely true, that that is what the coroner said, that but for what the sheriff was telling him what the case was about, they would not have ruled it a homicide. And that sheriff's information wasn't new, and isn't new. It existed then. So why did they do it? Maybe they did it because this man was Tasered in his own home, thrown to the ground at the foot of the poor, deceased Ms. Clarkson—"

"Broken nose, and two black eyes, and fifty thousand volts of electricity shot through me, unarmed, inviting the police into my house," Phil broke in again, now definitely echoing Lenny Bruce.

Abramson again attempted to silence him with a subtle shushing gesture with her hand. "Now, *maybe* this has something to do with that [decision to file murder charges]," she said. "But I shan't speculate on the motive for prosecutors, never having seen to put people away or hurt them, I have no idea."

She turned the focus back to Phil's strongest defense point, the gunshot residue findings. The very fact that Lana's hands had been covered with gunshot residue indicated that the gun had been in her hands when it was fired, Abramson said. And the fact that there was none on Phil's hands or even his clothes indicated that he hadn't been holding the gun, she said. She didn't mention the evidence that seemed to indicate that Phil might have washed up afterward, however, and none of the reporters brought it up.

What about Desouza's evidence, the "I think I shot someone" statement?, someone asked.

"Well, I won't say how I'll deal with it," Abramson said, "although I have a very good way to deal with it. But I will tell you, he said [Desouza], he claims that while he's sitting inside a closed car, with the radio on—"

"Asleep," Phil added.

"Asleep," Abramson agreed. "Phillip, please, darling, I do wish you wouldn't say anything! At five o'clock in the morning, with a fountain going right next to him—"

Abramson interrupted herself, to explain Phil's penchant for speaking out. "You can't stop a starring talent from being a starring talent, you just can't!" she said. "But it's okay, I don't mind—"

"I should stop now?" Phil said, clearly playing to the crowd.

"You have to stop me, darling, and I have to stop you," Abramson said. "My point is, this is the situation, it is five o'clock in the morning, this man [Desouza] has been up for who knows how many hours, inside a closed car, there is a loud fountain right next to him, the radio is going in the car, he claims he hears something. He then opens the door of the car—he doesn't turn off the radio or the fountain—and claims he sees Mr. Spector in the doorway. What he says he heard—and by the way, this gentleman is from Brazil. His native language is Portuguese. He is not perfect in his English. I will not say he is illiterate, he is not. I will not say he is stupid, he is not—"

"But he *is* illegal!" Phil cracked.

"Well, that's a different issue," Abramson said.

"Yeah, he's an illegal alien," Phil continued. "And he was threatened with deportation."

"Exactly," Abramson said. "He is undergoing deportation proceedings but the district attorney's office has interceded on his behalf. And these are important considerations about who gives the police what they want to hear. He claims, in one of his many statements, that what he heard Mr. Spector saying, and listen to this, 'I think I shot someone.' Now, we know now, unquestionably, that this young lady was shot with a gun, inside her mouth, past her lips, past her teeth, because there's no damage to her lips, there's no bullet tracing on her teeth, the coroner's office looked for that specifically. He is claiming that someone who did that would then say, 'I *think* I shot someone?' "

Abramson's rhetorical question implied that anyone in their right mind would know for certain that they'd shot someone under those circumstances. The problem, she said, was that Desouza wasn't proficient in English.

"And his native language is, and this is all I'm going to say about it, is a Romance language," she said. "For those of you who understand Romance languages, who understand pronouns, who understand phrasing, for people whose native language is other than English, I think you can see that this case is—*blechhh!* And let me say that they had that statement from this witness on February 4. The autopsy report did not conclude homicide until September 20. That witness may mean that this entire case hinges on one letter: the letter 'I.' That's it."

In other words, Desouza had simply misunderstood Phil. What he'd really said was something like, "Someone shot herself."

But none of this answered the most salient questions: why, if he had discovered Lana Clarkson dead or dying of a self-inflicted gunshot wound, hadn't Phil immediately called 911 himself? Who put the bloody holster back in the drawer next to the chair Lana was found sitting in? Who wiped the blood on the diaper found in the bathroom? Why did he change his bloody coat? Why didn't he tell this story about Lana Clarkson's supposed suicide—apparently with his own gun—

when the Alhambra Police first arrived? Why did he delay admitting the police to his mansion, the circumstance that led to his being Tasered?

All of these questions, and others like them, made Phil's story of what happened on the fateful night seem wobbly, maybe even manufactured.

So, as the spring of 2004 wound into the summer, the two sides jockeyed over Phil's ultimate fate. At last Phil was back in the public eye, at the center of attention once again (although, during one of his first appearances before Uranga, Phil's media thunder was upstaged by Michael Jackson, who had just been charged with child molestation). Here was an ending, all right, one that even Mitchelson had pointed out was "gripping." It was just that it would take years, the way the California courts worked, and, the way Abramson was threatening to defend the case, before it might get to a jury. But as Mick Jagger might have told Phil, time was on his side.

So the question of Phil's innocence or guilt was really one that could not yet be determined—not with the finality that comes with a jury's verdict.

Was Phil telling the truth—that Lana Clarkson had chosen his Castle to kill herself? Or was this just another chapter in the legend? Was this another thing that Phil wished would have happened, or had said happened, even if it hadn't? Or was it just another lie? Would Phil beat the rap—not the music, but the one from the gavel?

For some, at least, there was no doubt as to what had happened in the Castle that night. The evidence was as clear as a bell—not the kind Phil used for the Wall of Sound, but one that was pristine: Lana Clarkson had wanted to go home, Phil wouldn't let her leave, and produced his gun to prevent it. That wasn't the legend, that was the history.

"This is a very simple case," said one investigator who was intimately familiar with all its details. "It's an interesting case, but it's still a simple case.

"Sometimes," he said, "a cigar is just a cigar."

Even in legend.

50

CODA

Over the three years since this book was first published, in September of 2004, there were a number of new, often-surprising developments in the case of *People of the State of California vs. Phillip Spector*. For one, Phil soon dispensed with Leslie Abramson's services, replacing her with noted New York lawyer Bruce Cutler.

Cutler had made his legal "bones" representing John Gotti, the so-called "Teflon Don" of the Gambino organized crime family in New York. With Cutler as his lawyer, Gotti had avoided conviction in three separate cases in the 1980s and 1990s. In a fourth case, Cutler was disqualified on technical grounds from representing Gotti, and the mob boss was finally convicted.

Employing a lawyer renowned for representing a notorious mobster probably appealed to Phil's self-image as a near mobster, or at least a persecuted rebel like Lenny Bruce. Cutler filed a motion to take over the case while Abramson was out of the country. Evidently taken by surprise, she announced that she'd been "forced to resign" for "ethical" reasons and refused further comment.

In the aftermath of the shooting, detectives from the Los Angeles County Sheriff's Department fanned out across the country, traveling from coast to coast, seeking out Phil's former associates and acquaintances. Week by week, they accumulated firsthand accounts of repeated violent rages by Phil, many of them involving guns. At the same time, the department's crime lab labored to interpret the evidence—most of it from Lana Clarkson's blood—scattered around the castle's foyer, in an effort to reconstruct what might have happened that night.

Probably the most important new development, however, was the decision of the Los Angeles County District Attorney's Office to present all this evidence to a county grand jury in September of 2004, almost 18 months after the shooting. Going to a grand jury permitted the prosecutors to present their evidence in secret, without challenge from the defense. Phil was soon indicted for murder, along with a "gun enhancement"—that is, an additional criminal count of using a firearm in connection with the underlying crime of murder—a charge that could add as much as ten years to his sentence, if convicted.

Thus, Phil was facing a possible penalty of at least 18 years in prison, and probably more. At the age of 64, the chances were very good that he would die while still serving this sentence. For all practical purposes, Phil was facing a form of the death penalty.

Phil was not happy with this move to the grand jury. He thought the prosecutors were cheating. Ordinarily, the case would have required a preliminary hearing, where Phil's lawyers could have cross-examined witnesses. By going to the grand jury, the prosecutors had eliminated this chance for Phil to rebut the allegations.

"The actions of the Hitler-like district attorney and his storm-trooping henchmen to seek an indictment against me, and censor all means of me getting my evidence and the truth out, are reprehensible, unconscionable and despicable," he said when the indictment was returned. In this statement, Phil seemed as cogent and coherent as he had ever been—one had to wonder: Had the authorities gone too far in charging him?

But what was the evidence?

By law in California, grand jury testimony is supposed to be released publicly within ten court days of transcripts of the testimony having been served on the person indicted. But despite his verbal assault on the "Hitler-like" district attorney's office, Phil didn't want these transcripts released. He sought and obtained a court order sealing them indefinitely. The news media responded with legal motions to unseal them.

In a hearing in early January of 2005, Bruce Cutler demanded that the transcripts remain sealed.

"This is poison!" Cutler bellowed, slamming the 1,000-plus pages of testimony down on the counsel table. In his inimitable style, frequently shouting, striding powerfully around the courtroom, gesticulating dramatically, the barrel-chested Cutler made the case that unsealing the evidence against Phil would irreparably poison the potential jury pool.

But after considering Cutler's argument, and the arguments from lawyers for the news media, Los Angeles Superior Court Judge Larry Paul Fidler ruled that the transcripts and most of the exhibits had to be unsealed.

The grand jury evidence was indeed "poison," it turned out. Over the previous months, the detectives had located at least five women who told them that, in the past, after nights of heavy drinking, Phil had pulled a gun on them and refused to let them leave. All said they'd had a casual, friendly relationship with Phil for months or years, until suddenly Phil flipped out and the guns appeared, along with a vituperative stream of verbal abuse. All five women told the police that they were terrorized, scared to death, and took steps to make sure they were never, ever alone with Phil again.

One woman, Dorothy Melvin, the former manager of Joan Rivers, told detectives that Phil held her at gunpoint in July 1993 at his Pasadena house, accusing her of having stolen something. At one point, Melvin contended, Phil had actually backhanded her across the side of her head with the hand that held a pistol. Phil demanded that she take off her clothes, and after she removed her jacket, searched her purse.

"What's this?" Phil asked, pulling a lipstick tube from the purse.

"It's lipstick, Phil," Melvin said.

"Get the fuck out of here," he then told her. But Melvin pointed out that Phil had her car keys, still in her jacket pocket. Phil fished the keys out of the pocket and threw them at her. "I told you to get the fuck out of here," he said.

Melvin ran to her car and jumped inside. She drove down the driveway to the wrought-iron gates that shielded the house from Arroyo Boulevard. The gates were locked. Just then, Melvin heard footsteps coming from behind, and noticed Phil running after her. He was holding a pump-action shotgun, and he racked it as he ran.

"I told you to get the fuck out of here," he told her when he reached her car.

"I can't, the gate's locked," Melvin told him, weeping, almost hysterical. She was sure that Phil was going to blast her out of her car with the shotgun.

"It's locked?" Phil asked quizzically. "Oh, okay, I'll open it." And he did. Melvin was stunned about the abrupt change in personality. One minute Phil was raving at her, the next instant he seemed perfectly normal. Then:

"I told you to get the fuck out here," he said once more, and Melvin put her foot to the pedal and sped through the gate.

A few blocks away, she stopped and called the Pasadena Police Department. Phil still had her purse. Not only did it contain her passport and the passport of Joan Rivers, there was $2,000 in cash in it. Police came. She told them she didn't want to press charges against Phil, she just wanted her purse back. Eventually, after two trips by police to Phil's house, the purse was recovered, but not before Phil was briefly handcuffed. But because Melvin didn't want to create bad publicity for Joan Rivers—and perhaps because the Pasadena police knew full well that Phil was a prominent citizen and taxpayer—no charges were ever filed.

Similar stories were told by others: Dianne Ogden, who had once worked for Phil as a part-time personal assistant, was eventually contacted by investigators for the district attorney's office. She told them that between 1982 and 1988, Phil had locked her in the La Collina house three different

times, and on one occasion, had put a pistol to her face, ordering her upstairs to his bedroom. There, Ogden would
later testify, Phil had tried to rape her, but failed, and instead
fell asleep. The following morning, she said, it was almost as
if nothing happened. Phil never spoke to her about the ugly
encounter, she said. It as if he had no awareness of what happened the night before—a classic example of an alcoholic
blackout.

Two weeks later, after another late night at Phil's house,
Dianne resolved to depart at the same time as others (including Allen Klein) to avoid a repeat of what had happened before. This time, Dianne said, Phil chased her down the
driveway with an Uzi, banging the weapon on her car window and shouting curses at her. She resolved never to see
him again.

A remarkably similar incident occurred with Melissa
Grosvenor, a New York waitress. Enamored of the slim, attractive Melissa, Phil invited her to visit him in California
and provided a ticket for her airfare. But Melissa noticed that
the ticket was one-way. Phil told her he thought they should
just hang out for awhile to see "how things go." Melissa,
against her better judgment, agreed. She flew out to California in early 1993.

After dinner, Phil brought her back to his house and began drinking. At about two in the morning, Melissa said she
wanted to return to her hotel, but Phil wouldn't let her leave.
He made her sit in a chair in the living room, put a gun to her
face, and told her she wasn't going anywhere. Then he put
the gun in a shoulder holster and began pacing back and
forth, verbally abusing her. Eventually Melissa, weeping,
terrified, jet-lagged, fell asleep in the chair, thinking all the
while that Phil was going to blow her head off.

And so, too, with Stephanie Jennings. A professional
photographer who had met Phil at a rock-and-roll awards
dinner in Philadelphia, Jennings had a brief intimate relationship with Phil. On several occasions, Jennings said, Phil
had drunk to excess and had refused to let her leave his
house. Then, in the spring of 1995, he'd invited her to a

rock-and-roll party in New York and arranged for her to stay at the Carlyle Hotel, where he also had a suite.

After the party—Phil got drunk—he sent one of his bodyguards down to Stephanie's room to demand that she join him. Stephanie declined; she was tired, she said—it was after 3 in the morning. A few minutes later, Phil himself came to her room and demanded that she join him. When she again refused, Phil reminded her that he was paying for her room.

In that case, Stephanie told him, she would pay for the room herself, and not only that, she would leave immediately. She began to gather her things, but Phil wouldn't let her. It appeared that Phil wanted to hold her belongings, including her expensive camera equipment, as "security" for the room charges. When Stephanie insisted on leaving anyway, Phil left, but came back a few minutes later, this time holding a pistol. He placed a chair in front of the door and brandished the gun in a threatening manner. Stephanie told him she was going to call the police, and dialed 911.

"You can call your mother if you want," Phil told her, "but it won't do you any good." Phil apparently hadn't heard Stephanie when she'd told him that she intended to call the police; he thought she was calling her mother in Philadelphia. The 911 operator came on the line, and soon a number of police officers arrived at the Carlyle. By then Phil had returned to his own suite, taking the gun with him. Stephanie was escorted by police to the train station; she thought the police were unsympathetic and that they believed she was a prostitute, an impression that infuriated her. No charges were ever filed against Phil.

And there were other incidents, not just involving women. At one point, Phil had gotten into an altercation with a parking valet at the Beverly Hills Hotel and pulled a gun. That resulted in a police report, but no charges.

The more police looked into the life and times of Phil Spector, the more they found instances of recklessness, usually involving firearms. All of this, the prosecutors decided, reflected a pattern of behavior, of motive, and as such, could be presented to warrant the conclusion that Phil Spector had indeed murdered Lana Clarkson, and that, in habitually brandishing weapons to terrorize women, he indeed had "an abandoned and malignant heart."

Finally, there was the evidence of what had actually happened on the night of February 3, 2003, when police had "literally stormed the castle," as Cutler later put it. Despite initial reports that Phil had said nothing upon his arrest, the opposite was true. Phil had begun talking almost from the minute the police arrived, and then seemingly hadn't been able to shut up.

As Alhambra police officer Mike Page told the grand jury, he'd reached the castle shortly after 5 a.m., to find DeSouza and the Mercedes waiting at the gate. After first surrounding the three-acre castle property to make sure no one could get away, Page and four other Alhambra police officers began making their way up the driveway, single file. The first officer in line, Brandon Cardella, held a "ballistic shield" in front of them, in case Phil came out shooting. Halfway up the driveway, Page and the others found a stairway up to the top of the hill, and took that shortcut. As they got to the top, they could see, through the windows, someone wandering around on the second floor. After securing the garage area, Page and the others advanced to the rear door of the castle. There they encountered Phil standing in the open doorway, his hands in his pockets.

"Take your hands out of your pockets!" Cardella shouted. Phil did it.

"Raise your hands!" Cardella commanded. Phil complied, then crossed them in front of his chest. He put his hands back in his pockets.

"Take your hands out of your pockets!" Cardella shouted again. Phil didn't seem to hear him, or understand why the police wanted this—to make sure he wasn't armed.

"You've got to see this," Phil said, and turned to go back inside.

At that point, fearing that Phil was going to get away and

barricade himself, Page fired a Taser dart at Phil. It had no effect. Phil kept moving. Page fired another dart, but that one didn't work either.

"Go!" Page shouted, and he and Cardella, followed by the other three officers, rushed after Phil and slammed him up against the wooden banister in the foyer of the house with the ballistic shield. Phil fell to the floor, on his stomach, while Page put a knee in his back and tried to handcuff him. Phil tried to wrestle his hands away, all the while screaming obscenities at the police. The other officers fanned out through the 22-room house, covering all the hallways with their guns in case there was someone else inside, perhaps armed and homicidal.

A few minutes into the scrum on the floor, Page realized that Phil might be saying something important, so he reached into his pocket and turned on a small tape recorder.

The recording that ensued was both dramatic and revealing, as Phil babbled away, alternately indignant and apologetic, while Page and the other officers were shouting to each other, in part to make sure they didn't wind up shooting each other in the candle-lit darkness. All the while, the background music once heard by Mick Brown floated through the surreal scene, shouts, grunts and profanity accompanied by strains of Bach.

The recorder came on in mid-sentence.

"Just ask me and I'll tell you," Phil was saying. "I'm not Robert Blake—what the hell is wrong with you? Oh, what the fuck is wrong with you? Oh, Jesus Christ. It feels good. What the hell is wrong with you?"

Page, Cardella and the other officers continued to call out to one another over the background music, making sure they had all the approaches covered. No one was paying any attention to Phil. The strings played on.

"What are you worried about?" Phil demanded. "What are you concerned about? Oh, God, LAPD works for me. What are you worried about? I can tell you what happened."

This brought Page's attention back to Phil, still writhing under his knee. Out of the corner of his eye, Page could see the body of Lana Clarkson, slumped in a chair, her face bloody and her eyes vacant with the look of death.

"Only if you want to," Page told him.

"If you're gonna arrest me, just tell me what happened," Phil said. "The dog was locked up . . . was a little schnauzer. What the fuck is wrong with you? Jay Romaine—he's a lieutenant in your fucking police department. What the hell is wrong with you people? Oh, Jesus Christ."

Page called in to his dispatcher. "Nine, be advised, we have one detained. We're clearing the house."

"Jesus," Phil said. "You know, you're acting stupid. Get the fuck off me! This is stupid. I'm sorry there's a dead woman here. But I'm sorry that this happened. I can explain it but if you'd just give me a chance. I mean, you know. What the hell are . . . you acting like assholes. You think you're so fucking important, man."

Page and the others continued communicating with their dispatcher about the progress of their search. At one point Phil realized they were looking through the house, and told the police they should ask him for permission first. They ignored him.

"Why are you standing on my head, asshole?" Phil shouted. "Jesus fucking Christ! I'm not drunk and I'm not stupid. I can tell you what happened. You don't have to handcuff me. I can tell you what happened. What's wrong with you people? Jesus Christ, the chief of police worked for me. If you want me to call him, I'll call him. I don't want to be an asshole. I'm sorry this happened. But, excuse me, I don't need to be tied up like a pig . . . why do you keep stepping on me? What the fuck? The gun went off accidentally. She works at the House of Blues. It was a mistake. I don't understand what the fuck you people is wrong with you . . . Oh God, I'm just gonna go to sleep. Would you like me to go to sleep? Do you have to step on my back?"

"I don't want you to get up," Page told Phil. "Just stay where you're at."

"No, but do you have to step on my back like an asshole? Jesus Christ, I mean it's a God-fucking disgrace. I mean, I

wouldn't step on your back 'cause you would probably . . .
Jesus Christ! I'm sorry this happened. I don't know how it
happened. It scared the shit out of me, that [it] happened. If
you're gonna arrest me, arrest me. I own this castle, I live
here, and I'm sorry this happened. And I see what happened."

Phil now said he wanted to call his lawyer.

Just before 6 a.m., Alhambra police officers Sean Heckers
and Derek Gilliam arrived at the castle. Gilliam was told to
go inside the house to help with the search of the house for
evidence, while Heckers was assigned to keep an eye on
Phil, who by this time had been placed in the rear of a patrol
car. About 6:30 a.m., Heckers rode with Phil to the Alhambra Police Station.

"He smelled of alcohol," Heckers recalled. "His de-
meanor was real relaxed, and he had real relaxed facial muscles, and somewhat lethargic in appearance." Once they
arrived at the station, Heckers performed a gunshot residue
test on Phil's hands, sealing the swabs inside the sterile en-
velope provided for that purpose.

At that point, the people at the Alhambra jail tried to
book Phil for arrest, but Phil refused to cooperate, growing
more belligerent by the minute. After a few minutes, it was
decided to put Phil into a side room in the hope that he'd
calm down. Gilliam, now back from the search, was assigned to sit with him.

As it happened, Gilliam was the nephew of Terry
Gilliam, the movie producer and Monty Python veteran.
Gilliam was told to simply stay with Spector, and most especially, not to ask him any questions. Phil was in an extreme
state of agitation.

"He was making very rude remarks," Gilliam said. "He
was belligerent, angry, almost being . . . very confrontational." Gilliam was asked if he thought Phil was drunk.

"Yes," Gilliam said. "He had slurred speech. He could
barely maintain his balance. Dry mouth, bloodshot eyes, and
he had this horrible odor." Phil soon began rambling on

about the music business, talking about George Harrison. Gilliam mentioned that his uncle had known George Harrison, that his uncle had been friends with him. Gilliam said he was only trying to get Phil to relax, so they could complete the booking process.

"How did he respond to your comment that your uncle was a famous person associated with Monty Python?" Gilliam was asked.

"He called me a liar," Gilliam said. " 'I basically have the rights to Monty Python,' " Gilliam said Phil told him.

Then, without prompting from Gilliam, Spector began to talk about the death of Lana Clarkson. He told Gilliam that there was a dead "girl" at his house, and demanded to know what the police were doing about it. Gilliam told him people were looking into the matter. Then Phil asked Gilliam what had happened; Gilliam said he didn't know because he hadn't been there. Gilliam noticed that Spector seemed to be talking mostly to himself. He repeated his question: "What happened at my house?" and Gilliam again gave a noncommittal response. Phil got frustrated, Gilliam said. He told Gilliam that the dead woman was a friend of his who worked at the House of Blues.

Phil continued to ramble, Gilliam said, muttering about the music business, dropping various names, saying he had to go to New York to produce a performance with Bono, that there were people he needed to get in touch with because of scheduled music videos.

"Sometimes he just didn't seem to be there," Gilliam recalled. Eventually Phil began to explain. Gilliam said he asked no questions, but that Phil volunteered his story.

"He said that the young lady began singing his songs, two of them, one being 'Da doo run run' [sic] and the other song by the . . ." Gilliam tried to remember the title of Spector's greatest hit, but couldn't think of it.

"Oh," Gilliam remembered, " 'You've Lost That Lovin' Feelin'.' He said that she took the gun into her hand and basically put it to her head, and this is how his hand was looking." Gilliam demonstrated by putting his index finger to his temple, using his thumb as the hammer. Of course, Lana Clarkson was shot in the mouth, not the temple.

"And basically [he] said, 'It went like this, *bang*,' and he . . . fell back into his chair, throwing his head back. And he sat there for about five seconds in that position . . . he said that she was singing the song, and continued with the process [singing, apparently]. He was real animated about it."

Phil reenacted this supposed suicide scene two or three times, Gilliam said. The last time, he didn't move for an extended period, and Gilliam became concerned "that maybe he had gone into some form of an attack [seizure] or something."

Phil next told him that Lana had somehow obtained the gun, and was waving it around, twirling it around her head. Phil said he told her to put the gun down, but she didn't. Then Phil said, "You don't pull a gun out on me," and smirked, according to Gilliam.

Gilliam now asked Phil if he was willing to cooperate with the booking people, and Phil said he was.

"He became very cooperative," Gilliam said. Phil then attempted to make a number of telephone calls, but apparently gave the jailers the wrong numbers. After the booking, Phil was placed in a holding cell.

By 11:30 that morning, Phil was beginning to sober up, at least slightly. He wanted to talk to his lawyer right away, he said. He also wanted to get out of jail. An Alhambra police detective, Esther Pineda, came to see him in the holding cell. She told him that Jay Romaine had come to the police department, as had Michelle Blaine. It also appeared that Rommie Davis was calling and wanted to talk to him. There now ensued a conversation between Pineda and Phil, in which it appears that Pineda confused Jay Romaine with Rommie Davis. When he learned that these people wanted to see him, Phil became obstreperous again. He insisted that he hadn't been able to speak to an attorney yet, and that while he wanted to tell Pineda what had happened, he wanted to talk to his lawyer first. The jailers insisted that

Phil had already had his allotted telephone calls; it wasn't their fault that Phil had given them the wrong number. Phil wanted to talk to his visitors, including Jay Romaine and Michelle Blaine. But Pineda said there wasn't time for that.

His frustration mounting, Phil lost his temper again. "I just want to talk to them so I can find out what the hell is going on," Phil told Pineda.

"Well, you're being charged with murder," Pineda told him.

"I'm being charged with murder?" Phil's disbelief was evident.

"Yes, that's one of the things that—"

"Of whom?" Phil interrupted.

Pineda admitted that she didn't know the name of the victim yet.

After more discussion of telephone calls—Phil said he hadn't been able to reach anyone, Pineda said the jail logs showed that he'd had his allotted two calls—Phil asked what was going on that morning at the castle. Pineda told him she didn't know, but again, that Phil was being charged with murder.

"This is the most bizarre nonsense," Phil said. "This is absurd. This is absolutely absurd."

Pineda had been using a tape recorder, and when Phil insisted that he wanted to speak to a lawyer, she turned it off. Then Phil made some sort of remark that caught her attention—something about an accident—and she turned it back on.

"What was it you were saying?" she prompted.

"You heard what I said," Phil shot back.

Pineda told Phil that Rommie Davis had called to say that Los Angeles criminal defense lawyer Robert Shapiro was on his way to the Alhambra jail. This appears to have stimulated Phil's aggressiveness.

"I want him down here," he said. "I'm gonna make you fucking people pay for this. This is bullshit. This is nonsense. You people have had me here for six fucking hours, maybe nine hours. And you have me locked up like some fucking turd in some fucking piece of shit. And you treat me . . . and you have me jerking around. And when somebody comes over to my fucking house who pretends to be security at the House of Blues and comes over to my house—remember, I *own* the House of Blues. Where this lady pretended to work, okay? And then just blows her fucking head open in my fucking house and then comes—and then you people come around and arrest me and bang the shit out of my fucking ass and beat the shit out of me and then you pretend and arrest me and then pretend like you're fucking Alhambra . . . and the mayor of Alhambra wants me to have Bono come and sing at the anniversary of—bullshit! This is nonsense. This is absolute fucking nonsense. I don't know what the fucking lady—what her problem is, but she wasn't a security at the House of Blues . . . and I don't know what her fucking problem was, but she certainly had no right to come to my fucking castle, blow her fucking head open, and [unintelligible] a murder. What the fuck is wrong with you people?"

It was clear to Pineda that Phil was getting wound up again. At that point, Rommie Davis's call to Phil was put through. Pineda decided to put Davis on the line, so Phil could tell her to get Shapiro down to the jail as soon as possible.

"I just want to get the fuck out of here," Phil told Pineda. And then, apparently, he told the same thing to Rommie Davis, because Shapiro soon arrived at the Alhambra police station and took up Phil's cause.

Later that day, Phil was taken to a nearby hospital, where he was tested for the level of alcohol in his blood. As of that afternoon's test, nearly twelve hours after the death of Lana Clarkson, Phil's blood alcohol level still registered at just under .08. One had to assume that at the time of the shooting, it had been much, much higher than that.

Later that evening, Phil posted his $1 million bail, signing over the deed to his castle as security. Shapiro hustled him away via the back door of the Alhambra Police Station, and Phil adjourned to a Los Angeles hotel until the news media heat died down. Eventually, other stories emerged, and Phil Spector and the murder charge against him faded from the public eye.

After a series of delays lasting years—Assistant District Attorney Sortino, the prosecutor, was made a judge; Bruce Cutler had to defend two former NYPD detectives accused of being secret mobsters in New York; Judge Fidler had to hear a serial murder case; and Sortino's replacements had to try a murder conspiracy case against a man accused of arranging a hit on former race driver Mickey Thompson—the trial of Phil Spector finally began in April of 2007, more than four years after Lana Clarkson was shot through the mouth.

By this point, Phil had broken with Michelle Blaine, eventually suing her for substantial sums that he claimed she'd misappropriated from "my money." He'd also sued Robert Shapiro, seeking a refund of the $1-million retainer Phil had paid. The Blaine lawsuit was later settled out of court, with Michelle returning some of the money Phil said she owed him. Shapiro said nothing doing—he'd earned his fee—and Phil dropped the case.

In the meantime, Phil had married again—this time to Rachel Short, a 26-year-old singer. Rachel would accompany Phil in all of his court appearances over the next few years, living proof that Phil did not really hate women. A joke made the rounds: as wedding gifts, Phil got a prenuptial agreement from Rachel; from Phil, Rachel got a bulletproof vest.

Late in April, the trial finally got underway.

By this point, the prosecution had advanced the notion that the blood evidence—a faint "mist-like" spatter of blood on the left-hand side of Phil's white jacket—showed that Phil had to have been standing within three feet of Lana Clarkson's mouth when the gun went off. Lana's blood alcohol level of .12, combined with the evidence of Vicodin, seemed to suggest that Lana was either barely conscious or asleep when she died. The prosecutors theorized that Phil had crept up to Lana while she was dozing in the chair in the foyer, put the gun in her mouth before she realized what was happening, and fired the pistol—if not intentionally, then recklessly.

The defense denied all of this. Drawing on experts Dr. Henry Lee and Dr. Michael Baden, they contended that "the science" would prove that Phil must have been at least six feet away when the gun went off, thus proving Phil's story about the "accidental suicide." The faintness of the blood-spatter pattern on Phil's coat would prove this beyond a reasonable doubt, the defense contended.

But forensic science is much less hard science than it is an art—the art of interpretation. There were all sorts of possible explanations for how the blood evidence, or lack of it, came to be distributed in the foyer of the castle that night: some explanations being "proof" of Phil's guilt, others tending to show he did *not* pull the trigger. Rather than proving anything, it was a matter of likelihood, of probabilities—in other words, *which* expert one chose to believe, and how likely their particular interpretation was.

It wasn't really *CSI*—in the real world, it's always more a matter of odds.

For Phil, the odds were: *You Bet Your Life.*

For the state of California, county of Los Angeles: The totality of the evidence—the long, unhappy history of Phillip Spector's predilection for guns and his deep-seated, compulsive desire for control over those capable of wielding emotional power over him; his storied life of manic highs and depressive lows, life as the so-called "mad genius"—only proved their point: Phil Spector had finally gone too far, exactly as had been predicted, years before.

Yet no one—not Annette Merar, not Marshall Lieb, not Ronnie Bennett Spector, not Larry Levine, not Dr. Kaplan, not the Kessel brothers, not Janice Zavala, or their surviving daughter, Nicole—in fact none of those who loved Phil Spector, or said they did, were able to pull him back to real life. Phil had long since left the land of ordinary people, and ascended (or descended) into a world of his own.

It was, as Carol Connors said as Phil's trial got underway, an American tragedy. To know Phil was to love him, but to know him was also to fear him.

Which was, perhaps, in the end, all that Phil had ever really wanted. If he couldn't get your respect, he'd take your fear—in fact, he would demand it. By 2007, the 67-year-old, one-time "Tycoon of Teen" had metamorphosed into the Old Man of Misery, if not murder. And while in real time it had taken fifty years to make the change, in another way, it seemed as if the transformation had happened only yesterday, right from the day Phil Spector first decided he wanted to make a record.

And although Lana Clarkson paid the heaviest price, finally reaching in death the stardom she had always sought, Phil Spector himself was the final victim of his own reckless success.

Index